Debbie

GW01044917

The Sacred In-Between

The sacred place was, and still is, an intermediate zone created in the belief that it has the ability to co-join religious aspirants to what they seek. An essential means of understanding this sacred architecture is through the recognition of its role as an "in-between" place, connecting humans to the understandings they seek and the gods they worship. By establishing the broadened contexts, approaches, and understandings of architecture through the lens of the mediating roles often performed by sacred architecture, this book offers the reader new insights into the forces behind these extraordinary buildings.

Written by a well-known expert in the field, the book draws on a unique range of cases including:

- Carl Jung's house in Bollingen (Switzerland)
- Native American earthworks, burial mounds, and effigy figures
- Tongdo Zen Buddhist Monastery (Korea)
- Saint Benedict's Abbey at Vaals (Holland)
- the Sokollu and Selimiye Mosques (Turkey).

The book concludes with reflections on the author's personal experiences at these effective, elucidative, and inspiring places, their continuing ontological significance and the lessons they can offer today. It makes fascinating and essential reading for anyone interested in sacred architecture.

Thomas Barrie is Professor of Architecture at North Carolina State University whose scholarship on the symbolism, ritual use, and cultural significance of architecture has taken him to sacred places around the world. He is an award-winning architect and the author of *Spiritual Path—Sacred Place: Myth, Ritual and Meaning in Architecture* (Shambhala Publications, 1996).

The Sacred In-Between

The Mediating Roles of Architecture

Thomas Barrie

Routledge
Taylor & Francis Group

LONDON AND NEW YORK

First published 2010
by Routledge
2 Park Square, Milton Park, Abingdon, Oxon, OX14 4RN

Simultaneously published in the USA and Canada
by Routledge
711 Third Avenue, New York, NY 10017, USA

Routledge is an imprint of the Taylor & Francis Group, an informa business

© 2010 Thomas Barrie

Typeset in Stone Sans and Univers by Keystroke, Tettenhall, Wolverhampton

All rights reserved. No part of this book may be reprinted
or reproduced or utilized in any form or by any electronic,
mechanical, or other means, now known or hereafter invented,
including photocopying and recording, or in any information
storage or retrieval system, without permission in writing from
the publishers.

British Library Cataloguing in Publication Data
A catalogue record for this book is available from the British Library

Library of Congress Cataloging-in-Publication Data
Barrie, Thomas.
    The sacred in-between : the mediating roles of architecture/Thomas Barrie.
        p. cm.
    Includes bibliographical references and index.
    1. Religious architecture. 2. Mediation between God and man.
    I. Title.
    NA4600.B36 2010
    726—dc22   2009037320

ISBN10: 0–415–77963–4 (hbk)
ISBN10: 0–415–77964–2 (pbk)

ISBN13: 978–0–415–77963–0 (hbk)
ISBN13: 978–0–415–77964–7 (pbk)

To everything architecture means – and does.

Contents

Illustration Credits

All drawings and photographs by the author, unless otherwise noted.

1.1: Tate Gallery, London/Art Resource, New York.

1.2: Isabella Stewart Gardner Museum, Boston.

4.4, 8.1: Courtesy of George Michell.

4.8, 9.9, 9.11, 9.12, 9.14, 9.17, 9.18, 9.22, 9.25, 9.29, 9.30, 9.35, 9.37: Photos by Aras Neftçi.

5.1: Art Resource, New York.

5.3: Drawing by Glenn Robert Lym, courtesy of Clare Cooper Marcus.

6.1, 7.4: Mondadori Electa.

6.2, 10.1: Drawings by Richard Tobias, from Spiro Kostaf (1985) *A History of Architecture: Settings and Rituals*, by permission of Oxford University Press, Inc.

6.5: Drawing by Rodney Castleden, from R. Castleden (1992) *Neolithic Britain*, Routledge, p. 240, fig. 6.3.

6.6: Photo by Andrew Crompton.

6.7, 6.8, 6.12: Drawing from Squier and Davis (1848).

6.11: From *Mound City Indian Ceremony* by Louis S. Glanzman.

6.13: Ohio Historical Society.

7.3: *The Amiens Trilogy, Part II: Revelation*, Columbia University, 1997.

7.8: Drawing by Tim Kiser.

7.9, 7.10, 7.12, 7.16, 7.19, 7.20: Photos by Shim.

7.17: Photograph © 2009 Museum of Fine Arts, Boston.

8.4: British Museum Press.

8.5: Cistercian plan by Villard de Honnecourt.

8.6: Vanni/Art Resource, New York.

8.10, 8.11, 8.13, 8.19: Courtesy of Saint Benedict's Abbey, Vaals.

9.2: Photo by Julio Bermudez.

9.3: Werner Forman/Art Resource, New York.

9.4: Erich Lessing/Art Resource, New York.

9.5: After Rowland Mainstone.

9.6, 9.7, 9.8, 9.10, 9.13, 9.16, 9.26: Drawings by Arben Arapi, from Gülru Necipoğlu (2005) *The Age of Sinan: Architectural Culture in the Ottoman Empire*, Princeton University Press, courtesy of Gülru Necipoğlu.

Every effort has been made to contact and acknowledge copyright owners, but the author and publisher would be pleased to have any errors or omissions brought to their attention so that corrections may be published at a later printing.

Acknowledgments

Writing is a solitary activity, but research depends on the assistance, generosity, and friendship of many. During the many years of field and scholarly research that resulted in this book, numerous organizations and individuals were essential to its success, but the following deserve special mention.

Two research grants from the Graham Foundation for Advanced Studies in the Fine Arts in 2001 and 2003, and a North Carolina State University Faculty Research and Professional Development Grant in 2005, provided essential support for the field research. A sabbatical at Lawrence Technological University in 2001 allowed me to frame the major issues of the book. A scholarly leave from NC State during the 2007–2008 academic year was crucial to the completion of the manuscript, and I am grateful to Dean Marvin Malecha and Professor Paul Tesar for their support.

The research in the United Kingdom and France was both successful and pleasant because of the assistance of old friends. In particular, the hospitality of Roger and Adrienne Stonehouse, Ian and Julie Hicklin, and Ray and Hassanah Burton is deeply appreciated. The C.G. Jung Institute in Zurich was instrumental to my research on Carl Jung's house in Bollingen and Daniel Baumann, an architect in Zurich, and Robert Hinshaw, publisher of Daimon Books, facilitated my field research. The monks at Saint Benedict's Abbey in Vaals displayed true Benedictine generosity during my stay there. In particular, Brother Hubertus opened the van der Laan archive and was instrumental in providing high-quality images of van der Laan's drawings. During the numerous trips to Turkey, many aided my work. Faculty at Istanbul Technical University, including professors Mine Inceoglu, Semra Ogel, Gunkut Atkin, Zeynep Kuban, and Arda Inceoglu, generously gave their time, and Aras Neftçi took the beautiful photographs of Sinan's buildings. Sevgi Parlak, a graduate student at ITU, provided consistent support – securing state permissions, obtaining resources, guiding, translating, and helping me to accomplish what alone I could not. The Korean field research would not have been possible without the generous support of Professor Jay Hwang of Chung-buk National University, and Professor Young-chul Chung of Kyungil University who over many years showed me paths that otherwise would have remained hidden.

Many conversations with colleagues, students, family, and friends have helped my understandings grow and deepen. Academia is a generous profession, and this book depended on the selfless assistance of those with the expertise and insights I lacked. Professor Robert Mugerauer of the University of

Washington and Professor Norman Crowe of Notre Dame University critically read the draft manuscript. Professor Alberto Perez-Gomez provided cogent criticism of the theory chapters and Professor John Hancock of the University of Cincinnati of the chapter on Native American earthworks, burial mounds, and effigy figures. Critical readings of drafts of the Korean monastery section were graciously supplied by Professor Jay Hwang and Professor Robert Buswell, Director of the Center for Buddhist Studies, UCLA. My colleagues at the Forum for Architecture, Culture, and Spirituality appeared at just the right time. John Orr, Catherine Eberhart, David Walker, and Marti Atkinson provided spiritual guidance when I needed it most. Julio Bermudez and Andrew Crompton graciously provided photographs on short notice. Katherine Ball and Liese Zahabi assisted during the book's completion. Special thanks to Fran Ford and the entire team at Routledge for their gracious and professional work.

Architecture and writing are lengthy and time-consuming endeavors. Throughout, my wife Lisa and sons Ian and Simon have provided much-needed patience, acceptance, and support. My gratitude for all that they bring to our collective lives is both timeless and immediate.

Chapter 1

Introduction

Sacred space constitutes itself following a rupture of the levels which make possible the communication with the trans-world, transcendent realities. Whence the enormous importance of sacred space in the life of all peoples: because it is in such a space that man is able to communicate with the other world, the world of divine beings or ancestors.

(Mircea Eliade)[1]

"How long wilt thou hide thy face from me?"[2] David cries in Psalms, a plaintive expression of the enduring religious theme of separation from the divine. "Why dost thou stand so afar off, O Lord?"[3] he asks, his question framing the perennial human condition of dislocation from larger contexts, broader knowledge, and deeper understandings. The disconnections may be spiritual, but they are often described spatially. In Taoism, the immortal gods reside on islands separated by vast waters. In Buddhism, unenlightened states are a "middle world" and texts describe a "crossing over" from delusion to enlightenment. In the first book of the Hebrew Bible, Adam and Eve are expelled from the place where God dwells and are separated by a gateway blocked by "cherubim and a flaming sword which turned every way."[4] The Christian Gospels contain a number of references to gateways and thresholds, physical boundaries that both separate and connect one to the divine. As Jesus asserted: "The gate is narrow and the way is hard that leads to life, and those that find it are few."[5]

What is required to bridge these seemingly unbridgeable gaps – to cross these narrow thresholds? This book argues that sacred architecture was conceptualized, realized, and utilized as a response to this eternal question, and believed to connect what was formerly discontinuous.

1.1
The Magic Circle, John William Waterhouse, 1886

Source: Tate Gallery, London/Art Resource, New York.

The Mediating Roles of Religion and Architecture

1.2
Religion is a mediator, its beliefs and rituals serve to interconnect the individual, the community, the understandings they seek, and the gods they worship. Annunciation, Piermatteo d'Amelia, *c.* 1475

Source: Isabella Stewart Gardner Museum, Boston.

Religious traditions insist that connections to deeper ways of being in the world are only possible through belief and participation in religion. The "holy" is the "whole" – the re-connection of humans with their god(s). Religious beliefs and practices from around the world, in all their variety, share the goal of connecting the individual to broader communal, cultural and theological contexts. The root word of religion is *reliquare*, "to bind together," suggesting its principal role of establishing connections with the divine. Hinduism views the ordinary world as *maya*, a scrim of illusion withdrawn only through the perspectives that religion provides. The term yoga means "to yoke" or "to bind together," and yogic practices served to join the separate individual with the universal "self." Religion, in this context, is a mediator, its beliefs and rituals serve to interconnect the individual, the community, the understandings they seek, and the gods they worship.

The principal argument of this book is that sacred architecture typically articulated an intermediary "position in the world" that was both physical and symbolic. Religion has traditionally articulated questions regarding the meaning and significance of human existence and mollified feelings of isolation and alienation. It has been intrinsic to the archetypal human endeavor of establishing a "place" in the world. Architecture has incorporated similar agendas – providing shelter, a meaningful place that embodies symbolic content, and a setting for communal rituals. Humans are unique because they are not only part of their environment, but actively and deliberately shape it – often in the service of cultural, socio-political, and religious imperatives. Sacred places were often precisely built at specific locations with the hope that connections would result and the otherwise inaccessible accessed. Throughout the book, I argue that sacred architecture performed, and in some cases continues to perform, a critical role in embodying religious symbols and facilitating communal rituals – with the goal of creating a middle ground, a liminal zone, that mediates between humans and that which they seek, revere, fear, or worship.

Religion and religious figures have traditionally been put into the service of mediating between humans and the knowledge or understanding they seek or the gods they worship. Similarly, sacred architecture was conceptualized and created as a physical and symbolic mediator, often in support of the religions it was built to serve. Just as scripture and mythology often describe the promise and potential of religion to join, to connect, to unveil, these themes were also symbolized by sacred architecture. In this context, analogous to scripture, prayer, worship, teachers, holy persons, oracles, shamans, and other mediums, sacred architecture was (and often still is) an intermediate zone believed to have the ability to co-join religious aspirants to what they sought. Moreover, communal rituals, as embodiments of myth, scripture, and belief, were another means of

1.3
The sacred place was (and often still is) an intermediate zone believed to have the ability to co-join religious aspirants to what they sought. The Western Wall, Jerusalem

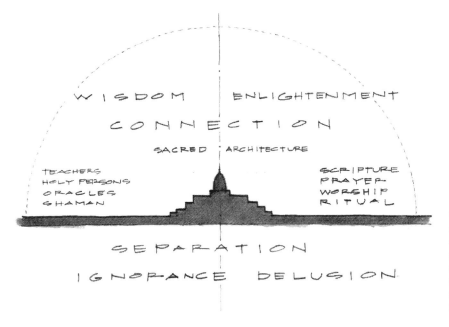

1.4
Analogous to scripture, prayer, worship, teachers, holy persons, oracles, shamans, and other mediums, sacred architecture was (and often still is) a means to establish revelatory links

connection where the architectural settings were vivified and completed. All were (and are) in-between places believed to provide bridges across liminal realms.

Context and Scope

This book positions architecture as a cultural artifact that responds to its social, political, economic, and environmental contexts and expresses a complex matrix of cultural beliefs and imperatives. In this context, it is presented as a communicative media that embodies symbolic, mythological, doctrinal, socio-political, and, in some cases, historical content. Moreover, it is often an active agent that performs didactic, elucidative, exhortative, and, in some cases, coercive roles.

The language or media of architecture serves to communicate its symbolic content to establish its often multiple, complex meanings. Central to the legibility of architecture is the active engagement it requires. One "reads" its content through deciphering its language to construct its meaning.[6] And because this engagement is context-dependent, this study includes pertinent social, cultural, political, historical, environmental, and liturgical settings that helped to shape the architecture. It recognizes that the deciphering of the symbolism of architecture often leads to deeper understandings of the culture that built it, and understanding its full context is essential to deciphering its meaning. Even though its meanings are often complex and subject to multiple interpretations, what we at times discover is the capacity of architecture to reveal a culture is equal to or exceeds textual or historical evidence.[7]

One early role of religion was to bind together a clan, tribe, nation, or culture in support of territorial and hierarchical agendas, which is why (both positively and negatively) religion, culture, and place are so inextricably connected. Architecture typically served these unified and multifarious cultural, religious, and territorial agendas. Even the most primordial of architectures, the burial mound, served to reinforce the continuity of the clan, the hierarchy of its leaders, and its territorial claims. Religious sites and edifices were rarely benign and typically served the political and social agendas of the organized societies that built them. The dark side of the declarative and didactic roles of architecture is its complicity in the reinforcement of social dictates and hierarchies. However, the incorporation of architecture's role in social coercion and territorial restriction in histories and theories of architecture can serve to deepen our understandings of its cultural significance. It can reveal the power that architecture did (and still does) possess.

This book establishes broadened contexts, approaches, and understandings of architecture through the lens of the mediating roles performed by sacred architecture. It examines a specific stratum of the layers of architectural history to provide heterogenous readings of its experiential qualities and communicative roles. I focus on sacred architecture because this particular "type" provides arguably the most accessible and diverse means to unpack the meaning and symbolism of architecture. In particular, sacred architecture was often the result of significant human and material resources – an indication of the value that it held. The book's focus, however, does not imply that other types of architecture do not perform partial or similar roles in particular settings. Some may – or may provide additional means and media of communication and engagement – but are outside of the scope of this study.

Definition of Terms

The term *sacred architecture* defines places built to symbolize the religious axioms and beliefs, communicate socio-political content, and accommodate the rituals of particular cultures within their specific historical settings. *God*, or *the gods*, is used both specifically and generally. In some cases, the religious and architectural orientation is toward a singular god – in others, the gods are diffuse or multiple. The term *divine* is applied to include objects of veneration or worship, such as divine ancestors or wisdom. *Content* refers to the *symbolism* embodied by the architecture, whereas *meaning* is the outcome of individual or collective understandings that result from participation in or with the architecture. Additionally, a *symbolic language* is the convention used to embody the *symbolic content*, which is also described as *communicative media* – all of which constitute an inclusive definition of *symbolism*.

The definitions and etymology of the term *mediate* and words related by meaning, use, and their roots, are necessary to establish our scope of inquiry. *Mediate* comes from the Latin *mediare*, which means to be "in the middle," and its Germanic root, *midja-gardaz*, means a "middle zone" that lies between heaven and earth. *Mediate* is an active verb that describes actions for bringing together separate parties, producing results, or synthesizing information. As such, it is understood as a dynamic activity that oscillates between discrete entities. Related terms include *mediating, mediator, media, mean, medial, median, mediant,* and *medium*, all of which include space and spatial relationships.

The act of *mediating* is to serve as an intermediary between separate positions. *Mediation*, in its current use, is a form of conflict resolution where a mutually agreed-upon solution is facilitated, but not imposed, by a third-party mediator. This definition is useful because of the necessity of participation of the separate parties to reach a conclusion. (The other current form of conflict resolution is arbitration where the third-party arbitrator provides a binding final decision, most likely favoring one of the petitioners and aptly called an "award.") These roles are distinguished from those of a *medium*, an agency (such as a person or material) through which something is accomplished. In the case of a person, a medium has the ability to connect otherwise inaccessible worlds, most popularly to communicate with the dead, as in a psychic medium. Turning to words that have more direct material and spatial implications, we note that a *medium* is also an environment where cultures or other growths can thrive or even a substance that acts between other substances, as in the use of a solvent medium in painting. In geometry, the *median* is the line that connects the vertex of a triangle to the midpoint of its opposing side – in anatomy, it is the line that divides bodies into two symmetrical parts. In mathematics, the *arithmetic mean* is a value at the center of all described values. Lastly, *media* (which is related to *medium*) is the means of communication and connection. Its current use defines all the means utilized to communicate information or content and print and broadcast media are the most common usages of this term. However, we should recognize that their hegemony is a rather recent development and that the media of the arts and architecture were at times predominant. That is why sacred architecture is often the most effective way to understand the beliefs of the religions that created it.

Aims of the Book

This book aims to contribute to the body of knowledge concerning the dynamic interactions sacred architecture requires, as well as its symbolism, ritual use, and cultural significance. Its intentions include framing broadened understandings of architecture. It positions architecture as a cultural artifact that expresses and influences the preoccupations, prejudices, values, and aspirations of the communal human endeavors we (inadequately) call culture. To do so, the book includes philosophical traditions that analogously express and influence cultural self-definitions and activities, and compares them to other cultural outputs – primarily religious beliefs and practices but also other creative media. It argues that architecture, like any communicative media, employs language that is accessible to a critical mass of participants while retaining sufficient nuance and variability of interpretation to facilitate personal resonances and connections. It recognizes that the language of architecture is primarily formal and scenographic and that through this media architecture is referential – leading one to connections with related cultural outputs, and thus contributing to individual and communal elucidation. It also suggests that because architecture provides the setting for communal activities, it consequently supports the most potent of human endeavors, the shared cooperative pursuit of knowledge, understanding, consciousness, and improvement.

In this book I focus on the more interstitial, hidden, and mysterious aspects of architecture to argue that traditionally it served as a media that incorporated and communicated content, engendered emotional and corporal responses and served to orient one in the world. This theoretical approach is consistent with more nuanced and multivalent understandings of architectural form and space, and includes a much broader context within which architecture performs and is experienced. It recognizes the power of architecture to re-veal ("un-veil"), to elucidate, and to transform – a concept intrinsic to architecture in the past, often misunderstood in the modern era, and essential that we reconsider today.

Theoretical Approaches

How do we effectively frame the issues and cogently establish reliable understandings of a cultural output as complex, nuanced, and ineffable as sacred architecture? First of all, we need to clearly establish the scope and limitations of our study and our methods of interpretation. Overall, I adopt philosophical approaches to understanding architecture, for, in the words of Hans-Georg Gadamer, "where no one else can understand, it seems that the philosopher is called for."[8] More specifically, I utilize comparative and intersubjective perspectives to synthesize a broad range of cultural contexts and the diverse communicative media, socio-political and religious agendas, and ritual uses of sacred architecture. It is in the "in-between" of the complex forms, media, agendas, and ritual uses that constitute sacred architecture that new understandings, from a contemporary perspective, might be gained. In this context, hermeneutical interpretive methodologies are put in the service of conceptualizing a "middle ground" of understandings and a holistic examination of predominant themes in sacred architecture. The process of analyzing certain aspects of the cultural outputs of the past, and applying current thinking to them, may establish interpretations that hold meaning for us today.

Pertinent aspects of phenomenology are put into the service of exploring the participatory agency of sacred places, the roles our bodies play in connecting with place, and the importance of embodied experience in deciphering place and its meaning. Together, hermeneutics and phenomenology are applied to structure and contextualize the ephemeral aspects of architecture. Similarly, Buddhist and American Transcendentalist philosophies are incorporated to bring attention to the poetic and immaterial aspects of architecture. In this manner, I hope to deepen the discussion of the interrelationship of place, experience, and meaning, and offer new methodologies for interpreting architecture. I do not comprehensively or exclusively apply any of these philosophies, perspectives, or practices, but utilize them in service of the book's comparative and integrative goals. Nor do I presume to find unequivocal answers, but within defined contexts, aim to comprehensively frame as many questions as appropriate and reach as many conclusions as possible.

The book interprets provocative, legible, and meaningful works of architecture by means of their morphology, symbolism, and religio-cultural agendas and aims to bring them alive as enduring (albeit changeable) cultural artifacts. From a hermeneutic perspective the enduring significance of sacred places lies in their historical understandings and experiential effects. From a phenomenological perspective, I argue that the sensual experience of architecture needs to be incorporated into any interpretations of its symbolism and meaning – it is only through the inclusion of the dynamics of spatial sequencing and serial symbolic content that more complete understandings can be achieved. Therefore, because this book focuses, in part, on the haptic, kinesthetic, perceptual, and emotional experience of place, most of the examples are those that I personally visited. At some, I spent extended periods of time and utilized sketching, measuring, observing (and, at times, participating in) rituals, walking, and sitting in silence as the means to connect with their presence. At all, I concentrated on the evocative and active nature of sacred places, and examined their more occulted and mysterious aspects.

The book positions architecture as a media and means of embodying symbolism. For example, the house that Carl Gustav Jung built in Bollingen, Switzerland, illustrates the making of architecture as an articulate symbolic activity. In this context, the media of architecture, similar to other arts, serves as a means to articulate concepts that otherwise would not find expression. Subsequent examples address the variety of media and means employed by sacred architecture in support of its mediating roles. Beginning with the primordial materials of earth and stone, I discuss how the earliest architecture articulated fundamental relationships and, in particular, an intermediate physical and metaphorical place. Other means are subsequently presented and illustrated through case studies – environmental appropriations and displacements, vistas and juxtapositions, surface and scenographic elements, spatial sequences, geometry and proportion, and their often potent distillations and combinations. In all, connections are established between the cultural intentions, symbolic agendas, and ritual requirements – and the architectural means utilized to achieve them.

Because this book focuses on the shared themes of the mediating roles of sacred architecture, it adopts pan-cultural and trans-historical perspectives. Therefore, it does not utilize a timeline or stylistic approach to the history of architecture or the traditional, evidence-based analysis of examples attendant to historicism. It benefits from focused studies of this type, but adopts a more homological and interpretive approach to the subject. There is much value in understanding the past not as a frozen artifact with fixed meanings, but as an accessible knowledge base that has contemporary relevance. That said, any study that aims to decipher the meaning of historical architectural sites needs to establish its context and scope through a modicum of historical and textual evidence. Therefore, I include appropriate scriptural sources and historical evidence as a means to reveal the pertinent events and cultural forces that helped to shape the architecture.

This is a deliberately ecumenical, multicultural book. I have included a range of examples drawn from most of the world's faiths. However, it is not a comprehensive work – some pertinent cultures and historical periods are under-represented, overlooked, or omitted. The descriptions and analysis that follow are selective, chosen because of their appropriateness to the subject and their potential to illustrate specific concepts, ritual uses, and historical perspectives. In some cases, I have deliberately chosen sites or buildings that, up to now, have not been afforded scholarship commensurate with their significance, to challenge the cultural prejudices that may have excluded them and redress their marginalization. Even though I often focus on an example's efficacy in facilitating meaningful interactions and connections for its users, I do not uncritically posit any as exemplars. Instead, I am much more interested in crafting a middle path of interpretation that identifies effective (and interesting) examples as worthy of scholarship in their own right, as a means to demonstrate particular interpretive methodologies, and hopefully offer concepts that can aid, in some fashion, contemporary architectural theory and practice.

This book recognizes the limits of understanding past cultures and their architectural artifacts, and the specific challenges faced when the author may be outside of the culture, language, or religion. However, the objective perspective gained by a supra-cultural position has the potential to discover new knowledge and interpretations. Recognizing and incorporating present-day methods of interpretation while directly engaging the physical presence of the architecture establish an analytical middle ground that mediates between past and present. This intersubjective position has the potential to integrate past and present contexts and reach new conclusions that have contemporary significance and value.[9]

I also recognize the risks of any study that attempts to establish parallels between a diverse number of examples. Because my diverse scholarly interests find their focus in archetypes, themes, and patterns, at times, important (or at least interesting) information, required in focused historical studies but inappropriate in holistic ones, has been omitted. Any enterprise that looks at architecture from new and syncretic viewpoints has a risk of misinterpretation or misappropriation, but one, I feel, that is justified by its larger goals. I have included detailed case studies, in part, to ameliorate the risks of generalization and de-contextualism attendant on thematic discussions but, more importantly, as a means to more thoroughly explore and explain particular issues. And because I address a broad range of examples and synthesize a number of theoretical approaches (instead of expanding on just one), this means that at times I must be a generalist, not a specialist. Because I am interested in what lies in-between, I do not claim expertise in any one thing. If I have any expertise, it lies in the interstitial – the space between styles, periods, or approaches.

By necessity, a focus on architecture as a cultural artifact leads to multiple interpretations. The contexts are diverse and expansive and our understandings often are nuanced and complex. What we often discover are conditions where multiple relationships are present. However, that everything may be in relationship to other things does not mean they are relative or are not subject to some versions of hierarchies of value. We do need to adopt a position, though it is incumbent on us to be cognizant of our reasons to do so, the types of choices, and the limitations that may result. Moreover, we need to confront contemporary cultural and theoretical prejudices and recognize the presumptions that we bring to any analytical and interpretive tasks. In architectural theory, subjective self-awareness of our motivations and the postulations of objective polemical positions, are not mutually exclusive. Making theoretical choices (and they are choices), reveals the contexts within which we operate and allows us to explore these dimensions in depth. Convictions provide focus, not *a priori* conclusions, and are the rational impetus for meaningful explorations and outcomes.

Philosophical and Interpretive Interests

With this in mind, the following summarizes the context of the book's philosophical and interpretive interests and trajectories:

- Religion, religious figures, ritual, and their architectural settings have traditionally been put in service of mediating between humans and the knowledge or understanding they seek or the gods they worship.
- Use and ritual are the means by which architectural settings are completed and vivified.
- Architecture is a cultural artifact that responds to its social, political, economic, and environmental contexts and expresses a complex matrix of cultural beliefs and imperatives.
- Architecture is a communicative media that contains and expresses symbolic, mythological, doctrinal, socio-political, and, in some cases, historical content. It is an active agent that performs didactic, elucidative, exhortative, and, in some cases, coercive roles.

- Architecture can only be fully understood through interpretations of the complex imperatives and contexts that inform its production. Hermeneutic, homological, and integrative perspectives and methodologies are effective means to establish an intersubjective middle ground.
- Understanding the ephemeral, mysterious, poetic, and immaterial aspects of architecture is essential to deciphering its content. The haptic, kinesthetic, and multi-sensory experiences of architecture are intrinsic to its significance and meaning. Applying phenomenological and related philosophical traditions are effective means to understand the synesthesia of architecture.
- The application of precedent and the pan-cultural and trans-historical aspects of architecture, as a means to codify and understand repeating, shared patterns in architecture, is an essential component of interpreting architecture. Understanding the morphology, structure, and space of examples and the typology of related design organizations and strategies are intrinsic to this process.
- Substantive understandings of architecture need to confront contemporary cultural and theoretical prejudices and recognize the presumptions that we bring to any analytical and interpretive task.

Each chapter provides the interpretive means employed or the common themes discovered regarding the mediating roles of sacred architecture. Chapters 2–4 provide an overview of the religious contexts, principal theories, and methodologies employed in this study. Chapters 5–9 utilize specific examples and case studies to illustrate the various aspects of the mediating roles that sacred architecture performs.

Chapter 2 identifies our bodies as mediators between oneself, others, and the environment (natural and built), and introduces the argument that it is only through the incorporation of the multi-sensory experiences of architecture that more complete understandings can be achieved. Phenomenology is presented as an antidote to contemporary visual biases and an effective methodology for including subjective experiences in critical inquiries. Hermeneutics is introduced as a means to effectively apply phenomenology and synthesize a broad spectrum of criteria in the analysis of architecture, and proposes that it is the reciprocal dialog of hermeneutics that can lead to more substantial readings of architecture. All of which serve to establish a theoretical "middle ground" to negotiate the diverse and multi-perspectival contexts of architecture.

Chapter 3 presents American Transcendentalism and Buddhism as philosophical practices that, because they require participation to communicate their content, provide methodologies and perspectives appropriate to interpreting architecture and our study. The chapter closes with the argument that the multiple aspects of architecture reveal its multifarious and nuanced cultural contexts, symbols, roles, and uses, and produces more complete, nuanced interpretations.

Chapter 4 provides an overview of the communicative and mediating roles of symbolism and how they are distilled and expanded in sacred settings. Meditating agents in religion – oracles, shamans, prayers, and rituals – are presented as analogous examples of the mediating roles that sacred architecture often performs and, in this context, architectural theories regarding the "in-between" are discussed. Interpretations of the shared symbolic language of the Medieval Western church, through the case study of Saint Foy in Conques, France, conclude the chapter.

Chapter 5 presents architecture as a participatory media through which humans may symbolize and render religious, social, and psychological conditions. The case study of Carl Jung's house in Bollingen, Switzerland, illustrates how Jung used architecture and other plastic arts as a means of "inner work" and personal transformation.

Chapter 6 discusses the paired environmental conditions of earth and sky as a metaphorical separation that architecture, from its earliest incarnations, was put in service of bridging. Neolithic European examples lead to the case study of Native American earthworks, burial mounds, and effigy figures to illustrate how, beginning with primordial architecture, symbolic and ritual places were created to define an articulate "place in the world."

Chapter 7 outlines the ways in which different path types served to define the boundaries of the sacred place, communicate symbolic narratives, and accommodate ritual activities. The case study of the Korean Zen Buddhist monastery Tongdo is presented in the context of the path as a mediator and the monastery as serving diverse symbolic and ritual agendas.

Chapter 8 addresses the roles of geometry and proportion in the dual agendas of integrating sacred architecture and joining it with the order represented by the cosmos. The modernist Saint Benedict's Abbey at Vaals, Holland, by the Dutch Benedictine monk Hans van der Laan, illustrates how the proportioning system he developed served to facilitate participation, to convey the orders it presents, and to symbolize the interconnection of the architecture with its larger contexts.

Chapter 9 argues that sacred architecture was often conceived as a cosmogram – perfected worlds that symbolized connection and completion. A discussion of the Pantheon in Rome and the Hagia Sophia in Istanbul leads to the Ottoman Era mosques by Mimar Sinan. The case studies of the Selimiye and Sokollu Kadirga Mosques are presented as potent amalgams of socio-political agendas, religious symbolism, ritual settings, and architectural expression.

The Conclusion posits new understandings of architecture and broadened perspectives regarding its role in materializing culture, incorporating symbolism, facilitating ritual, and deepening its impact through the sensual experiences it provides. It repositions architecture as a much more active agent in expressing and influencing a culture, and insists that, as a predominant cultural output, architecture is more important and influential than is commonly recognized in our time and culture. It argues that architecture is didactic and elucidative – it communicates content, often at multiple levels and means for a diversity of audiences over a range of time. The most successful architecture reaches a broad spectrum of constituents and remains relevant long after the culture that produced it has lost its relevancy. In this way, it transcends culture and time, and exists, like all great art, in a more timeless manner. Hermeneutic, phenomenological, American Transcendentalist, and Buddhist interpretive and reflective methodologies and philosophies are revisited and positioned as a means to expand contemporary discourses on the meaning and significance of the built environment. The discussion of the mediating roles of sacred architecture is broadened by considerations of the potency of "im-mediate," or unmediated experiences. Lastly, elements of an authentic and engaging architecture are outlined, and suggestions posited regarding the lessons for contemporary practice the interpretive methodologies and examples might offer.

Finally, it should be stated that this is fundamentally an optimistic book. It argues that architecture and the built environment can make our lives, and those of succeeding generations, better, more satisfying, and meaningful. It does so by examining appropriate examples of sacred architecture with a particular focus on the sacred center as a place where connection, understanding, and transformation are believed to be possible, and the setting for the most momentous and significant transitions of human life, including personal transformation. Chapter 11, Closing Thoughts, provides reflections on my personal experiences at sacred places that have, at times, been affective, elucidative, and inspiring, and their continuing ontological significance. Louis Kahn reflected that the city was a place where one might discover who we want to be – an observation that suggests the potential of the built environment to change our lives for the better. The promise of effective (and affective) architecture to inform us, improve us, and transform us is at the heart of every optimistic theory of architecture.

Chapter 2

The Middle Ground of Interpretation

Phenomenology, Hermeneutics, and the Sensory Experience of Architecture

> To live is to dance with an unknown partner whose steps we can never wholly predict, to improvise within a field of forces whose shifting qualities we might feel as they play across our skin, or as they pulse between our cells, yet whose ultimate nature we can never entirely grasp or process in thought.
>
> (David Abram)[1]

The Senses as Mediators

To recognize the roles that our senses play in negotiating the built environment is to remember that human existence is fundamentally sensual. Humans are sentient beings – from the Latin *sentire*, which means "to feel." We engage the world through all of our senses that serve as an interface between our surroundings and ourselves. In complex and coordinated ways, we engage the natural and built environment through sight, touch, hearing, smell, and taste – as a means to "make sense" of them. However, according to the poet and naturalist Diane Ackerman, "The senses don't just make sense of life in bold or subtle acts of clarity, they tear reality apart into vibrant morsels and reassemble them into a meaningful pattern."[2]

We can understand our senses not as isolated sense organs, but as an integrated system, and our perceptions as multi-sensory experiences. The psychologist J.J. Gibson argued that the senses are not passive receptors but acquisitive ones actively engaged with the environment, and he outlined five "perceptual systems" – visual, auditory, taste–smell, basic orienting, and haptic.[3] His contributions are significant because they describe integrated systems that are not merely processors of information but, one might say, active aspects of us. All of which serves as an antidote to the contemporary prejudices of Western culture that tend to separate (not integrate) functions, regard perception as information processing, and predominantly rely on vision over other senses.

If there is any part of our physiology that is merely an information processor when it comes to a sensual engagement with the world, it is the brain. Our brains are not sense organs; they are only recipients of messages from our sensory systems. In this regard we can view our cognitive functions as translators

2.1
Perception and experience are multi-sensory – our multifarious senses engage architecture in a synesthesia of connections and meanings. Cathedral of Notre Dame, Amiens, France, begun thirteenth century, view of nave

of sensory input, whereas the body is a transducer (from the Latin *transducere*, which means "to lead across"). However, what we really have is an integrated system, at times referred to as "body–mind" but perhaps more effectively defined as "embodied consciousness." Diane Ackerman suggests that the "mind doesn't really dwell in the brain but travels the whole body on caravans of hormone and enzyme, busily making sense of the compound wonders we catalogue as touch, taste, smell, hearing, vision."[4] In Buddhism, the mind is often described as a sixth sense, an integral component of all of our sense organs, but with its own specific functions.[5] Our engagement with the world can be understood as a symphony of choreographed senses – a holistic system of being. Together they constitute a unified sense organ that, for functional, pleasurable, and meaningful reasons, is primed to deeply engage the world.

The Multi-sensory Experience of Architecture

Steen Eiler Rasmussen succinctly summarized the multi-sensory experience of architecture when he stated: "it is not enough to see architecture; you must experience it."[6] Juhani Pallasmaa argues that architecture engages our senses, which leads to a deeper ontological engagement with the world.[7] He reminds us that perception and experience are multi-sensory – our multifarious senses engage architecture in a synesthesia of connections and meanings. For Pallasmaa, there is "an architecture that also recognizes the realms of hearing, smell and taste."[8] In auditory experience, "the space traced by the ear in the darkness becomes a cavity sculpted directly in the interior of the mind," and though "our look wanders lonesomely in the dark depths of the cathedral . . . the sounds of the organ makes us immediately experience our affinity with the space."[9] He describes the other senses in evocative prose that brings these often hidden aspects of architecture alive. "The nose makes the eyes remember," the "door handle is the handshake of a building," and "highly polished colour or wood surfaces frequently present themselves to the unconscious appreciation of the tongue."[10] Pallasmaa's "delicious" prose reminds us that there is much more to the experience of architecture, especially buildings that, whether consciously or unconsciously, invite a deep and sensual communion with their spaces. To "taste" a building is to take it deeply into ourselves, to make it part of us. Thus we may appreciate the intimacy of meaningful connections through the media of architecture, a coition between space and ourselves.[11]

Stating the obvious point that our experience of being, of inhabiting our places, is sensual, is often a defense against the "ocular centrism" of contemporary culture and architecture. Pallasmaa describes the "pathology of everyday architecture" as attributable to "ocular bias,"[12] and states: "modernist design has housed the intellect and the eye, but has left the body and other senses, as well as our memories and dreams, homeless." An architectural culture distinguished by "self-expression, detachment and alienation,"[13] has, for Pallasmaa, resulted in an "architectural autism"[14] of withdrawal from the meaningful, sensual world. The hegemony of vision as a cultural phenomenon has been thoroughly established by Pallasmaa (who cites contemporary philosophers such as David Levin[15]), to the extent that it is not useful for our purposes to provide further scholarship (or complaints). It is more useful to recognize that, for many reasons, the dominance of vision in nearly all cultural productions, including some of the more egregious examples in architecture, is too often "sense-less."

We can elaborate on Pallasmaa's fruitful discussion of the multi-sensory experience of architecture as a means to more clearly frame the discussion regarding the often subtle but deep ways sacred architecture engages our senses, connects with us, and leads us to subsequent connections. First, we must recognize the power of the visual and the fact that physiologically we are pre-dominantly visual creatures. Architecture and, in particular, sacred architecture provides dynamic visual experiences. Movement, approach, shifting views in concert with gradations and modulations of light and shadow, present an ever-changing panoply of images that entice and engage us. Whereas I would suggest that we are all, more or less, fluent in the language of vision, for physio-logical and cultural reasons, we are less versed in either engaging or critically examining our other senses, to which I now turn.

The relationship between seeing and touch is well known – we tend to touch things as a means to confirm or augment what we see. Textually rich environments – rough or smooth, soft or hard – invite our intimate caresses and respond by revealing what we cannot see. The engagement of our ears and hearing with the built environment is a gradient from gentle nuance to brash cacophony. If we are quiet and still, we can gauge space and our relationship to it through its auditory qualities. Quite simply, a small space feels compressed, and a large one expansive due to its relationship to the space inside, and mechanisms of, our ears, independent of sound. We see and touch textures and materials, but of course, they also affect the auditory qualities of a space. And sound, from echoing footsteps, to hushed whispers, to vibrating musical crescendos, all help us to measure, to "read" and thus connect with, an arch-itectural setting. Sound is also connected with memory. The Japanese Zen monk Shunryu Suzuki recalled, after returning to his home monastery Eiheiji, how deeply sounds affected him. "I heard the various sounds of practice – the bells and the monks reciting the sutra – and I had a deep feeling. There were tears flowing out of my eyes, nose, and mouth!"[16]

The relationship between smell and memory and its ability to construct meaning is also well known, but not often the subject of architectural scholar-ship. From the Song of Solomon, to Proust, to Baudelaire – Western literature includes examples where smell is the dominant sense. Baudelaire describes the relationship between memory and the smells of his lover's hair as:

> Blue hair, the night's outspread pavilion,
> The blue of boundless heaven you restore;
> Upon your downy twisted locks undone,
> I seek the sweet intoxication
> Of cocoa-nut oil, mingled musk and tar.
>
> For long, for ever, in your heavy mane
> The sapphire, ruby, pearl I'll scatter free,
> So that I'll never plead to you in vain:
> You my oasis, flask elysian
> From which I drink long draughts of memory![17]

2.2
Textually rich environments –
rough or smooth, soft or hard
– invite our intimate caresses
and respond by revealing
what we cannot see. Jonas
Salk Institute for Biological
Studies, La Jolla, CA, Louis I.
Kahn, 1965, view of arcade

The childhood smell of home, for most of us, was a first, distinctive, and encompassing phenomenon of primary ontological importance. Place, the feeling of "being home," and smell are intrinsically and intimately intertwined. The familiar smells of particular sacred places also have this ability to speak to us about "home."[18] When we speak about the taste of architecture, we need to include empathy. Much of our engagement with architecture is not through

2.3
Much of our engagement with architecture is not through direct contact, but through the act of empathy, of emotionally responding to an object, image, or space from a distance. Great Mosque, Bursa, Turkey, fourteenth century, central fountain

direct contact, but through the act of empathy, of emotionally responding to an object, image, or space from a distance. In this sense, we may be said to taste the refreshing water gushing from the courtyard fountain, or imbibe the cool, hard marble on the altar as we press our face to the floor in prayer. Sensually rich architecture provides settings where we intimately engage in intercourse, literally a "running between" or co-joining, between us and the other.

The experience of sacred architecture takes us out of the everyday. Similar to the experience of wild nature, we enter a different environment where our senses are confronted by the complexity and profusion of images and surface decoration typical of many sacred places. Sacred places are sensual places, however incongruous this may seem considering the beliefs and practices of the dominant Western religions. Through a choreography of space and sequence, light and shadow – in consort with smells, sounds, touch, and, in some cases, taste – we are engaged, brought to the present, and thus prepared

for connections outside of ourselves. Just as sacred architecture deliberately choreographs space and sequence for desired affects, the other senses are engaged as well – to heighten the intensity of our experience through the mediation of our senses. There are, of course, many built environments that engage the senses. The studied picturesque of eighteenth-century English narrative gardens, influenced by the ideas of the sublime, aimed to heighten experience through sensual and associative means. Others may be said to assault our senses – open-air markets, Middle Eastern souks, and busy restaurants come to mind. An afternoon spent at a French Saturday market or in the Grand Bazaar in Istanbul leaves one sensually exhilarated, but there is an important difference between sensorially rich environments and the sacred. It is in sacred architecture that the sensory is joined with the symbolic and brought to life through ritual.

2.4
The experience of sacred architecture takes us out of the everyday. Similar to the experience of wild nature, we enter a different environment where our senses are confronted by the complexity and profusion of images and surface decoration typical of many sacred places. Court of Lions, Palace of the Alhambra, Granada, Spain, fourteenth century, detail of façade

Phenomenology

Phenomenology is a 100-year-old European philosophical tradition that from its founding promoted the inclusion of subjective experiences into the objective sciences. Its assertion that subjective experience can be objectively applied in philosophical inquiry is pertinent to any discussion regarding the sensory experience of architecture and it has substantially informed postmodern theoreticians with an interest in this aspect of architecture. Edmund Husserl

(1859–1938) is recognized as the first to outline the philosophy of phenomenology, but it is most popularly known through the writings of Martin Heidegger (1889–1976) and his principal treatise *Being and Time* (1927).

A number of principal themes define the phenomenological project. Foremost is its challenge to scientific positivism, which has dominated the physical and social sciences, and prejudices the objectively measurable, and marginalizes that which is not subject to scientific metrics. According to the contemporary philosopher (and magician) David Abram, "Phenomenology is the Western philosophical tradition that has most forcefully called into question the modern assumption of a single, wholly determinable, objective reality."[19] In scientific rationalism, the subject is neutral, objective, and anonymous as a means to eliminate the compromising prejudice of personal opinions or pre-assumptions. The subject, in essence, is a means of recording and analyzing data through the agency of the intellect. René Descartes (1596–1650), and in particular his *Meditations on First Philosophy* (1641), is regularly cited as the framer of this scientific worldview and, by extension, the so-called scientific method.

Phenomenology challenges the hegemony of scientism and insists that the subject is always part of any scientific inquiry. The early phenomenologists argued that maintaining a distance between subject and object denied the subjectivity that is intrinsic to any cognitive activity and truncated the ability to fully experience (and subsequently understand) the observed phenomenon. It is only by recognizing and contextualizing the subjectivity we bring to any analytic enterprise can we fully engage the work at hand. In other words, phenomenology aimed to establish an objective understanding of subjectivity. It has been described as "a radical way of doing philosophy, a practice rather than a system" and positioned itself, counter to positivism and empiricism, as a holistic approach that stressed the "mediating role of the body in perception."[20]

In architectural theory, however, it is the phenomenological battle cry of a return of "back to the things themselves" that has been predominantly emphasized. As a postmodern enterprise, architectural phenomenologists attack what they perceive to be a theoretical field truncated by the same alienated formal scientism that Husserl and others rebelled against. Phenomenology is posited as a means to more substantially understand architecture and as an antidote to the distanced, academic discourse that has dominated the humanities during the postmodern era. Heidegger has held a privileged position in architectural phenomenology and, even though he seldom wrote directly about architecture, *Being and Time* and "Building, Dwelling, Thinking" have proven to be highly adaptable to theoretical arguments regarding the meaning and experience of architecture and place.[21] Heidegger's terms of *Dasein* ("There-Being") and *In-der-Welt-sein* ("Being-in-the-World") have enjoyed a wide variety of interpretations and applications.

That architectural theoreticians who have found inspiration in Heidegger have made important contributions to the field is indisputable and this book will utilize many of their important findings. However, the over-emphasis on Heidegger has resulted in the marginalizing or exclusion of other, perhaps more important voices – philosophical and theoretical views that this book endeavors to incorporate. At times, the reactive positions of phenomenology's champions result in an exclusive, anti-objective polemics that is counter to its inclusive foundations.[22] It is important to recall that Husserl, for example, established a philosophy and means of inquiry that aimed at a quantifiable "science of experience." Central to his approach is the interaction and interpenetration of our bodies with the environment that he describes as follows:

> The Body is, in the first place, the *medium of all perception*; it is the *organ of perception* and is necessarily involved in all perception. In seeing, the eyes are directed upon the seen and run over its edges, surfaces, etc. When it touches objects, the hand slides over them. Moving myself, I bring my ear closer in order to hear. Perceptual apprehension presupposes sensation-contents, which play their necessary role for the constitution of the appearances of the real things themselves. *To the possibility of experience there pertains, however, the spontaneity of the courses* of presenting acts of sensation, which are accompanied by a series of kinesthetic sensations and are dependent on them as motivated: *given with the localization of the kinesthetic series in the relevant moving member of the Body is the fact that in all perception and perceptual exhibition (experience) the Body is involved as feely moved sense organ, as feely moved totality of sense organs,* and hence there is also given the fact that, on this original foundation, all that is thingly-real in the surrounding world of the Ego has its relation to the body.[23]
>
> (Capitalization and italics in original)

For Husserl, the "thingly-real" (a term we will adopt to describe the sensate real), is apprehended by the "ego" through the "medium" of the body. Husserl describes this "ego" in Kantian terms as "transcendental," a disembodied essence removed and inaccessible to scientific means of analysis. In other words the subject, through the mediation of the body, understands the object. On the other hand, Maurice Merleau-Ponty (1908–1961), who was interested in the integration of mind and body, conceptualized an embodied consciousness termed the "body–subject," and the interrelationship of the "body–subject" and the object.[24] Both of their postulations are applicable to the interpretation of sacred architecture. Through Husserl we can appreciate the intimate participation of the body, our bundle of integrated senses, as a mediator between our memory and cognition – and the built environment. Merleau-Ponty helps us to understand the interrelationship of embodied consciousness and the environment, the realm of more ephemeral, intuitive, and psychic phenomena central to what might be described as the "religious experience."

The postmodern architectural theoretician Christian Norberg-Schulz (1926–2000) made important contributions to architectural theories that focus on the phenomenal aspects of place. Even though his writings on phenomenology rely almost exclusively on Heidegger (and in particular the short essay "Building, Dwelling, Thinking") for its phenomenological foundations,[25] his architectural applications and interpretations of Heidegger provide useful and applicable theories regarding the roles and meaning of architecture. Norberg-Schulz is primarily interested in the "psychic implications of architecture rather than its practical side" – the ability of architecture to "keep and transmit meanings" in the service of helping humans establish an "existential foothold" and thus to "dwell" meaningfully in the world.[26] The meaning and significance of architecture, often described simply as "place," are a result of its cultural and environmental contexts. Norberg-Schulz is not interested in multiple contexts or interpretations of cultural productions through the media of architecture, but of describing "meaning" itself as an antidote to the limitations of formal and functional analysis. "Place" he connects with action (as in to "take place"), as a means to describe an authentic engagement with the world. Phenomenology, according to Norberg-Schulz, "was conceived as a 'return to things,' as opposed to abstractions and mental constructions."[27] It is equated with the "poetic dimension," and positioned as a bulwark against the hegemony of scientism. He often stresses that "The place is the concrete manifestation of man's dwelling, and his identity depends on his belonging to places."[28]

There is an aspect of Romantic longing found in Norberg-Schulz's writings that may limit, but certainly does not negate, their appropriateness to contemporary architectural issues and the subject of this study. In fact, a certain Romantic strain is understandable in a theory that overly relies on Heidegger for its extra-disciplinary inspiration and sources. It is useful to be reminded by Norberg-Schulz, through the lens of Heidegger, that man "dwells" between heaven and earth, an "in-between" zone, the "gathering middle" in Heidegger's terms, that mirrors man's existential setting. Within this physical and philosophical liminal zone, man builds as a means to "order reality" and the "primary purpose of architecture is hence to make the world visible." This is a perspective, regardless of its sources and limitations, that succinctly summarizes an important theoretical position that is essential to understanding sacred architecture as a mediator.

Alberto Perez-Gomez brings additional and appropriate perspectives to cultural, phenomenological, and symbolic interpretation of architecture. Perez-Gomez provides a view sympathetic to Norberg-Schulz's when he states: "Architecture offers societies a place for existential orientation. As representations of meaningful action, it contributes to an understanding of one's place in the world."[29] Perez-Gomez is similarly critical of the formal and material prejudices of contemporary architecture when he argues that "materialistic and technological alternatives for architecture – however sophisticated and justifiable they may be, in view of our historical failures – do not answer satisfactorily to the complex desire that defines humanity."[30] Perez-Gomez makes clear the necessity of reclaiming meaning and experience in architecture. He laments the "modern epidemic of empty formalism and banal functionalism,"[31] and dismisses contemporary advanced digital media investigations. "Made possible by powerful computers and ingenious software," he writes, "the new algorithmic magic creates novelty without love, resulting in short-lived seduction, typically without concern for embodied cultural experience, character and appropriateness."[32] Beauty and meaning are interdependent for Perez-Gomez, and it is clear that for him much contemporary work has neither. What is needed is an architecture that provides an antidote to our materialistic and technologically prejudiced culture.[33] Perez-Gomez's linking of the erotic tension of delay and fulfillment with the anticipation and attainment of increasingly sacred spaces provides an important perspective on architectural settings that were created as propitious places where human and divine might be co-joined. The role that our bodies play in deciphering place and content is often undervalued or forgotten, as well as the power of the ephemeral, the mysterious, and the poetic to transform our view of the world. But as the author asserts, "The experience of the poetic, like sexuality, jolts us and can change our life."[34]

Juhani Pallasmaa's challenge to the "asertonic gaze" of "ocularcentrism" is predicated on his insistence on a reintegration of all the senses regarding the experience and significance of architecture. Implicit is the assertion that the more the formal and visual language dominates, the more truncated our depth of experiences becomes. The distance between sensual experience and place is mirrored by the narcissistic and nihilistic separation of architects from the physical places they conceptualize. The antidote, for Pallasmaa, is a reconsideration of the importance that all the senses play in our palpable and concrete interactions with the built environment. He asserts: "It is difficult to think of a nihilistic touch."[35]

Pallasmaa's articulation of the problems produced by the prejudices (and progress) of contemporary architectural culture and their potential resolution, provides helpful considerations regarding the ability of architecture to deeply engage us and make meaningful connections beyond our initial contact. When he states: "Architecture is the art of reconciliation between ourselves and the world, and this mediation takes place through the senses," he suggests a double mediation – our senses connect us with the place and the place connects us with the "world." Powerful, sensual architecture "touches" us, and once contact is established, connects us to psychic and symbolic territories that are both broader and deeper. The sensual place is where this profound engagement is imagined and is possible. For Pallasmaa, "architecture is engaged with fundamental existential questions in its way of representing and structuring action and power, societal and cultural orders, interaction and separation, identity and memory," and "the timeless task of architecture is to create embodied existential metaphors that concretize and structure man's being in the world."

These are timely and useful perspectives that appropriately question contemporary cultural prejudices and define the deeper phenomenological, ontological, and symbolic roles played by architecture. They suggest that architects have a responsibility to recognize these broader contexts and create meaningful places in service of them. According to Norberg-Schulz, it is incumbent on us to strive to create places where humans can "dwell." In the words of the architectural theoreticians Kent Bloomer and Charles Moore,

> The landscape of the human inner world of landmarks, coordinates, hierarchies, and especially boundaries serves, we believe, as the only humane starting point for the organization of the space around us, which, more than being perceived, is inhabited by us.[36]

Hermeneutics

Phenomenology can be understood as a counterpoint to a predominant contemporary worldview described, in part, by positivism and scientism. This is conveniently illustrated by the philosophy of Descartes (as many have pointed out), which doubts the veracity of the thinking mind and thus prejudices the "rational facts" of a measurable world. The obverse of the statement *cogito ergo sum* – "I think, therefore I am" – is that without the agency of our mind, we do not exist, thus establishing a world that exists independent from us that can only be effectively studied from an objective position. Only in this way can cultural traditions and individual preferences be eliminated. The scientist becomes an anonymous transducer of data.

Phenomenology rejects the scientific separation of subject and object and re-inserts individual perspectives into scientific and scholarly activity. However, this immediately raises the question – how does one engage, study, and understand a world that is no longer bifurcated by the terms objective and subjective? If this new understanding depends, in part, on relative, individual perspectives, is there any chance of establishing a modicum of objective truths? Hermeneutics, a branch of phenomenology, aims to provide answers to these questions and methodologies to reconcile them.

Hermeneutics emerged from eighteenth-century theological scholarship and is attributed to the Protestant theologian Friedrich Schleiermacher (1768–1834). Schleiermacher challenged the prevailing rationalism and conservatism of his time (exemplified architecturally by the Neo-Classicism of Karl Friedrich Schinkel). Its impetus was the belief that objective readings of scripture were isolating the text in its historical context and compromising its ability to maintain contemporary relevance.[37] Hermeneutic methods were developed to re-introduce the importance of interpretation as a means to re-vivify the meaning of scripture in its present setting and re-present it as a living document. Contemporary hermeneutics has been influenced by postmodern perspectives that posit three essential points: (1) "reality" is not given, but is constructed by human agency; (2) meaning is always dependent on its context; and (3) no one perspective should be privileged, because contexts are endless.[38] These three areas of constructivism, contextualism, and multi-perspectivalism are essential to understanding hermeneutics and its applications to architectural interpretation.[39]

Hermeneutics aims to dissolve the cultural and historical distance of objective "readings" and insists that any substantial understandings require the engagement of a researcher with their subject matter. Engagements of this type, by necessity, are the result of an individual's corporal and intellectual participation with their enquiry. It is the difference between analyzing a traditional dance as an historical artifact and interpreting the same dance from a contemporary perspective (and even as a participant). Because contemporary interpretations emerge from multiple individuals (and contexts), multiple subjective positions result. We no longer have the solitary, anonymous scientist (or historian) translating empirical data to arrive at a unitary, objective conclusion, but numerous interlocutors producing collective responses to the observed or experienced object. The findings are therefore found between the subjects – an intersubjective realm that mediates between individuals and their findings, and between the findings themselves. It is through the recognition of multiple interpretations that new and potentially hybrid or integrated understandings can be established.[40]

Ken Wilber addresses hermeneutics from the perspective of comparative religion. He describes "Phenomenological-Hermeneutics" as "emphatic interpretation," where to take the object into oneself, to enter the circle "in a particular historical context," is required. This engagement has the potential to discover "the nature and meaning of mental acts *as* mental acts" and because a "mental event" or "concept" refers to other "entities" which in turn do the same, we are now involved in an "intersubjective circle of symbolic meanings." According to Wilber, hermeneutics is the branch of phenomenology that is particularly focused with interpreting intersubjective meanings. It is a "dialogical dance" where one connection leads to another – a spiraling sequence of intersubjective connections otherwise known as the "hermeneutic cycle." The monological gaze of science is predisposed to *describe* – the dialogical activity of intersubjectivity leads to *understanding*.[41]

Contemporary hermeneutics is most closely associated with the work of Hans-Georg Gadamer (1900–2002).[42] Gadamer challenged the "monological gaze of modern science" and insisted that "human knowledge" and "human practice" depend on "tradition and its prejudices" much more than scientific models allow. Gadamer's philosophy is positioned between the scientific rationalism of Descartes and the relativism of postmodernism. The concepts and methodologies of hermeneutics, outlined in *Truth and Method* (1960), recognize that knowledge is gained as a relative condition of multiple (but not unlimited) aspects. A presentation of art is both declarative and dialogical and in this manner art is always contemporary because we have the ability to engage it in the present. For Gadamer, "The genuine reception and experience of a work of art can exist only for one who 'plays along,' that is, one who performs in an active way himself."[43] This, for Gadamer, is a counter-project to the historicizing of art, which, through its reduction of art to historical and stylistic categories, effects the distancing of the individual and the work.[44] Gadamer, taking his inspiration from Plato, argues that Greek tragedy may *present* the human condition, but the spectator *participates* in it:

> The spectator does not hold himself aloof at the distance characteristic of an aesthetic consciousness enjoying the art with which something is represented, but rather participates in the communion of being present. The real emphasis of the tragic phenomenon lies ultimately on what is presented and recognized, and to participate in it is not a matter of choice.[45]

In one of his later essays, Gadamer points out that traditionally art was intrinsic to its religious and cultural contexts:

> As far as so-called classical art is concerned, we are talking about the production of works which in themselves were not primarily understood as art. On the contrary, these forms were encountered within a religious or secular context as an adornment of the life-world and of special moments like worship, the representation of a ruler, and things of that kind. As soon as the concept of art took on these features to which we have become accustomed and the

work of art began to stand on its own, divorced from its original context of life, only then did art become simply "art."[46]

Gadamer insists that the "truth" can just as potently be found in art as in science. However, when art distanced itself from its contexts, it became "art for art's sake." As an individual, largely idiosyncratic output, modern art subsequently lost the communal, shared meanings it had possessed (and communicated) in the past. Because art is now isolated from its broader cultural contexts, its power to lead us to meanings outside of the work is diminished. Therefore, contemporary culture has difficulty believing that art (and architecture) have any meanings beyond themselves; thus the usefulness of Gadamer's view regarding architecture as a cultural artifact and its significance and meaning.

Lindsay Jones, like Ken Wilber, approaches hermeneutics from the position of comparative religion, but with a clear focus on sacred architecture. The hermeneutic method, according to Jones, occupies a middle ground between the positivist insistence of unitary "once-and-for-all meanings," and the post-structuralist embrace of infinite progressions of relative signifiers. Jones challenges contemporary scholarly conventions that either apply empirical models to establish certainties of architectural history or those that do not accept any fixed meanings.[47] According to Jones,

> If we are to secure any empirical reliability, with respect to the ways in which specific buildings are actually experienced, we must find a way to transcend this preoccupation with the formal attributes of buildings and this misplaced confidence in the one-to-one correlation between buildings and their meanings.[48]

But that, "Contemporary critical theorists and historians of religion" provide no certainty but often seem most interested in "making the familiar strange." For Jones, hermeneutics possesses the ability to make "the strange familiar,"[49] and Heidegger and Gadamer figure prominently in his work. From a Heideggerian perspective, hermeneutics is both relational and ontological and demands the active engagement of the person with the subject matter. Jones insists that the subjective perspectives we bring to any theoretical undertaking are not only unavoidable but also essential. Referencing Gadamer, he argues that "pre-understandings" (Gadamer's term), "make understanding possible." All understanding is "episodic" and "subjective," and is an "ontological event" that requires a "hermeneutical perspective" to be able to synthesize historical textual evidence with a broad range of more subjective sources.[50] In this way, more complete and diverse understandings of places and their uses can emerge.

The architectural theoretician Robert Mugerauer states that "all understanding is interpretation, that is, contextual," a position that guides his applications of hermeneutic models to decipher architecture and the built environment. He argues that because any analytical activity includes our own prejudices it is necessary to remove the "prejudice against prejudices" in the work of "interpreting environments." This "broadening of our context" seeks to understand the past through incorporating the present, a position that depends on recognizing the limits of traditional scholarship to understand past cultures and their artifacts, while also limiting the breadth of contemporary contexts. In essence, we move to a middle ground between past and present – a mediation between the historical and the contemporary. The result, referencing Gadamer, is a "fusion of horizons, where the past and present contexts come together to make something new of living value," and that may "help us to deal with our contemporary problems."[51]

The application of hermeneutical perspectives and methodologies establishes a middle ground of interpretation – it is neither the linear progression of historical facts in traditional research, or the diffuse, uncentered relativism of post-structural analysis – but seeks the truth in the middle of multiple perspectives. What distinguishes hermeneutics is the self-conscious participation of the interpreter with their object of study. According to Gadamer, interpretation is a method, but also a very human process of inquiry that is fundamentally dialogical. All of which leads to deeper engagement and understanding or, in Gadamer's words, "the work that goes on in a Platonic dialog . . . points towards the One, toward Being, the 'Good,' which is present in the order of the soul, in the constitution of the city, and in the structure of the world."[52]

This study is not exclusively phenomenological or hermeneutic, and recognizes what these methodologies often omit and their limitations regarding a clarity of outcomes. However, it benefits from the important contributions these related philosophies and methodologies can make in establishing a broadened context for the understanding of architecture and, in particular, sacred architecture. It is a "middle way" that includes but goes beyond formal and historical analysis while setting limits on relative subjectivity. It does so by establishing intersubjective connections between the sacred place, its embodied experience, the discrete historical, cultural, environmental, political, liturgical, and religious contexts, and the shared transcendental aspects of the "human condition." Fundamental relationships are established between the architecture, its diverse contexts, and our experience of it. Analogously, especially in the case of sacred places, the architecture serves to "make sense" of our relationship to "the world." And so we have a three-fold or, one might say, triangulated dialog of the interpreter, the architecture, and the world – each providing aspects of the whole within the structure of hermeneutical inquiry.

In summary, I will utilize the following approaches that are included in, but not limited to, phenomenology and hermeneutics:

- incorporating the multiple contexts of sacred architecture;
- applying methodologies that mediate between place, multiple contexts, and ontological significance;
- recognizing the limits of thoroughly understanding the artifacts of past cultures;
- focusing on sacred architecture as living works available for contemporary engagement;
- establishing structural frameworks as a means to contextualize the findings;
- suggesting contemporary lessons offered by historical artifacts.

Chapter 3

Practices of Connection

Applications of Transcendentalist and Buddhist Philosophies

The experience of the beautiful, and particularly the beautiful in art, is the invocation of a potentially whole and holy order of things, wherever it may be found.

(Hans-Georg Gadamer)[1]

Perhaps one of the most important contributions that contemporary hermeneutics brings to interpreting the built environment is that its methods are a means of personal connection and even transformation. When we engage in a dialog with a work of art or architecture, we seek in essence to apply present understandings to the unknown as a means to deepen our understanding of the work, ourselves, and our position in the world. The moments when we understand something deeply and are subsequently changed by this new perspective, is one of hermeneutical interpretation.[2] As Gadamer reminds us, "Always present when we experience something, when unfamiliarity is overcome, where enlightenment, insight and appropriation succeed, the hermeneutical process takes place in bringing something into words and into the common consciousness."[3]

Hermeneutic methods of interpretation can be viewed as a philosophical practice. In this context, it is a means to personally engage art, architecture, and other cultural productions – a reciprocal action that requires that one directly engages their object of study as a means to achieve deeper understandings. There are other philosophical traditions that aim for the personal, profound, perspicacious, and even prescient internal experiences of engagement and connection, and therefore may be able to provide appropriate models regarding the dual (but not separate) aspects of philosophy and practice. Two philosophical traditions and spiritual practices, American Transcendentalism and Buddhism, are discussed next in the context of the profound experience of "being" and its connection to setting or place. These are sources that were more concerned with cultivating meaningful internal and external connections than one often finds in post-Renaissance Western philosophical traditions. A remarkable characteristic of these latter traditions is the absence of any philosophical *practice* coupled with the philosophical *system*. This was a clear departure from the formative roots of Western philosophy, such as the Pythagorean School and the Hellenistic Epicureans and Stoics, where a separation of philosophy and practice would have been incongruous at best.[4]

Even though Transcendentalism did not include specific spiritual practices, it did seek deep engagement with oneself and one's surroundings – intentions or practices that cultivated self-improvement and served to confirm the philosophy itself. Buddhism, on the other hand, provides a detailed philosophy regarding a deep and direct engagement with the world, and provides specific practices as a means to do so. Aspects of these two examples are applied to broaden the discussion regarding the mediating roles of place (and specifically sacred architecture) and the agency of our embodied consciousness in making these connections. Sacred places, either by intuition or design, are often multi-sensory, psychic engagements; therefore, traditions that focused on similar agendas may contribute to our understanding of the intentions and outcomes of exchanges of this type.

Transcendentalism

American Transcendentalism was an intellectual movement of mid-nineteenth-century New England that viewed itself as an antidote to the conservative, Eurocentric intellectual climate of Harvard College and the Cambridge intelligentsia. It was a loose group of intellectuals and Unitarian ministers that never coalesced into a unified school of thought, nor lasted very long, but came to make significant contributions to philosophy and religion. Its beginnings were modest. The founders of the Transcendental Club, Henry Hedge, George Putnam, George Ripley, and Ralph Waldo Emerson, first met in Cambridge in Massachusetts in 1836. Inspired by Kant's "transcendental idealism," they believed that the human intellect unrestrained by preconceptions and cultural limitations had the ability to perceive, engage, and experience the world deeply and authentically. America as a young democracy, birthed but separate from European religion and culture, was viewed as the perfect setting for a new philosophy. America at this time was expanding its boundaries and settlements and Transcendentalism was similarly inclusive and expansive. "Transcendent," from which their name is derived, is from the Latin *transcendere,* which means "to cross a boundary," an accurate description of its heterodox, liberal foundations.

Central to their philosophy was the importance of individual experience and the value of the subjective. According to one Emerson biographer, "Transcendentalism taught – teaches – that even in a world of objective knowledge, the subjective consciousness and the conscious subject can never be left out of the reckoning."[5] Henry David Thoreau, known for the precise observations of nature recorded in his journals, insisted that "the purest science is still biographical."[6] The championing of the subjective is not surprising given that George Ripley saw himself as a disciple of Friedrich Schleiermacher, the eighteenth-century theologian credited with founding hermeneutics. Ripley considered Schleiermacher to be the foremost of theologians and devoted part of his career to translating his works into English. The hermeneutic principle that one needs to participate in their object of study appears throughout Emerson's thought. His essay "History," with its emphasis on interpreting history from a contemporary perspective is as much a tutorial on how to read history. When he writes that "when a thought of Plato becomes a thought to me, when a truth that fired the soul of St. John, fires mine, time is no more,"[7] he makes the case that true understanding is firmly positioned in the present.

Emerson's essay "Nature" was published the same year that the Transcendental Club was founded and described the ability of a transcendent intellect to deeply engage the world. "Nature," for Emerson, included the entire "material" world but found its most potent images in the abundance of the natural world. The pure and interpersonal intellect, named by Emerson the "Over-soul," dissolved boundaries of thought and preconception and intimately communed with its surroundings. He wrote:

> [I]n the woods, we return to reason and faith. There I feel that nothing can befall me in life – no disgrace, no calamity (leaving me my eyes), which nature cannot repair. Standing on the bare ground – my head bathed by the blithe air and lifted into infinite space – all mean egotism vanishes. I become a transparent eyeball; I am nothing; I see all; the currents of the Universal Being circulate through me; I am part and parcel of God.[8]

Emerson in his essay of 1842 entitled "The Transcendentalist" stated that "what is properly called Transcendentalism among us, is Idealism; *Idealism as it appears in 1842*" (italics added). This short essay concentrates on distinguishing "idealists" from "materialists," the former incorporating the subjective – the latter only the objective. According to Emerson, the idealist "transfers every object in nature from an independent and anomalous position without there, into the consciousness."[9] Intuition was the means to fully and unselfconsciously engage reality – it was the ultimate mediator between the intellect and the objects it engages through the senses. Emerson insists that we "respect the intuitions" and give them, "all authority over our experience."[10] He called for engaged, un-mediated experience as a counter-project to objective materialism and arid intellectualism. "Life," for Emerson, "was something not to be learned, but to be lived."[11]

Nature, for Emerson, mediated between humans and a broader, deeper reality, the "Universal Being" of which all are a part:

> In the instant you leave far behind all human relation, wife, mother and child, and live only with the savages – water, air, light, carbon, lime and granite . . . I become a moist cold element. Nature grows over me. Frogs pipe; waters far off tinkle; dry leaves hiss; grass bends and rustles; and I have died out of the human world and come to feel a strange, cold, aqueous terraqueous, aerial ethereal sympathy and existence. I sow the sun and moon for seeds.[12]

Emerson's contemplative, connecting practice involved solitary sojourns through the nature that surrounded his home in Concord and, in particular, the property that he owned at Walden Pond. It was his younger friend Henry David Thoreau, however, who came to practice a philosophy that was both Epicurean and phenomenological though the agency of his simple, self-constructed hut on Walden Pond. In Thoreau's two and a half years at Walden, the simple hut where he lived symbolized his contemplative practices, deeply influenced by Eastern thought of which both he and Emerson were very knowledgeable. In *Walden*, the book that resulted from Thoreau's practice of essential engagement with "nature," he insisted that an authentic life could only be lived in the here and now.

Buddhism

Being present in the moment is a theme that is central to most contemplative traditions and appears throughout *Walden*. Thoreau describes an evening walk around the pond. "This is a delicious evening, when the whole body is one sense, and imbibes delight through every pore. I go and come with a strange liberty in Nature, a part of herself."[13] Thoreau, in recalling the experience of the body as "one sense," described a synesthesia of connection in the moment. For Thoreau, living in the moment connected one to his or her surroundings and constituted an authentic life.

Of all the traditions of contemplative practices, Buddhism may provide the most extensive and detailed system for engaging the present moment as a means to transcend the limitations of self and achieve deeper connections with the environment, others, and aspects of the "divine" within and outside us. Included in the vast canon of the Buddha's teachings are the "Seven Factors of Enlightenment," where three "energizing" qualities of "investigation," effort ("energy"), and "rapture," along with three "calming" qualities of "tranquility," "concentration," and "equanimity" contribute to create the most important, which is "mindfulness."[14] For Buddhists, mindfulness is a practice cultivated in meditation and applied to daily life as a means to understand the transitory nature of all physical and mental phenomena and therefore, logically, the ephemeral nature of what we consider to be "the self." We suffer, or experience *dhukka*, as outlined in the "Four Noble Truths," because we grasp, or try to hold on to things in a world where everything is subject to change.[15] The realization and acceptance of the inevitabilities of sickness, old age, and death and their incorporation into a larger interdependent context, are understood as part of the process of enlightenment.

The Buddhist Pali Canon, compiled approximately 100 years after the Buddha's death, is a vast, philosophical system that is divided into three major sections known as the "Three Baskets" – the Discourses (*Sutta*), Disciplines (*Vinaya*), and Philosophy (*Abhidhamma*). Since its founding 2,500 years ago, subsequent Buddhist sects, schools, and teachers have added considerably to the initial texts. The result is a philosophical system that in breadth and depth rivals the Western traditions that continue to hold privileged positions in contemporary (Western) philosophical discourses and architectural theory. That contemporary architectural theory, for the most part, has ignored the Buddhist philosophical system, has resulted in a truncation of opportunities to develop new perspectives on the experience and meaning of place. In particular, the emphasis on practice in Buddhism means that those who developed their particular contributions to its philosophy (which are as varied as in Western traditions) did so based, at least in part, on their own personal engagement with the questions they posed. As the other examples in this chapter demonstrate, the direct engagement of the person with the object of investigation is not limited to Buddhism, but, as I intend to illustrate, finds a particularly potent home there.

All of the major sects of Buddhism include varieties of what might be called mindfulness practices. The Forest Lineage School of the Theravada sect, found mostly in Southeast Asia, practices *Vipassana*, known in the West as "mindfulness" or "insight" meditation. Monasteries in Thailand, for example, include a campus of simple huts where some of the monks spend a considerable amount of time in solitary meditation. Emulating the historical Buddha who described himself as simply "one who has woken up," monks practice moment-to-moment awareness. As articulated by the Thai monk Achaan Chah, "Proper effort . . . is the effort to be aware and awake in each moment, the effort to overcome laziness and defilement, the effort to make each activity of our day meditation."[16] Zen Buddhism is a Mahayana sect that first developed in China but came to find its most potent expressions in Medieval Korea and Japan. Typical of most schools of Buddhism, Zen developed highly systematic monastic practices designed, in part, to dissolve the boundaries of self. Japanese Zen is best known in the West for its insistence on direct engagement in the world. The founder of the Soto School of Japanese Buddhism, Dogen Zenji exhorted his students to "Think only of this day and this hour, for tomorrow is an uncertain thing; and no one knows what the future will bring. Make up your mind to follow Buddhism as if you had only this day to live."[17]

Buddhist practices are too varied and nuanced to effectively summarize or characterize, but can be understood, in part, as a means of direct engagement with one's mind and the environment. Contemporary Buddhist teachers provide an accessible source for understanding particular aspects of its vast philosophy. Mindfulness practice, as described by the contemporary Vipassana teacher Jack Kornfield, can lead to deeper connections to our senses and surroundings:

> As we continue to reestablish and focus our attention, new levels of understanding will come into view. Eventually, mindfulness can get so precise that we can separate the process of perception, hearing the first vibration at the ear, followed by a moment of knowing its pleasant quality, followed by a moment of recognition – "bird song" – followed by an image of a bird and then a desire to hear more. We can learn to pay such fine attention that our whole solid world reveals itself to be a flow, and interactive process of body and mind, a dance of many moving pieces. What at first appears as just our "self" hearing a "sound" opens to show us moments of sense perception, moments of feeling, and moments of recognition and response. In this way, the very solidity of our world can be dissolved. Through very careful attention we can experience new levels of the

instantaneous arising and passing of the whole body and mind. As we "dissolve," so do the boundaries between "us" and the "world outside," and we can come to experience the unity and nonseparation of all things, and find a freedom not limited by any of them.[18]

Through the practice of meditation and the mindfulness it can bring to everyday life, connections are established to broader psychic and environmental contexts. One is more part of one's surroundings when limited self-conceptions are dissolved, allowing for fuller and deeper sensory experiences of place. At the least one cultivates a more connected, peaceful, and meaningful life, at best, one is led to enlightenment and the capacity to lead others. Monastic practices may have been generally ascetic, but rarely were they sense denying. This is perhaps best illustrated through the Zen-imbued poetry known as *haiku*, where self, setting, and emotion are synthesized through an elegant economy of words, as we find in the poem by Issa (1762–1826):

> A lovely thing to see:
> through the paper window's hole,
> the galaxy.[19]

or Matsuo Basho (1644–1694):

> Dusk –
> Temple bells quieting,
> Fragrance rings from the night-struck flowers.[20]

Meaning in Architecture through Connection

One definition of the "meaning" of architecture is its ability to lead one to more substantive understandings of the experience of being human. As Lindsay Jones cogently states, "The daunting fact . . . is that buildings in and of themselves do not 'mean' anything!" but only "in the negotiation or the interactive relation that subsumes both the building and the beholder – in the ritual-architectural event in which buildings and human participants are involved."[21] It is through the practice of participation with sacred architecture (for Jones, through ritual), that its often-nuanced meanings are accessed. It is the capacity of sacred architecture to connect us with a deeper understanding of ourselves, our relationship to others, and to our place in the cosmos, that is the principal subject of this book. Therefore the philosophical systems we have just outlined, and in particular their specific iterations of practice, inform the analyses of the case studies that follow.

Meaning in architecture can be understood as the result of an intimate connection (whether it is individually or collectively) that engages us sensually and intellectually. Sacred architecture often provided potent settings to facilitate the deep internal and external connections intrinsic to the religious experience, and therefore need to be understood in this context (as opposed to so-called textual readings of symbolism, or other theoretical positions that maintain an intellectual and physical distance from the work). Emerson promulgated a deeper engagement with the material world he called "nature" as a means to live a more authentic, ethical life. He and his fellow Transcendentalists articulated philosophical positions that endeavored to establish direct and meaningful connections with the human experience of embodied consciousness. "Nature," for Emerson, was the medium through which one viscerally engages the world to reveal its inherent divinity. The Transcendentalists had little sympathy for objective materialism or intellectualism, but were interested in the means to achieve engaged, direct experience. Thoreau states in *Walden*:

> To be a philosopher is not merely to have subtle thoughts, nor even to found a school, but so to love wisdom as to live according to its dictates, a life of simplicity, independence, magnanimity, and trust. It is to solve some of the problems of life, not only theoretically, but practically.[22]

Philosophical traditions, such as Transcendentalism, that maintain the primacy of connection through their sensual orientation or direct practices, can inform our task of understanding the multifaceted and multifarious meanings of sacred architecture. According to one Transcendentalist scholar: "In its deepest reaches Transcendentalism was a quest for authentic religious experience. It rejected forms, creeds, rites and verbal explanations and sought to penetrate to the heart of things by a direct, immediate encounter with reality."[23] In Emerson's case, the Transcendentalist interest in the "thingly-real," was realized through the practice of engagement with the physical environment. As he wrote in his *Journal* in 1837:

> Miracles have ceased! Have they indeed? When? They had not ceased this afternoon when I walked into the wood and got into bright sunshine, in shelter from the roaring wind. Who sees a pine-cone or the turpentine exuding from the tree, or a leaf, the unit of vegetation, fall from its bough, as if it said, "the year is finished," or hears in the quiet, piney glen the chickadee chirping its cheerful note, or walks along the lofty promontory-ridges which, like natural causeways, traverse the morass, or gazes upward at the rushing clouds, or downward at a moss or a stone and says to himself, "miracles have ceased?"[24]

Transcendentalism was interpretive in spirit and practice, insisting on an active engagement with scripture that reveals the influence of Schleiermacher's hermeneutics. Its religious orientation was ecumenical and heterogenous – a much more liberal philosophy than the "liberal religion" of Unitarianism from which many Transcendentalists emerged. Their Kant-influenced idealism earned some a reputation of aloofness, but did not prevent many members from engaging in ambitious solitary or communal experiments, or of committing themselves to the social concerns of their day. It was a philosophy that insisted on a thorough immersion in life without resorting to orthodoxy or dogmatism.

Emerson insisted that each individual has to find his or her own means of accessing the universal:

> His thought – that is the universe. His experience inclines him to behold the procession of facts you call the world, as flowing perpetually outward from an invisible, unsounded centre in himself, centre alike of him of them, and necessitating him to regard all things as having a subjective or relative existence relative to that aforesaid Unknown Centre of him.[25]

The consonances between Transcendentalism and Buddhism are well known and reveal the openness Emerson and his contemporaries had to philosophical systems outside of European traditions.[26] In both philosophies, attitudes regarding the value of a depth of engagement with the world and multifaceted perspectives regarding the world are explicit. The Buddha's last instruction to his disciples was that his teachings should be the teacher:

> Rely on the teaching, not the teacher.
> Rely on the meaning, not the letter.
> Rely on the definitive meaning, not the interpretable meaning.
> Rely on wisdom, not on ordinary consciousness.[27]

The Buddha consistently demonstrated his heterogenous approach through his teachings, which were typically aligned with the personality, presuppositions, and level of development of the student. According to Buddhist scholar Donald Lopez, the Buddha's methods of teaching were "facultative rather than dogmatic with regard to the acceptance of his teachings. He adjured his followers to adopt only what they found to be apodictic."[28] As described in a Buddhist text:

> Just as grammarians
> Begin with reading the alphabet,
> The Buddha teaches doctrines
> That students can bear.[29]

The subsequent hermeneutic "retrieval of meaning" by Buddhist scholars and practitioners defines, in part, Buddhist philosophy, and the Buddha's didactic methods continue to provide models for contemporary Buddhism. Buddhist texts often describe vast and complex cosmologies and Buddhist practitioners are exhorted to cultivate multi-perspectival understandings. The principal means to cultivate the "enlightenment" of multifaceted connections is to practice a mimesis of the Buddha's path of enlightenment. In other words, through the practice of meditation and other spiritual means, one is able to more and more deeply engage with the world and achieve increasing levels of understanding (or "enlightenment"). The levels of the *dhamma* are attuned to the level of the practitioner and accessing the different levels of the Buddha's teachings is dependent on one's degree of enlightenment.

If we accept that architecture, and in particular sacred architecture, is a fundamental means for humans to articulate their physical, psychic, and spiritual

position in the world, then philosophies that aim for more direct and heterogenous engagements with the world can serve to inform our understandings of
the agency that architecture performs. Ken Wilber argues that multiple
perspectives are necessary to achieve understanding because "meaning is always
context dependent and contexts are boundless." His integrated approach
emphasizes the "intersubjective" over the "objective," the "dialogical" over the
"monological," the "structural" over the "empirical," and "systematic networks"
over "representational images."[30] In the case of sacred architecture, which was
often built in stages and for a variety of cultural, social, political, and religious
goals, the multifaceted approaches formulated by Wilber (and others) are
necessary to achieve the broader perspectives required for understanding sacred
places. Substantive interpretations of sacred architecture depend on recognizing
the variety (and often conflicting) imperatives that produced it and the application of heterogenous means to understand it.

Christian Norberg-Schulz argues that: "The place is the concrete manifestation of men's dwelling, and his identity depends on his belonging to
places."[31] For Norberg-Schulz, the primary role of architecture was to "order
reality," and the history of meaningful architecture was one of "intermediary
objects" that served to "gather the contradictions and complexities of the life-
world" and render them accessible and understandable.[32] In this context,
architecture served the primary human need to understand our lives as having
significance and meaning. Religion and, by extension, the architecture built to
serve it, have traditionally been the media by which humans have articulated
their understanding of the cosmos and their relative position within it. The multi-
perspectival and connective emphasis of Transcendentalism and Buddhism can
serve to expand our discussion regarding architecture as a mediator. By recognizing multiple aspects of a work of architecture, we may reveal its multiple
cultural contexts, symbols, roles, and functions and thus gain more complete,
nuanced interpretations. Philosophical and spiritual practices of connection can
help us to more fully understand the means by which sacred architecture entices,
engages, and elucidates its users, which range over type and time.

Juhani Pallasmaa argues that the "existentially mediating task" of architecture serves in part to integrate our inner worlds and outer experience. It is
through our interactions with, and connections to, architecture that our dislo-
cations may be reconstructed or, in other words, made whole. The holy leads to
greater wholeness. The making of architecture can also be a means of connection and self-development. Henry David Thoreau effectively utilized the medium
of architecture to express and manifest his prescient philosophy regarding an
essential and authentic life. It was through the agency of the architecture of his
simple dwelling on Walden Pond that he was able to articulate positions that
ranged from material costs to social criticism to cosmological perspectives. It is
instructive that the medium of architecture served as a means to fully engage
his thesis and thus either confirm or disprove his philosophy. He asserted:

> [I] went to the woods because I wished to live deliberately, to front
> only the essential facts of life, and see if I could not learn what it
> had to teach, and not, when I came to die, discover that I had not
> lived.[33]

The mediating role of hermeneutics suggests that only through occupying a position between the multiple aspects of sacred architecture can substantial understandings be established. It also requires that one, in essence, "take a position," as a means to reveal the presuppositions one brings to the places we seek to understand and to focus our inquiry. Additionally, for one to write with an understanding, or even authority, about engagement with the physical, experiential, and psychological world, one needs to bring practices of moment-to-moment being to places – and experience them accordingly. This is not to suggest a definable expertise (that is why it is called "practice"). Instead, it is a regular appreciation of embodied consciousness and its reciprocity with the soul – the sense of being in the world. Emerson and Thoreau, for example, are accessible and engaging, in part, because they write from the perspective of experience. Contemplative practices, in all their forms and traditions, aim to quiet the mind as a means to allow our senses to more directly engage the world. Ken Wilber, a longtime student of contemplative practices, describes an experience that resonates with the hermeneutical, phenomenological, Transcendentalist, and Buddhist practices we have outlined:

> Raindrops are beating, a large puddle is forming, there on the balcony. It all floats in Emptiness, in purest Transparency, with no one here to watch it. If there is an I, it is all that is arising, right now and right now and right now. My lungs are the sky; those mountains are my teeth; the soft clouds are my skin; the thunder in my heart beating time to the timeless; the rain itself, the tears of our collective state, here where nothing is really happening at all.[34]

This book contends that architecture that is designed with sensory impacts in mind, as many sacred sites were, is also a medium of mindful engagement and connection to the broader (and often unrecognized) contexts of which we are an intrinsic part.

Chapter 4

Mediating Elements

Symbolism, Religion, and the In-Between

> What the book is to literacy, architecture is to culture as a whole.
> (Dalibor Veseley)[1]

Traditionally, architecture articulated its creator's place in the world and therefore can best be understood as a symbolic activity. That the history of architecture can be fruitfully interpreted through the lens of symbolism is well established. What is surprising is that not more historians and theoreticians have done so.[2] Even in contemporary cultures that are dominated by heterogenous and positivist hegemonies, architecture continues to perform symbolic roles, however nuanced, subtle, and multifarious they may be. A variety of content is communicated by sacred architecture, including historical, textural, didactic, exhortative, coercive, and empathetic, and a number of means including surface and scenographic elements, spatial sequences and symbolic narratives, vistas and juxtapositions, environmental appropriations and displacements, and geometry and proportion (all of which is often enriched by communal rituals). Often the capacity of the symbolic content to engender shared (though often diverse) meanings depends on the synthesis of content and the means by which it is communicated. The communicative efficacy of sacred architecture is the result of its content structuring meaning. In other words, analogous to literature, the construction of the content, and one's engagement with it, lead to meaning.

A broad range of formal, scenographic, spatial, cultural, historical, and experiential considerations are necessary to substantially interpret sacred architecture. Formal analysis is an essential component but, if addressed in isolation from other aspects, presents an incomplete picture.[3] It is not enough to explain *what* the architecture is – its form, spaces, materials, and organizations – but *why* it is and *how* it is experienced.[4] That said, because architecture is, in part, a media of material and space organized to serve specific agendas and functions, we need

4.1
A broad range of formal, scenographic, spatial, cultural, historical, and experiential considerations are necessary to substantially interpret sacred architecture. Saint Foy, Conques, France, 1050–1120, view of nave

to understand its formal and material characteristics. There are, of course many established methodologies to this end, including plan typologies, spatial compositions and relationships, texture and surface, and geometry and proportion – all of which are utilized in this study. However, even though formal characteristics may be identified and discussed individually, this should not be done independent of the larger contexts of the historical and cultural background and present-day experience. What is required is an understanding of the content communicated through the media of architecture, how this communicative capacity is expanded through use and communal rituals, and the resulting meaning. Meaning should not be understood as a static "reading" of the artifact, but as a dynamic inter-relationship of form, surface, space, cultural setting, and experience. The symbolic media of architecture provides one component of depth in a multivalent system of relationships.

A more complete understanding of symbolism can broaden our interpretations regarding the mediating role that sacred architecture typically performs. Symbols serve to mediate between states of comprehension – their meaning is designed to elucidate and enrich the experience and significance of our lives. Carl Jung defined symbols as the means by which humans represent "ideas that lie beyond the grasp of reason" and "because there are innumerable things beyond the range of human understanding, we constantly use symbolic terms to represent concepts that we can't define or fully comprehend. This is one reason why all religions employ symbolic language or images."[5] Gadamer recalls the Greek root word *sumbolon* ("token of remembrance"), and its relationship to *tessera hospitalis*, an ancient Greek practice where a host would present half of a broken object to his guest to commemorate the event:

> [The host] kept one for himself and gave the other half to his guest. If in thirty or fifty years time, a descendant of the guest should ever enter into his house, the two pieces could be fitted together again to form a whole in an act of recognition. In its original technical sense, the symbol represented something like a sort of pass used in the ancient world: something in and through which we recognize someone already known to us.[6]

He concludes that through the symbol, "the particular represents itself as a fragment of being that promises to complete and make whole whatever corresponds to it."[7] These are useful perspectives to explain why architecture has expansively employed symbolism and the mediating role it plays in establishing meaning. Furthermore, a clear rationale for the importance of symbolism is essential in a cultural and theoretical climate that remains mistrustful of the significance of the more ephemeral, referential, and interpretive aspects of architecture. E.B. Smith made an argument (and complaint) in 1956 that still resonates today, when he stated:

> The problem of presenting a convincing exposition of symbolic intent that is seldom specifically stated is made difficult by the modern conviction that architecture, apart from its figurative sculptures, has always been created for utilitarian and aesthetic reasons. Even

when dealing with the buildings of the Middle Ages, there has been a prevailing tendency to disregard the political issues involved in the symbolism and to minimize the spiritual connotations as mystic, vague, and nonessential to appreciation. This means that architectural symbolism will continue to seem artificial as long as the buildings that embodied it are divorced from the history of ideas, and as long as it is assumed that the motivating factors of architectural creation were always, as they are today, only structural necessity, utility, decorative desire, and a particular kind of taste.[8]

The Symbolic Agendas of Architecture

Traditionally, the arts have used two- and three-dimensional symbols. For example, Christian iconography utilized symbols of purity, devotion, and spirit to deepen the content of the annunciation and make its meanings accessible to the viewer. The arts have also presented symbols spatially and temporally – music and dance have presented their content serially, and myths and folk tales weave symbols into a narrative. The media of architecture, especially in sacred architecture, similarly employs a symbolic language. The surfaces and spaces of sacred architecture embody content that is expanded and enriched through the dynamics of one's ever-changing perspectives. Rudolf Arnheim applied the psychology of art to the experience of architecture to argue that the "asymmetry of experiential space," produces a dynamic sequence of objects and spaces that are revealed (and assimilated) over time.[9] Steven Holl argues that:

> Architecture, more fully than any other art forms, engages the immediacy of our sensory perceptions. The passage of time; light, shadow and transparency; color phenomena, texture, material and detail all participate in the complete experience of architecture. The limits of two-dimensional representation (in photography, painting or the graphic arts), or the limits of aural space in music only partially engage the myriad sensations evoked by architecture. While the emotional power of cinema is indisputable, only architecture can simultaneously awaken all the senses – all the complexities of perception.[10]

One of the potent components of spatial sequences in sacred architecture is serial symbolic narratives that unfold temporally. Sacred architecture is arguably the most extensive and potent application of symbols, because here symbols are not only representational but spatial and temporal. The symbolism is communicated in multivalent ways – a powerful synthesis of the various communicative media. Unlike iconography, for example, the scene is not apprehended passively, but is dynamically moved to, through, and around. Architecture expands on the temporal narrative of listening to a myth through a sequence of spaces that often link the components of the "story." As early as the appropriation of caves for art by the Paleolithic peoples of Europe, humans recognized the potential of space and sequence to deepen symbolic meanings.

4.2
Sacred architecture is arguably the most extensive and potent application of symbols, because here symbols are not only representational but spatial and temporal. Wells Cathedral, United Kingdom, fourteenth century, Chapterhouse stair

Since our earliest days as cognitive creatures, humans have invented symbols; hence our use of them reflects the expansiveness of our minds and psyches. Symbolism was essential to the religious beliefs of archaic societies and served, in part, as a means for them to explain their position in the world. The sentient and ephemeral nature of human existence is a bountiful font of artistic output. "The production of a work of art throws a light upon the mystery of humanity," said Emerson.[11] The arts have traditionally addressed enduring questions of existence and meaning, using symbols to articulate the incomprehensible and perhaps make it visible – to establish meaning amidst the mystery of existence; and to explain natural phenomena and our relationship to them.

Symbols occupy a middle ground, an in-between area bridging the known with the unknown, and can be understood as mediators between the present and the past; the individual and the collective. Sacred texts often describe the way to enlightenment as obscure and arduous. In the *Upanishads*, it is a "sharpened edge of a razor, hard to traverse, A difficult path is this – poets declare!"[12] Symbols often represent an in-between zone, placed between the profane and the sacred – ignorance and understanding. Connections across rivers – bridges, rafts, ferries – are found in many myths and sacred texts. Sir Lancelot must

4.3
Symbols often represent an in-between zone, placed between the profane and the sacred – ignorance and understanding. Tongdo Buddhist Monastery, Korea, view of One Vehicle Bridge

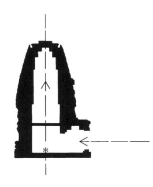

4.4

The form, scale, and placement of the architecture often serve to establish formal hierarchies and underline the significance of the sacred place. Cave, mountain, and cosmic axis symbolism in the Hindu temple

Source: Courtesy of George Michell.

traverse the sharp edge of the sword bridge to rescue Queen Guinevere from the castle of King Death,[13] and in Islam the bridge to heaven is described as being as narrow as a sharp sword. As we find in the *Bhagavad-Gita*, "*Jnana Yoga or, Path of Wisdom*," "Be thou the greatest of all sinners, yet thou shalt cross over all sin by the ferry-boat of wisdom." The *dhamma* or teachings of the Buddha are viewed as a bridge between delusion and enlightenment. "By me is made a well-constructed raft," said the Buddha. "I have passed over to Nirvana, I have reached the further bank, having overcome the torrent."[14]

Sacred architecture utilizes a broad range of surface and spatial media to perform its symbolic functions. The form, scale, and placement of the architecture often serve to establish formal hierarchies and underline the significance of the sacred place. External and internal surfaces serve to communicate symbolic content, and spatial relationships and sequences choreograph its dynamic serial experience. Sacred architecture is often pedagogical[15] and employed to affect, coerce, or transform its participants. In this context its ontological significance serves as an agent to transform an individual's perspective and engender spiritual insights. All of which is typically broadened and deepened through ritual.

Particular physiological and psychological responses are often engendered by sacred settings, consistent with their symbolic agendas. It is important to recognize that symbolic representation is only one of the means employed to communicate content and elicit responses. A critical understanding of the more intangible, ephemeral, and immaterial aspects of sacred architecture is essential to reveal the full breadth of its effects. Two- and three-dimensional symbols in the Medieval Church effectively communicated Biblical content and social conventions, but it was the modulation, quality, and hues of its light that viscerally underlined its religious themes. Any space that heightens or deprives the senses can produce feelings of discomfort or ease, anxiety or peace. A cadence of light and dark as one ambulates through a series of spaces can serve to underline feelings of passage and progress toward the goal. Modulating the quality of light can also produce feelings of comfort or discomfort, depending on its intensity and whether one gradually approaches the luminous or is abruptly plunged into darkness. Similarly, the scale of the form and spaces of the architecture can produce empathetic feelings ranging from grandeur to insignificance.

The belief in personal improvement through the positive experience engendered by sacred architecture is a popular and predominant position. What is less prevalent is the dark side of the politically motivated and socially coercive roles of some places. In this study, we are primarily concerned with how the medium of architecture served to communicate content and produce responses, emotions, and outcomes, and so consequently places that invite and inspire or coerce and oppress have equal interest.[16] The fact is, many places do both, and more, and that is what makes them particularly potent. In the case of the Western Medieval Church, the potency of its themes of trial, transformation, and redemption depended on complementary symbols of sin, judgment, and damnation.

Sacred places are typically viewed as peaceful settings for the cultivation of devotion and spiritual connection, and many are. However, they were often more complicated where architecture was also put into the service of reinforcing the social structures and political hierarchies of their time. Hadrian's Pantheon in Rome may exist today as an ontologically significant place, but in its time it also reinforced imperial authority and symbolized the hegemony of the Roman military and political world.[17] The Hagia Sophia in Istanbul (Constantinople), heir to Imperial Rome, was not dissimilar in its appropriation of symbols of power, most clearly by the omphalos stone located in the nave that demarked the symbolic center of the Byzantine world and where imperial investitures took place. The formal elements and materials of mosques in the post-Byzantine Ottoman Empire unambiguously communicated the station of the patron of a particular building. (For example, it was only imperial mosques that could have more than one minaret, a theme that reached its conclusion in the six minarets of the "Blue Mosque" in Istanbul.) William Coldrake argues that the form and placement of building elements of Japanese Medieval architecture clearly described the social and political strata of the military aristocracy. The form of the gateways to residential compounds, for example, unequivocally represented the status of the inhabitants inside. He goes on to argue that:

> [T]he relationship between architecture and authority, therefore, goes beyond signs and symbols. In manifesting authority, architecture can serve as a potent tool for political and social engineering or for profoundly affecting religious belief. We may readily acknowledge the power that a work of art of ineffable beauty has to move us, but what of the power of a work of architecture of sublime proportions to convince us? A beautiful building can move, inspire and beguile its beholders with the visual language of architectural form in the same way as a charismatic orator can move, inspire and beguile an audience with words.[18]

Historical scholarship has typically applied archeological and textual evidence as the principal means of establishing the use and meaning of architecture. Because scientific models have been emphasized in historical and cultural studies, architecture has at times been relegated to a secondary position. However, these Classical research methods miss aspects of cultures and religions that only sacred architecture can reveal.[19] The difference is the recognition that extant and active religious sites are alive places, where content is communicated through the media of the architecture (in all of its surface, formal, and spatial aspects), and further vivified through rituals. The media of architecture is both a means of communication and a medium of spiritual engagement. These two aspects are not separate, but can be understood as part of the integrated agendas of sacred architecture as a mediator – an intermediary believed to co-join separate worlds. Our understandings of sacred architecture are enriched and expanded by the inclusion of their past and present active roles, and the dynamic interplay of place and participant.

Types of Religious Mediators

Our study is primarily concerned with the mediating roles of sacred architecture. However, because of their architectural implications, the variety of means employed by religious traditions in the service of establishing connections with the divine is pertinent to our discussion. An examination of religious figures, spiritual teachers, oracles, medicine men, magicians, shamans, and other spiritual mediums reveals their roles as mediators between two otherwise separate states. Jesus states in the Gospels, "No one comes to the father except through me,"[20] and in a direct architectural metaphor, "I am the door; if any one enters by me, he will be saved."[21] Jesus is a rabbi, or teacher, described in the Gospels as both man and god, and thus mediates between both worlds. This relationship is made explicit in Paul's "First Letter to Timothy" in which he states, "For there is one God, and there is one mediator between God and men, the man Jesus Christ."[22] A similar figure is found in Mohammed, to whom in his cave retreat on Mount Hira the angel Gabriel made his appearances to bring him the word of God. Gabriel interceded between God and Mohammed who subsequently served as intermediary between God and humans. His solitary cave became a dynamic place connected to divinity and the revelations that he received became the foundations of Islam.

Oracles have traditionally performed the role of bridging the known with the unknown – the present with the future. The Delphic Oracle was said to enter into a deep trance as she sat inside the inner sanctum of the Temple of Apollo at Delphi. The tripod upon which she rested was placed above a chasm from which vapors rose from the earth, a medium that induced her receptive state. However, her utterances, received from a hidden world, were often in ambiguous cipher that needed to be translated by priests (who served as additional intermediaries).[23] Similarly, traditional shamans, medicine men, magicians, sorcerers enter into different states to connect with hidden, separate worlds. Sometimes this is self-induced through spiritual practices or psychoactive drugs; or comes unbidden in the form of distress and illness. The initiation of one Siberian shaman includes a journey to a place that contains all human illnesses where he is ritually dismembered and, after three years, "re-membered," the last piece, his head with new eyes and opened ears to facilitate his access to the spirit world.[24]

In shamanic initiation there are consistent themes of death and rebirth – the former personality is destroyed and the shaman is reborn as a new person with special powers. The journey to the spirit world also describes spatial relationships – there is a distinct place of spiritual power that shaman have the ability to access. There are propitious locations for shamanic initiation – most occupy a liminal zone such as mountain summits or the remote wilderness utilized by the North American Plains Indians during vision quests. The shaman, both physically and psychically, occupies a liminal zone between worlds and mediates between the spirit and corporal worlds, often utilizing the media of words and music as a means to induce trance-like states and make divine connections. According to David Abram, the shaman serves as an "intermediary between the human community and the larger ecological field," and is an "exemplary voyager in the intermediate realm between the human and the more-than-human worlds, the primary strategist and negotiator in any dealings with the Others."[25]

The experiences of the spiritual lives of holy men and spiritual teachers are distinguished by the trials of passage from one state of being to another. As we read in the Story of Job when this pious man is tested by his God, "Man is also chastened with pain upon his bed, and with continual strife in his bones." But later we learn that, "If there be for him an angel, a mediator, one of a thousand to declare to man what is right for him," he will pass safely, as Job ultimately does. Scripture and religious teachings are similarly believed to provide linkages to God. Jesus' Sermon on the Mount is propitiously delivered at a place between heaven and earth and was transmitted from God through the medium of Jesus. Similarly, the Buddha after his enlightenment brought the *dhamma*, or teachings, to his disciples; and Moses brought the Ten Commandments down from Mount Sinai, the word of God in a legible medium. Mohammed brought the Koran, the laws of Islam that for Muslims complement the teachings of Judaism and Christianity; and Lao Tzu left his teachings with a border guard as he rode off into obscurity. Catholicism includes the concept of apostolic succession, an unbroken chain leading back to Jesus and God. In Buddhism, the tradition of *dhamma* transmission created a lineage of teachers, guides along the way to enlightenment.

4.5
Prayer, ritual, and architecture perform roles as intermediaries to the divine. Main Temple, Beomeo Monastery, Korea

When religious devotees pray, either silently or aloud, the words repeated are placed as an offering, an in-between place between the petitioner and the divine. The medium of prayer establishes a connection that, it is hoped, is reciprocal. *The Way of the Pilgrim* is an eighteenth-century account of a Russian pilgrim, who states: "It is prayer that must come first and foremost, for without prayer no other good work can be performed and one cannot find the way to the Lord." For this mystic, simply repeating the prayer: "Lord Jesus Christ, have mercy on me!"[26] was the medium of salvation. Many Christians offer the Lord's Prayer, a medium given by Jesus in his Sermon on the Mount, as a means to connect with God. For Roman Catholics, repetitive prayers of supplication serve as the medium of repentance; and devout Muslims offer daily prayers, standing and kneeling shoulder to shoulder in the mosque, facing the holy city of Mecca – the center of the Islamic world.

Prayer, ritual, and architecture perform roles as intermediaries to the divine, but there are other media as well. Religious rituals throughout the world's faiths are powerful settings where the congregation is joined together in hopes of achieving new understandings or connecting with the divine. Music, sung and played, often is part of the ritual – hymns sung during a Protestant service, the Psalms sung by Medieval monks throughout the days, nights, and weeks, or Buddhist chants as a meditative medium. Hindus, among other faiths, consider water to be a liminal media. The Ganges in Varenasi is a pilgrimage destination, a medium of cleansing and, for some, final passage. Pushkar is a holy city where pilgrims ritually bathe in its holy lake, as part of their pilgrimage to its holy places including a rare temple dedicated to Brahma. For some Christians, the Eucharist is a medium of renewal and redemption. The ritual of ingesting bread and wine, symbols for the "body" of Christ, is a symbolic connection to God through his intermediary. Its practice actually began in the first Christian "house churches," in which worship culminated with a shared meal. Now it is distilled to a concise symbolism, the wafer and wine liminal materials that perform a double mediation of binding the celebrants to each other and to the god they seek.

Scriptures also perform mediating roles – they promise new understanding and even relationships with God, which are revealed through an inculcation of their meaning. The enduring theme of the hidden, veiled, or obscured condition of the divine as a result of human ignorance, is mitigated by the belief in the possibility of scripture to lessen this separation. Some sacred texts directly describe blindness and revelation to illustrate the thin veil that often separates a world split between humans and the divine. In the Gospel of Luke, as two disciples "were walking and discussing together, Jesus himself drew near and went with them. But their eyes were kept from recognizing him."[27] Jesus' disciples do not recognize him after he is resurrected – they are blind to him even when he is right next to them. Only later when Jesus blessed bread at the table for them, "their eyes were opened and they recognized him."[28]

The In-Between

Understanding architecture as a dynamic set of articulate relationships is central to the argument of this book – an approach that is consistent with a more nuanced and multivalent understanding of the reciprocal relationship of form and space in architectural theory. Herman Hertzberger provides an antidote to the formal prejudices of typical architectural analysis through his emphasis on the "in-between." Thresholds, for Hertzberger, provide the most potent condition of the "in-between":

> The threshold provides the key to the transition and connection between areas with divergent territorial claims and, as a place in its own right, it constitutes, essentially, the spatial condition for the meeting and dialogue between areas of different orders.[29]

Aldo van Eyck describes the "twin-phenomena" of dynamic spatial relationships, where "binary" conditions of "open-outside, closed-inside, closed-outside (i.e. open, closed, small, large, many, few, outside, inside, in any combination)" can be understood and their "meaning . . . clarified."[30] For Robert Mugerauer, the in-between is both spatial and metaphorical, as in the archetypal house porch that provides "a transition in spatial form and meaning. The shift is from 'the rest of the world' to another place or manner of being. The porch joins different worlds."[31] All emphasize the importance of the in-between as an essential third place that co-joins others, and the reciprocal agency of architecture as essential to its significance and meaning.

Any act of building articulates a place that is between others and an essential measure of its success is its ability to complete or unify its larger context.[32] According to Christopher Alexander:

> When you build a thing you cannot merely build that thing in isolation, but must also repair the world around it, and within it, so that the larger world at that one place becomes more coherent, and more whole; and the thing which you make takes its place in the web of nature, as you make it.[33]

Stephen Holl describes the ability of architecture to "bring things together" as follows:

> Beyond the physicality of architectural objects and practicalities of programmatic content, enmeshed experience is not merely a place of events, things, and activities, but something more intangible, which emerges from the continuous unfolding of overlapping spaces, materials, and detail. Merleau-Ponty's "in-between reality" is then perhaps, analogous to the moment in which individual elements begin to lose their clarity, the moment in which objects merge with the field.[34]

Articulate relationships, of course, depend on both a clear definition of its elements and the establishment of critical distances between them. The delimiting of boundaries was often the first task of sacred places – in-between zones that distinguished the sacred from the profane.[35] The center is consecrated as the only or most propitious place for contact with the otherworldly – all that is inside is legible, meaningful form; everything outside is formless, undefined, and meaningless. From sparse stone circles to elaborate complexes, the marking of a place to distinguish it from other places is a fundamental human and architectural act. Paradoxically, it is through separation that connection is believed to exist. The sacred place, separated from the profane, now is viewed as a liminal place that mediates between the profane and the sacred. The sacred enclosure is a place of power where divine ancestors, spirits, or divinities are believed to be mysteriously present, embodied in the architecture and often evoked through ritual.

Sacred mountains were believed to be potent mediators between humans and their gods, a symbol when translated into architectural form that resulted in one of the most enduring architectural motifs. Most significant cultures utilized the symbol of the world mountain in their sacred architecture, though it is also found in preliterate cultures. Summerian Ziggurats replicated the cosmic mountain and symbolized a pathway to god. The Late Sumerian Ziggurat of Nippur (2050–1950 BCE), dedicated to Enlil, the god of air, was a five-tiered intermediary between earth and sky. A temple at its summit was built to accommodate the divine, and its ceremonial stairs connected the below with the above. The Egyptian stepped pyramid-tomb of King Zoser in Saqquara, also

4.6
Sacred mountains were believed to be potent mediators between humans and their gods, a symbol when translated into architectural form that resulted in one of the most enduring architectural motifs. King Zoser Funerary complex, Saqquara, Egypt, Third Dynasty, *c.* 2680 BCE, view of Pyramid and Heb Sed Court

had five tiers – precise geometry for the specific task of symbolizing the connection of heaven and earth mediated by the divine ruler.

Hindu pilgrimage sites are located throughout India. Many are associated with sacred rivers such as the Ganges in Benares, but there are also many mountain sites. Pushkar, a holy city located at the edge of the desert in Ragistan, is an important Hindu pilgrimage destination. This small, peaceful city is built around a holy lake that is surrounded by temples and bathing *ghats*. Its most important temple is dedicated to Brahma, one of only a few in the world. Brahma is the god of creation who is often depicted with four faces, which symbolize the four quarters of the world, and so a temple to him suggests a powerful center. His female counterpart is Sarasvati and, located on the summit of a mountain that rises next to the city, is a temple dedicated to this goddess of learning and a patron saint of married women.

The temple is known as a pilgrimage site primarily for Bengalis, who travel to Pushkar to pray at Sarasvati's shrine, and as a portentous shrine for women who make offerings and prayers for their families and for the long lives of their husbands. The rough stone path is initiated by a temple dedicated to Durga, the goddess of judgment and death, and rises vertiginously until reaching the masonry temple at the summit of the conical mountain. The temple itself is pure white, with a spire painted blue like the sky above, its crenellated form recalling the mountain it completes. A statue of Sarasvati is there, dressed in opulent robes, her eyes glowing brightly in the gloom. Pilgrims enter the shrine, ring a bell and offer prayers and offerings to the goddess.

4.7
"The mountain is the bond between Earth and Sky. Its solitary summit reaches the sphere of eternity, and its base spreads out in manifold foothills into the world of mortals. It is the way by which man can raise himself to the divine and by which the divine can reveal himself to man." Pushkar, India, view of Sarasvati Temple with Durga shrine in foreground

Mediating Elements

The temple, set on its rocky height, perches uneasily in an in-between zone, mediating between two worlds. Here, an irruption is created, and a bridge from the earth to heaven believed to be established. Its critical formal position suggests the portentous settings of sacred mountains described by René Daumal in *Mount Analogue*, in which

> [t]he mountain is the bond between Earth and Sky. Its solitary summit reaches the sphere of eternity, and its base spreads out in manifold foothills into the world of mortals. It is the way by which man can raise himself to the divine and by which the divine can reveal himself to man.[36]

According to George Michell, the Hindu temple is designed to bring about contact between man and the gods; "it is here that the gods appear to man."[37] It is a place of transcendence where the god is believed to respond to prayers, to elucidate, and to improve one's understandings and life. Accordingly, the architecture is an active agent that acts to dissolve the boundaries between man and the divine.

Similar to mountains, remote locations of religious communities have traditionally served to symbolize their roles as intermediaries between the secular world and the divine. The in-between position of a sacred place symbolized its liminal position, as well as accommodating the practical value of separation from others as a means to more closely approach the divine. The agrarian sites of Cistercian abbeys, for example, served the dual function of satisfying the functional needs of the order's contemplative and self-sustaining agendas while symbolizing the exemplar of the Gnostic Desert Fathers. Korean Zen Buddhist monasteries, as we will observe later, were founded as mountainside hermitages for similar, practical reasons, while simultaneously symbolizing the contemplative traditions of the Zen Patriarchs.

Attendant to the clear delimiting of sacred space are the approaches, paths, thresholds, and paths to enter it. Ritual processions are a symbolic journey from outside to inside, edge to center, profane to sacred, and from one mode of being to another. The effective choreographing of approach, threshold, spatial sequence, and arrival has a long and recognized history, especially in religious architecture. The spatial sequences and symbolic narratives of the entry paths of sacred places often symbolized shared beliefs and facilitated communal rituals. In particular, it replicated the path of the hero–redeemer figure who appears in the mythology of many religions and cultures.[38] However, though the spiritual journey is a powerful theme in the world's religions, it is the sacred place itself where the most important events happen. The Jews traveled through the wilderness for forty years – a period of great significance – but it was the founding of Jerusalem that is the predominant event. Jesus developed his teachings during his ministry and suffered along the path of Calvary, but it was at Golgotha where his word became manifest. The Buddha engaged in six years of spiritual exploration before finally sitting down under the Bo Tree and attaining enlightenment.[39]

Sacred sites are often animated places, vivified by the anticipation of, or belief in, the presence of gods, divine ancestors, or spirits, their dynamism further deepened through ritual activities. All of the world's religious traditions utilize rituals, which are tied to annual calendars and typically mark significant historical and mythological events.[40] (Often rituals commemorate events that happened at a sacred time.) Just as the architecture was typically believed to serve as a receptor and vessel for the divine, it is also built to receive its creators in hopes of bringing the two together. In this aspect the architecture is unfinished until its ritual use completes its totality. Architecture built to serve ritual, as sacred architecture nearly always is, needs those individual and communal rituals to complete them – they depend on humans to animate their spaces and articulate their meaning.[41] The meaning of the architecture is deepened and broadened through ritual – the architecture becomes the setting for ritual performance and the re-enactment of mythic themes and stories. Through ritual, each participant becomes part of the myth, occupying a liminal place between the sacred and the profane, the present and the past, and humans and the god(s) they worship. This sacred time, set in a sacred place, serves as a bridge to the divine and a portentous setting for transcendent experiences.

Ritual is a medium of transition from one mode of being to another. Just as life passages, such as puberty, marriage, and death, are often negotiated by ritual, sacred architecture serves a similar linking function. Devotional sites receive the religious aspirants they are built for, and serve as the setting for individual and communal rituals – both setting and ritual serve as mediators between participants and the transformation they hope for. In many cases the body shapes or is shaped by the architecture, as in the act of circumambulating the sacred center. Additionally, seasonal rituals establish a temporal setting for the "ritual-architectural event"[42] that is both episodic and eternal. In all, the sacred place, the ritual, and their interrelationship, create an irruption in the mundane world. Through place and action – setting and ritual – participation and belief – a liminal place is created that promises a link with the divine. Always, the enactment of the ritual needs a setting, otherwise it loses its potency and risks

4.8
Devotional sites receive the religious aspirants they are built for, and serve as the setting for individual and communal rituals – both setting and ritual serve as mediators between participants and the transformation they hope for. Suleymaniye Mosque, Istanbul, Turkey, 1548–1549, Mimar Sinan, communal prayer facing the *qibla* and *mihrab*

Source: Photo by Aras Neftçi.

4.9

The setting of sacred architecture is critical to its power and meaning. Pueblo Bonito, Chaco Canyon, New Mexico, *c*.929–1085 CE, view of the Great House showing kivas

becoming meaningless. Whether it is a temporary altar, a simple forest clearing or an immense temple, the sacred setting provides the stage for ritual and, it is presumed, a threshold to the gods or the understandings that are sought.

The subterranean kivas created by the Anasazi of the North American Southwest were carefully delineated spaces that provided potent settings for rituals. The Anasazi were an enigmatic people whose origins and abrupt disappearance remain mysterious. (We do not even know what they called themselves, as the term "Anasazi," which means "ancient enemies," was given to them by the Navaho.) They are best known for their cliff houses at Mesa Verde that were built toward the end of a culture distinguished by its sophisticated architecture and arts. At the beginning of the second millennium the Anasazi had completed a series of "cities" connected by a road system that linked an extensive trade network (by 1300 CE the culture had mysteriously dispersed). The most significant cities are found in Chaco Canyon in present-day New Mexico, a linear canyon that at its height held over 10,000 inhabitants. Pueblo Bonito was the largest and comprised four stories, 800 rooms, 37 kivas, built with ingenious stone masonry and arranged in a semi-circle around a south-facing central courtyard.[43]

According to Hopi mythology, the Anasazi believed they emerged from the womb of the earth at the center of their world. Rituals served to connect this primordial myth with the present, ensuring the continuity of the culture. Pueblo Bonito was apparently divided into "winter people" and "summer people," each responsible for rituals associated with their half of the year. In the courtyard there were two great kivas – presumably one for each of the clans. These large, round, subterranean rooms were the center of religious life and the settings for initiatory rituals. Here, mystery plays would be enacted, potent vehicles for the indoctrination of boys into the religious duties and rituals of their clan that were essential to its future. The walls of the kivas were constructed of stone and covered with a wooden roof – a prototypical form reminiscent of early Mesa Verdian pit houses. The walls had low stone banquettes where the participants would sit, above which were offertory niches. At its center there was a fire pit, and next to it an opening called a "sipapu" or "path from the navel." For the young initiates, the scene must have been terrifying at times. The large space would have been dark and clouded in smoke – the men beating out rhythms with loose floorboards at their feet. At its climax masked performers would appear to burst from the "sipapu," re-enacting their people's mythical birth from the earth; a reclamation of the past that established meanings for the present.

The setting of sacred architecture is critical to its power and meaning. Often sacred rituals were linked with specific sites – sacred centers such as Mecca, Jerusalem, and Varenasi have an annual round of events. Initiation rites, often in the form of mysteries ritually transmitted from teacher to initiate, typically depended on specific architectural settings.[44] Often a place is consecrated as sacred following the appearance of the divine. When Jacob rests his head on a stone and sleeps in the desert at Bethel, he dreams about a ladder upon which angels are descending and ascending to heaven. God appears above it and speaks to him, promising him his holy presence. When he awakes, Jacob marks this place, setting up the stone as a "pillar" and anointing it with oil. "How awesome is this place" he cries, "This is none other than the house of God, and this is the gate of heaven."[45]

Sacred architecture employs a variety of means to establish a place that is both separated and connected to its contexts. A symbolic language, delimitation of place, articulate approach, entry and path sequence, geometry and proportion, and diverse representational media are employed – often in concert – in the creation of the sacred place. These were the means employed by the Medieval Church to fulfill diverse ecclesiastical, political, and social agendas, as discussed in the following example.

The Symbolic Media of the Western Medieval Church: Saint Foy in Conques

Part of architecture's efficacy as a mediator is its ability to physically structure symbolic narratives or, in other words, temporal scriptural readings in physical form. Both scripture and architecture describe religious histories, ideas, beliefs, and practices – one through words, the other through built form, surface, and organization. The linear organization of the Western Medieval Church, for example, can be understood as a rendition of the central Christian theme of trial and redemption. In this context, the western front and tympanum established a place of judgment presided over by Christ; the nave and aisles elongated the journey to the sanctuary and typically contained the Stations of the Cross; and the sanctuary itself was a place of redemption. The act of ambulation by the devout engaged the body and intellect to communicate understandable and palpable meanings.[46]

A shared symbolic language was the media utilized by the Medieval Christian Church to promulgate its social, political, and religious messages. The architecture and sculpture of its churches were its primary means to deliver the Church's distilled communications with the mostly illiterate populace of the Middle Ages – that life was perilous, the punishment for sin was eternal, and redemption was only accessible to the saved. The church of Saint Foy and, in particular, the carved tympanum over its entry doors, are one of the most potent examples of the power and content of this message. The small remote village of Conques (in the Aveyron region of Southwestern France) is an unusual location for an important pilgrimage church.[47] However, it was situated between important churches on the Via Ponensis – one of four Medieval pilgrimage routes that traversed France en route to the Cathedral of Saint James in Santiago de Compostella in Northwestern Spain – and the relatively small church and monastery became a very important pilgrimage destination during the Middle Ages.

Its history actually begins during the reign of the Roman Emperor Diocletian (284–305 CE). As the story goes, a 12-year-old girl who had recently converted to Christianity was ordered by the provincial authority to renounce her beliefs. She was tempted by the promise of marriage and the pleasures of a worldly life. When she piously refused, she was martyred by being burned alive (and thus is often depicted holding a brazier). After the Roman Empire was swept away by internal and external forces, Louis the Pious, King of Aquitaine, placed Conques under his protection. Datus, a shortening of Deo-datus or "God-given,"

4.10
Saint Foy, Conques, view of west front

founded a hermitage there in the first millennium, and soon attracted a number of followers. Eventually a small church was built and a monastery dedicated to the ideals of Saint Benedict established. The relics of Saint Foy, as the martyr was called, were transferred here in 866 CE, and soon after a series of miracles were reported, that further established the power of this isolated place.[48]

The abbey church, its compact plan the result of the steep slope of the site, was begun in the twelfth century. Though the church's size was limited, its height was not, and its nave is distinguished by an unusual 1:2.5 width to height ratio. Otherwise it is a typical pilgrimage church with generous aisles flanking the nave that led to the ambulatory and the sanctuary, where originally the treasures of Saint Foy were displayed. Similarly, large transepts provided room for pilgrims to watch masses celebrated at the center of the crossing, and the upper arcade of the three-tiered nave would have accommodated what, at times, would have been an overflow of devout pilgrims.[49] The greatest treasure of Conques is arguably the church itself and, in particular, the carved, relief

4.11
The semi-circular tympanum depicts Christ in Judgment, a common theme of pilgrimage churches. Saint Foy, Conques, view of tympanum

Mediating Elements

4.12
Saint Foy, Conques, view of
left tympanum

4.13
Saint Foy, Conques, view of
right tympanum

sculpture of the tympanum at the western front. A pilgrim arriving at Conques may have approached the church by means of the main street named for Charlemagne and passed through one of the original Roman gates that formed part of the town's fortifications. Approaching the western front of the church the tympanum would have come into view – its brightly polychromed narrative sculpture located between flanking towers. Here the dualistic worldview of the Medieval Christian Church was concretized and the power and peril of God were revealed to Medieval pilgrims.

The semi-circular tympanum depicts Christ in Judgment, a common theme of pilgrimage churches. Here, the world is definitively split between good and evil. Christ sits on a throne at the center, flanked above by angels, two of which blow horns announcing the Second Coming and Day of Judgment. On his left, the damned descend into the jaws of an open-mouthed monster and enter a hell of myriad horrors presided over by a grimacing Satan, their way to redemption blocked by fierce, armed angels. The horrors, punishments for the Seven Deadly Sins, are described in a detailed visual language that would have been understood by all. An adulteress awaits her fate, roped at the neck to her lover; a drunkard vomits his wine; a money forger is forced to drink the molten metal of his counterfeit currency. No one is exempt – monks and kings are subject to eternal punishments as well – all dictated by a placid Christ who commands on a banner above "Away from me accursed ones." On Christ's right side, in contrast to the chaos and horror of hell, the scene is one of calm and peace. The Virgin Mary leads the saved, including St. Peter, Datus, and Charlemagne, to heaven. Below the dead rise from their coffins and at Christ's feet their souls are weighed (by an angel on one side and a dishonest-looking devil on the other). Paradise is depicted as repeating bays of columns and arches, the central arcade framing Abraham who sits holding two children. Above him is Saint Foy, kneeling before God, her hands in prayer, mediating on behalf of the saved.

Saint Foy in Conques was an important stop along the Via Podensis. The journey through the sacred spaces of the church replicated at a smaller scale the pilgrim's journey and its themes of trial and redemption. At Saint Foy one can imagine the pilgrims passing under the left hand of Christ to enter the church, its message of foreboding and peril explicit. Then, suddenly, the richly colored and decorated grandeur of the soaring nave of this richly endowed church would slowly be revealed, its gloom suffused with incense. Passing the sanctuary, the golden treasury of Saint Foy would glow in the polychromed light created by the stained glass windows. All of which was presided over by Saint Foy herself, martyr and savior, an exemplar of Christ's dictate that to be saved one must first die. Exiting, the pilgrims might have passed through the door located below Christ's right hand – symbolically saved and reborn. Christ, strategically located at the center of the tympanum, mediates between good and evil – sin and salvation. As a human incarnation of God, the "son" of the father, he occupies the middle ground between humans and God and it is only through him that God is manifest and salvation made possible. "I am the way, and the truth, and the life; no one comes to the Father, but by me," was understood in both its physical and spiritual contexts.

In both sacred scripture and architecture, the content is often highly structured. In the text, language is codified and the narrative ordered in a consistent and coherent manner. Similarly, the architecture presents a legible and structured formal and symbolic language. This does not mean that the content in either media is static, objective, and uniform. Indeed, the power of both scripture and sacred architecture is that they are multivalent. Because their content is nuanced and subject to multiple interpretations, each individual has the ability to "read" the content from an individual perspective and can find their own particular interpretation (or, in religious terms, path to god or personal transformation). The sacred, in both word and material, is portentous; a medium that provides bridges to the expanded contexts established by the religions that created them.

Chapter 5

Symbolic Engagements

The Media of Architecture

Life, so-called, is a short episode between two great mysteries, which yet are one.

(C.G. Jung)[1]

Saint Foy employed architecture to embody the textual, religious, and social messages of the Medieval Church. Its full meaning was revealed through the serial tableaux that unfolded as pilgrims ambulated its spaces. The participatory nature of places like Saint Foy illustrates the dynamic interchanges they required. One was presumably affected, even changed, by the communicative media of the architecture and the meanings it delivered. We now turn to a closer examination of the communicative media of architecture through a discussion of the discursive roles that art and architecture have played, and continue to play, in establishing connections, structuring meaning, and at times facilitating personal transformation.

According to Karsten Harries, myths and architecture share the roles of representing the world so that "it no longer seems indifferent to our needs, arbitrary and contingent, but is experienced as a place we can call home."[2] One can expand this definition to include all the arts. Architecture may be the principal means by which humans articulate places in the world, but its "existentially mediating task"[3] could logically be applied to two- and three-dimensional art, literature, and other expressive and narrative forms. In this manner, we can deepen our discussion regarding architecture as a communicative media. In this chapter, we will examine art as a *media of communal activity*, and its application as part of a *means of personal development*. We will then turn to the Swiss psychiatrist Carl Gustav Jung's[4] house in Bollingen, Switzerland, to present, by means of an individual, secular example, the diverse symbols and communicative capacity of architecture and its roles as a *medium of transformation*.

Art as a Media of Communal Activity

The very earliest of art forms found in the Paleolithic cave paintings of Southern Europe were the means for the hunting societies that created them to concretize their world and describe their place within it. The best-known site at Lascaux, France, was created approximately 30,000 years ago at the very beginnings of human history. The appropriation of caves has been cited as the first architecture that satisfied the archetypal human need for shelter and refuge.[5] They were not limited to utilitarian uses, however, but became places of symbolism, narrative, and ritual. Inside the dark recesses of Lascaux is a remarkable series of paintings, which not only used the rock surfaces as a "canvas" but also transformed the textures and forms for spatial effects. The paintings were created over time and over generations – a palimpsest of images by a range of "authors" – a "sanctuary" for the "worship" of the beasts its creators depended on.

Lascaux was the result of acts of devotion to the life-sustaining force of the animals the Paleolithic peoples hunted and depended upon for their survival.[6] Throughout the cave galleries animated figures appear. The images of the Swimming Stags in an inner chamber called the Nave are partially in relief and the stags appear to tread water above the surface of a projecting ledge. Dynamism and movement are present elsewhere, and there is a sense of passage as a sequence of tableaux unfold throughout the cave. At the entrance, the passage narrows, then expands into the great Hall of the Bulls. Here one immediately confronts an image of four large bulls; three sideways, the fourth facing forward as if it just noticed your presence. Moving on, the path splits, one leading to the Axial Gallery, the other the Shaft of the Dead Man. The latter, located at the bottom of a precipice, shows a mortally wounded bison in a strong, dignified pose. Next to him is a dead man with a bird's head and an erect penis. These have been called symbols of power, of the soul, of fertility, and of the endurance of life beyond death.

5.1
The images of the Swimming Stags in an inner chamber called the Nave are partially in relief and the stags appear to tread water above the surface of a projecting ledge. Cave painting, frieze of Swimming Stags, Lascaux Caves, Perigord, Dordogne, France, Paleolithic

Source: Art Resource, New York.

The paintings, rendered in mineral earth and charcoal, symbolized the strength, dignity, and divinity of the animal gods – all gathered together and stilled for a moment in the space of sacred time. Their animated yet inert figures perhaps became easy targets for the spears of the men who gathered there, props for a ritualized hunt where the risks were known and the outcomes sure. Perhaps the paintings magically dispelled time, depicted past and future events of the hunt to prepare the hunters for the rigors and challenges to come and communicated legible information regarding the skills necessary for a successful hunt.[7] In this context, the cave was a physical setting that mediated between humans and their gods, an intermediary between the ritual and the act, and a liminal zone between the past and the future.[8] Reciprocal communal acts of creation and ritual enactments, in their earliest forms such as Lascaux, served the purpose of integrating the community for a common purpose. Within the sacred enclosure the creative/re-enactive rituals bound the initiates to the clan and underlined their place within it. Much like the Neolithic sites we will discuss later, Lascaux has engendered a plethora of speculations and conclusions regarding the motives of its creators and the meanings it held for them. The recognition that none can be definitively established does not lessen the importance of Lascaux (and places like it). What's important and useful are the meanings it holds for us today, especially in the context of our shared human condition of seeking to understand our position in the world, and the role that art plays in these perennial inquiries.

Art as a Means of Personal Development

One aspect of artistic activities important to the focus of this chapter is that their creation was often believed to be a means of connection and personal transformation. From Medieval Christian illuminated manuscripts to the design of Zen gardens in Medieval Japan (commonly understood as manifestations of the level of enlightenment of the monks who created them), the production of sacred art was often devotional and developmental. The paintings at Lascaux were put into the service of articulating questions germane to their time – a role, in all of the diversity of contemporary forms, art continues to play. Contemporary art therapy recognizes the roles art has played in symbolic activities. Its primary focus is the transformative potential of art to assist individuals along the path of self-understanding and integration.[9] The therapeutic use of art, usually in conjunction with "talk therapy" and "active imagination," owes much to the pioneering work of Carl Jung. Psychotherapy, especially the depth psychology developed by Jung, aims to access the unconscious areas of the psyche and, through the media of talk and awareness, to understand them more. If memories or feelings have been repressed, these therapies aid in accessing them and determining what significance they currently hold. In this manner, the analysand, through the guidance of the analyst or the media of art (or both), reconnects with sublimated emotions to integrate them into their consciousness. Art therapy, similar to the role the analyst plays in accessing the unconscious, artistic endeavors, if skillfully guided, can serve as a medium of connection and engagement. Artistic activity and the art created mediate between levels of consciousness, materializing what was formerly hidden.

Carl Jung recognized the potential of art to act as a medium of psychological discovery and development. He used two- and three-dimensional media to explore themes of archetypal symbolism during his own self-analysis, and encouraged his patients to do the same. Most succinctly, during a period of over thirty years, Jung built a house on Lake Zurich, an act of building integral to his process of psychological and spiritual maturation.

Carl Jung's House in Bollingen: Architecture as a Medium of Transformation

Architecture and the Unconscious

Carl Jung used painting, sculpture, and architecture as an integral part of his own "inner work" (a Jungian term used to describe the psychotherapeutic process). During the time he characterized as his "confrontation with the unconscious" he produced a series of narrative mythological paintings and mandalas that were later collected in what came to be known as *The Red Book*.[10] Because they had no relationship with his past, Jung believed they were manifestations of what he termed the Collective Unconscious.[11] Mandalas took on a special importance to Jung at this time as "cryptograms concerning the state of the self."[12] For Jung, the years of intense artistic output were the most important of his life where "everything essential was decided."[13] He also worked in stone and wood, but architecture, which often appeared in his dreams, was the most productive media.[14] Home and houses served as both refuges and departure points for creative and symbolic explorations. According to Robert Mugerauer, "Jung's own lifelong journey to selfhood was intertwined with his psychological concerns and houses, both imaginary and concrete."[15] In middle age, he began to build the first of a number of structures of a private retreat in Bollingen outside of Zurich on the shores of Lake Zurich.

Clare Cooper Marcus writes that Jung's house illustrated "our complex symbolic relationship with the homes we live in." Marcus documented the symbolism of our homes through testimonials given by people who described personal feelings about their houses at certain periods of their lives. Often their inner world was mirrored by feelings about their home environment, or they transformed their homes in ways that did. Marcus argues that certain repeating themes or archetypes associated with specific parts of the house emerged from the research:

> The unconscious often chooses houses, buildings, and secret rooms as symbols. The basement, or cellar is often a metaphor for the unconscious, of something hidden that needs to be explored, whereas the attic or roof or opening to the sky often reflects a desire to explore transpersonal realms or spiritual directions.[16]

When Jung was a child, meaningful play often involved houses. He created a secret place on a beam in the attic of his home (forbidden to children because of its rotten floorboards) where he kept a totemic figure he had carved from a wooden ruler. He made a bed for the figure in a pencil case where it lay along with a special painted stone, and eventually a number of "scrolls" of paper. Jung recounted that in the attic he felt "safe, and the tormenting sense of being at odds with myself was gone." Periodically he secretly

> clambered up on the beam, opened the case, and looked at my manikin and its stone. Each time I did this I placed in the case a little scroll of paper on which I had previously written something during school hours in a secret language of my own invention. The addition of a new scroll had the character of a solemn ceremonial act.[17]

When Jung and his mentor Sigmund Freud traveled to America together, he had a dream about a multi-storied house that was to prove significant for himself, as well as his relationship with Freud.[18] In the dream, Jung is

> in a house I did not know, which had two stories. It was "my house." I found myself in the upper story, where there was a kind of salon furnished with fine old pieces in rococo style. On the walls hung a number of precious old paintings. I wondered that this should be my house, and thought, "not bad." But then it occurred to me that I did not know what the ground floor looked like. Descending the stairs, I reached the ground floor. There everything was much older, and I realized that the house must date from about the fifteenth or sixteenth century. The furnishings were medieval; the floors were of red brick. Everywhere it was rather dark. I went from one room to another thinking "Now I really must explore the whole house." I came upon a heavy door, and opened it. Beyond it, I discovered a stone stairway that led down to the cellar. Descending again, I found myself in a beautifully vaulted room which looked exceedingly ancient. Examining the walls, I discovered layers of brick among the ordinary stone blocks, and chips of brick in the mortar. As soon as I saw this I knew that the walls dated from Roman times. My interest by now was intense. I looked more closely at the floor. It was of stone slabs, and in one of these I discovered a ring. When I pulled it, the stone slab lifted, and again I saw a stairway of narrow steps leading down to the depths, these too I descended, and entered a low cave cut into the rock. Thick dust lay on the floor, and in the dust were scattered bones and broken pottery, like the remains of an ancient culture. I discovered two human skulls, obviously very old and half disintegrated. Then I woke up.[19]

Jung's break with Freud was followed by an intense period of his confrontation with the unconscious. Jung carefully reviewed the details of his life to see if they could reveal the cause of his "psychic disturbance," but felt bereft of any means to understand the "constant inner pressure" that he was experiencing. He finally concluded that, "'since I know nothing at all, I shall simply do whatever occurs to me.' Thus I consciously submitted to the impulses of the unconscious." A childhood memory from when he was ten or eleven and had built "little houses and castles" out of bottles, stones, and mud evoked a "good deal of emotion," and led him to engage in similar play on the shores of Lake Zurich at the family home in Kusnacht. Most days after lunch (and before seeing his afternoon patients) he would work on a "village" composed of stone and mud cottages, a castle, and a church, the latter finished with a pyramidal red stone altar that recalled the "underground phallus" of a childhood dream.[20] For Jung, "it was a painfully humiliating experience to realize that there was nothing to be done except play childish games," but that through his engagement with the ritual of building, he "was on the way to discovering my own myth. For the building game was only a beginning. It released a stream of fantasies which I later carefully wrote down." Subsequently, whenever he felt at an impasse, he "painted a picture or hewed stone. Each such experience proved to be a *rite d'entrée* for the ideas and works that followed hard upon it."[21]

The Building of Symbols

Some years later Jung was to use architecture and associated artwork for similar aims at the house he constructed on the shore of Lake Zurich, outside of the city in the village of Bollingen. Jung purchased the land in 1922 and began work on the first structure, a stone tower, in 1923 just after the death of his mother. Jung had worked closely with his cousin Ernst Fiechter on the design of the family house in Kusnacht – the center of his busy family and professional life. Plans for a private retreat came in the early 1920s, when his professional life was very busy.[22] The property he eventually purchased in Bollingen was not Jung's first choice, but one that he recognized as propitious.[23] It is a small house, an amalgam of parts that were constructed over a 32-year period and completed in 1955, six years before Jung's death. At the time, it was more remote from Zurich than it is now.[24] Otherwise it looks much the same as it did when it was Jung's family camp and spiritual refuge. Its small scale makes it feel like a child's house, evoking images of the building rites he had performed years earlier.

When Jung began work on the first tower, his plan was to construct a round, one-story primitive hut with a fireplace in the middle, the "maternal hearth" of archetypal family dwellings. Jung was very clear that the house would never have electricity or plumbing (and it still doesn't). A primitive country retreat may have been practical, but it had symbolic aspects as well. It was a place of primal simplicity where the separation from his external life was clear and participation in the mundane tasks of living was possible. Jung's primitive hut allowed him to live in "modest harmony with nature," and he described the virtues of simple acts:

> I have done without electricity, and tend the fireplace and stove myself. Evenings I light the old lamps. There is no running water, and I pump the water from the well. I chop the wood and cook the food. These simple acts make man simple; and how difficult it is to be simple![25]

5.2
Jung House, Bollingen, Switzerland, 1923–1955, view from lakeside

The archetypal primitive hut is an enduring symbol of an essential authentic building that has a long architectural lineage. The first architectural theoretician Marcus Vitruvius Pollio equated the first dwellings with the founding of language, political discourse, and civilization, and the eighteenth-century French Jesuit priest Marc-Antoine Laugier posited it as an exemplar.[26] Simple dwellings have often symbolized separate sacralized places where contact with inner or outer divinity is possible. The cave dwellings of the Gnostics, later replicated in the troglodyte dwellings and churches in Cappadocia, Turkey, deliberately shed the comforts of the world, presumably to focus on devotion. Remote hermitages have enjoyed a special status as places where the enlightened master retires for contemplation and connection with the divine. The Hermit Scholar's retreat of Taoism found potent expression in paintings of the Southern Sung period, and in Medieval Japanese temples and tea houses. The Medieval Japanese tea master Sen no Rikyu (1521–1591), is known for his insistence that the only authentic tea ceremony was the *soan-no-yu* performed in a small, austere hut.[27] We have already mentioned Thoreau's simple hut on Walden Pond and how it served as a means for the philosopher to concretize the essentials of life, and came to represent the essence of Transcendentalism's insistence on spiritual authenticity. Thomas Merton built a simple concrete block hermitage at the Abbey of Gethsemani in Kentucky, which in a letter to a friend he described as follows, "One works there, cutting wood, clearing ground, cutting grass, cooking soup, drinking fruit juice, sweating, washing, making fire, smelling smoke, sweeping, etc. This is religion."[28]

Symbolic Engagements

Jung's analysis of his dream of the multi-storied and multi-aged house was that it represented a "kind of image of the psyche," where each level constituted a particular aspect of consciousness. The ground floor "stood for the first level of the unconscious," and the cave, "the world of the primitive man within myself – a world that can scarcely be reached or illuminated by consciousness."[29] Jung often dreamed of unknown rooms in houses, which represented yet to be discovered aspects of his personality.[30] Jung's house at Bollingen became a potent media that he used to "achieve a kind of representation in stone of my innermost thoughts and of the knowledge I had acquired," and each subsequent addition took on the symbolic qualities of the dream that held so much importance to him. At this stage of his life (and inner work), "words and paper . . . did not seem real enough" – he needed to make a "confession of faith in stone" beginning with the construction of the first tower.[31]

5.3
The stages of Jung House, Bollingen

Source: Drawing by Glenn Robert Lym, courtesy of Clare Cooper Marcus.

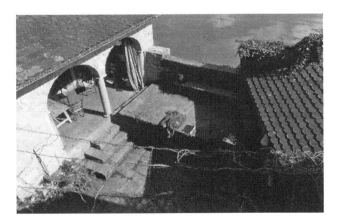

5.4
Jung House, Bollingen, view of courtyard from central tower

5.5
Jung House, Bollingen, view of final central room (on left)

Jung's original plan for a round single-story structure with a "hearth at the center and bunks along the walls," was modeled on huts he would subsequently see in Africa. For Jung, "Primitive huts concretize an idea of wholeness, familial wholeness," but he soon realized that this ideal was "too primitive" and decided to build a two-story structure instead. The first building was completed in 1923, but each stage of construction was both an end and a beginning. The completion of the first tower elicited feelings of "repose and renewal," but soon Jung became aware that "it did not yet express everything that needed saying, that something was still lacking," and so in 1927 he began construction on the central part of the house and a "tower-like annex." Four years later the second tower was expanded to accommodate a private place of "spiritual concentration." In 1935, Jung again felt that the house was unfinished and in need of another component. He added a courtyard between the house and the lake that included an open loggia with a large fireplace.[32] This fourth component represented a quaternary, a "fourth element that was separated from the unitary threeness of the house" and symbolized wholeness.

Each of the buildings was constructed over a period of twelve years in four-year intervals, a temporal symmetry that matched the quartered organization of the house. It would be twenty years before Jung would build the final room over the central section of the house. This room was extroverted, a much lighter construction of wood with large windows that overlook the lake. It represented his "ego-personality," and "signified the extension of consciousness achieved in old age." When Jung built this room following the death of his wife, he felt that he had become "his own person." Emma Jung had lived the lighter part of life for Jung, leaving him to wrestle with the darker parts of his personality. Now, in old age, he felt as if he were "being reborn in stone," and that the last room was a "symbol of psychic wholeness."

Paintings and Carvings

Jung later stated that he had no preconceived plans for the house, or the ability to reflect on its ultimate meaning until after it was completed. The first tower, built out of solid stone, served as a refuge during the time he was buffeted by doubts and psychic instability. Its original entrance is marked by an inscription that states "VOCATUS ATQUE NON VOCATUS DEUS ADERIT" ("Summoned or not, the god will be there"). The same statement is found at the entrance to the house in Kusnacht, and refers to the Delphic Oracle's answer to the Lacedaemonian's plans for war against Athens. For Jung, the oracle's meaning was that "the god will be on the spot, but in what form and to what purpose?" It served to remind his patients at Kusnacht that they were embarking on a path to the divine (in all of its aspects) – a sentiment he applied to himself at the original tower at Bollingen.[33]

The lower room of the first tower is dark and introverted with a round dining table at its center. Its plan is quartered – the entrance in the east, the stove north, most of the windows west, and a niche in the solid south wall. At the northeast side of the room, a narrow, curving stair leads upstairs to three bedrooms. On the wall of one upstairs room Jung painted a mandala. He had begun

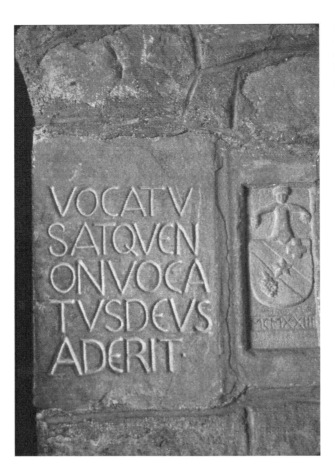

drawing and painting mandalas in 1916 and felt that they helped him to "emerge from the darkness" of his inner work of the time.[34] Mandalas are typically quartered compositions that include imaginary gateways and passages. They have served as two-dimensional representations of the spiritual path and have spatial and architectural implications.[35] For Jung, mandalas were "cryptograms concerning the state of the self . . . my whole being – actively at work,"[36] and symbolized the "wholeness of the personality." It was through the media of their creation that he realized

> all the paths I had been following, all the steps I had taken, were leading back to a single point – namely to the mid-point. It became increasingly plain to me that the mandala is the center. It is the exponent of all paths. It is the path to the center, to individuation.[37]

In another room in the upper floor of the first tower, Jung created a painting that featured Philemon, recalling one featured in his *Red Book*. Philemon first appeared to Jung in a dream and he described him as derived from the figure of Elijah and colored by Hellenistic and Gnostic elements.[38] Philemon was

5.7
"Philemon and other figures of my fantasies brought home to me the crucial insight that there are things in the psyche which I do not produce, but which produce themselves and have their own life." Jung House, Bollingen, painting of Philemon by Jung in an upper room of the first tower

introduced to Jung through Goethe's *Faust*[39] and served as his guide along the pathways of his inner work:

> Philemon and other figures of my fantasies brought home to me the crucial insight that there are things in the psyche which I do not produce, but which produce themselves and have their own life. Philemon represented a force which was not myself. In my fantasies I held conversations with him, and he said things which I had not consciously thought . . . Psychologically, Philemon represented superior insight. He was a mysterious figure to me. At times he seemed to me quite real, as if he were a living personality . . . what the Indians call a guru.[40]

The importance this figure held for Jung illustrates the influences that informed his work, including architecture as both a media and symbol of inner transformation. In Goethe's *Faust*, the pious Philemon and Baucis are murdered by Faust so that their land can be used for his technological plans. Jung viewed himself as an "advocate and avenger" of Philemon, which reveals his proclivity toward the revelation of the hidden but ever present reality described in Gnostic writings and the power of place. In Greek mythology, Philemon and Baucis welcome into their simple hut the gods Jupiter and Mercury, disguised as wayfarers, after all of the inhabitants of Phrygia had turned them away.[41] Even though they are very poor, the couple welcome the gods to their hearth and generously feed them. The wayfarers finally reveal themselves to the couple and punish their neighbors by flooding the valley. At Philemon and Baucis' request, their primitive hut becomes a temple that they tend until their death.

5.8
Jung House, Bollingen, trickster figure on the base of the first tower

Similar to art, working with stone was Jung's *rite d'entrée* for working out ideas and through the medium of stone, Jung transformed shifting, "troublesome things" into "steady and durable" objects. Similar to depictions of swimming stags at Lascaux, Jung's chisel responded to the existing surfaces of the stone. Like a sculptor uncovering the figure inside, Jung's carvings allowed his stones to speak – a metaphor of timelessness and the anima of natural materials. The alchemy of uncovering the images inside the stone replicated the psychological process of revealing the unconscious aspects of his personality.

Stones at the base of the first tower contain a number of associative and narrative images. One depicts a trickster, an aspect of Mercury (who accompanied Jupiter on the earthly travels that brought them to Philemon and Baucis). Mercury was Jupiter's favorite traveling companion, known for being shrewd, resourceful, and entertaining. He was a complicated character, however, who was a trickster and thief but also served as the guardian of travelers, including leading the dead to Hades.[42] An adjacent figure of a woman reaches out to milk a mare. Written in Latin is the passage "May the light arise which I have born in my body." This carving reflects Jung's interest in the feminine (and his animus), and anticipates the coming age of Aquarius (under the constellation of Pegasus), where it is believed that attributes associated with the feminine will become more recognized and accepted.[43]

5.9
"May the light arise which I have born in my body." Jung House, Bollingen, woman and mare on the west base of the first tower

5.10
"Time is a child – playing like a child – playing a board game – the kingdom of the child. This is Telesphoros, who roams through the dark regions of this cosmos and glows like a star out of the depths. He points the way to the gates of the sun and to the land of dreams." Jung House, Bollingen, stella

Outside of the courtyard and near the shore of the lake is a stone stella also carved by Jung. The origins of the stone illustrate the often-prescient thoughts and actions of Jung. He had ordered a load of stones for a garden wall, but when they arrived the cornerstone was discovered to have been incorrectly quarried. When the mason gave orders for it be returned, Jung cried out, "No, that is my stone. I must have it!"[44] It appears that he recognized the potential of the stone to reveal answers to the questions he was asking and felt afterward that its arrival was miraculous.[45] He referred to it as the *Lapis Philosophorum*, the Philosopher's Stone, which is "loved by the wise," and "despised by fools,"[46] and on the side of the stone that faces the lake carved alchemical quotations in Latin that suggest they are the words of the stone itself:

> I am an orphan, alone; never the less I am found everywhere – I am one but opposed to myself. I am youth and old man at one time, I have known neither father nor mother, because I had to be fetched out of the deep like a fish, or fell like a white stone from heaven. In the woods and the mountains I roam, but I am hidden in the inner-most soul of man. I am mortal for everyone, yet I am not touched by the cycle of aeons.

Jung's choice of the stella form was consistent with his use of stones. Greeks placed stellae as way-finding markers along roads and trails (typically featuring the figure of Mercury).[47] Another intriguing connection to Greek civilization and, in particular, the Hellenistic Age, is apparent in a passage carved on another face of the lakeside stella. It is entitled "Homunculus" and, this time in Greek, reads:

> Time is a child – playing like a child – playing a board game – the kingdom of the child. This is Telesphoros, who roams through the dark regions of this cosmos and glows like a star out of the depths. He points the way to the gates of the sun and to the land of dreams.

The homunculus is the reflection we see of ourselves in another's eye – a symbol perhaps of the interdependence of the collective unconscious. Telesphoros was a Hellenistic healing deity associated with Asclepeius and was typically depicted as a boy whose face is hidden in the shadows of a hooded cloak.[48] The Hellenistic Greeks built a number of significant Asklepeions – hospitals where physical and psychic diseases were treated by exercise, music, bathing, visualization, and the analysis of dreams.[49] An important center was at the Hellenistic and later Roman city of Pergamon on the Aegean coast of present-day Turkey, and contains a treatment building that has remarkable synchronicity with the architectural and psychological work of Jung.[50] The treatment building, dedicated to Telesphoros, was reached by means of a long, underground passage called the *crypto-portico*. Patients would first bathe in the mineral baths near its entrance and then descend steps where water coursed down either side. The passage had openings in its vaulted roof where physicians would whisper encouraging words "from the gods."

The treatment building of Telesphoros was cylindrical with a solid cylinder at its center, from which vaults spanned the surrounding ambulatory. Water ran

5.11
Asklepeion, Pergamon, Turkey,
Hellenistic and Roman, view of
the *crypto-portico*

5.12
Asklepeion, Pergamon, view of the Telesphoron, sleeping chambers are on the right

through channels in the floor of the ambulatory, filling its spaces with relaxing sounds. Patients would sleep in individual chambers, after praying to the gods for dreams that would aid in the cure of their illnesses. The *crypto-portico*, or "hidden passage" led to this place of mystery. Inside the treatment building the gods would speak through dreams that would be analyzed by the physicians. Only then could a diagnosis be made and a treatment prescribed. Jung makes no mention of the Asklepieon at Pergamon (or other related sites) in his autobiography, which raises the intriguing question of whether he knew about it, or other Greek and Roman hospitals of this type. However, a cylindrical building dedicated to a mysterious god who points to the "land of dreams," where the dreams of patients would be analyzed certainly suggests a potent reciprocity between Pergamon, Bollingen, Jungian psychology, and the transformative role of architecture.

Architecture as a Medium of Transformation

Art and architecture have typically served as potent means for humans to materially articulate otherwise vague, ephemeral understandings of their "place in the world." The largely intuitive Paleolithic paintings of Southern Europe resulted in concrete representations of the world by the hunting societies that created them. One painting found in a cave in Northern Spain shows the imprint of a painted hand that was pressed into the surface of the rock. It is a simple statement of presence and may be understood as an expression of the reciprocity of self-awareness and place. Powerful images such as these still affect us today because they depict the archetypal human condition of self and other that our ancient ancestors perhaps were just becoming aware of. Because creative activity broadens our intellectual and emotional reach, it has the ability to transform us. The personal growth that results from creative acts and our understandings of the works themselves, are reciprocal.

By the agency of art and architecture, Jung explored temporal, terrestrial, and personal realms of consciousness. He was especially interested in the reconciliation of the different aspects of his personality – conscious and unconscious – intellectual and earthy. In his student years, he became aware of a split in his personality – what he called Number 1 was his rational side, disconnected from any historical context; Number 2, his intuitive personality, that had an affinity with the Medieval ages. He described his "life work" as having "revolved around the study of opposites."[51] Robert Mugerauer argues that, "In Jung's lifelong struggle to unite these two contradictory dimensions . . . dreams involving houses and built environments played a persistent and decisive role," and "houses were intimately connected with Jung's self-realization."[52] Jung's interest in alchemy was based, in part, on the exploration of dichotomies this early scientific practice engaged in. Bollingen expressed the physical and psychic splits symbolized by alchemy, most potently through the juxtaposition of the "maternal hearth" and the "spiritual tower." The former represented (and accommodated) Jung's earthy, animal side and was centered on the original tower building – the "spiritual retreat" of the second tower symbolized his intellectual, rational self. Here in stone his *anima*, or feminine side, and *animus*, masculine side, were co-joined – a conjunction of opposites.

Bollingen allowed Jung to connect with his environment and the present moment in ways that were inaccessible to him in his busy and intellectually demanding professional life. He used the house as a solitary retreat – doing most of his writing there and raising a flag when he wished to be left alone. But it was also a place to be with family and friends, a place of convivial meals and activities. Jung valued direct experiences and wrote:

> The older I grow the more impressed I am by the frailty and uncertainty of our understanding, and all the more I take recourse to the simplicity of immediate experience so as not to lose contact with the essentials, namely the dominants which rule human existence throughout the millenniums.[53]

As a young man, Jung's disagreements with his minister father regarding the latter's insistence on faith over reason precipitated Jung's interest in cultivating a more direct connection with life and the divine.[54] He enjoyed cooking and Barbara Hannah (a patient and biographer) recalled an evening where Jung prepared a meal for Toni Wolff and herself:

> It was very cold and Jung was cooking in his original round kitchen in a long Oriental robe which he often wore in cold weather. He looked like a picture I had once seen of an old alchemist at work among his retorts . . . Jung was entirely engrossed in some absorbing cooking and in watching the fire. (He was a most unusually good cook and used in those days to cook the most complicated dishes. I remember one sauce with no fewer than sixteen ingredients!)[55]

Jung built a "house like those of mediaeval times with thick stone walls and small windows, so that when you are inside you are contained; if you want to see more you can go out."[56] Most spaces at Bollingen feel introverted, intimate and enclosed. For Barbara Hannah, "It seemed to be back in the Middle Ages, with the lamp and the firelight making a small illuminated circle in what struck me that evening as a huge circular circumference of darkness."[57] However, the later constructions of the courtyard, loggia, and upper room of the central structure are clearly extroverted, framing views of the lake and the sky. These last additions were completions of both the architecture and Jung's spiritual and psychological development that served to integrate the conflicted aspects of his personality. After the death of his wife, Jung felt the "inner obligation to become what I myself am." Once again, architecture was used in service of his process of individuation (his term for psychological and spiritual integration). Jung realized that the original central structure was himself, hidden between the "maternal" and "spiritual" towers. When completed, it represented his "ego-personality" and "signified an extension of consciousness achieved in old age." There was symmetry to the building programs at Bollingen, beginning after the death of his mother and completed following the death of his wife.[58] Jung worked on Bollingen episodically and intuitively, "always following the concrete needs of the moment." He described the process as "a kind of dream," and only when it was completed did he recognize that "all the parts fitted together and that a meaningful form had resulted" that symbolized his now integrated self. As E.A. Bennet reflected, "This is really C.G. in stone, the expression of himself, quite apart from the world."[59]

In Jung's lifelong struggle to reconcile his outer and inner worlds he employed a number of what might be described as "practices" – scholarship, scientific analysis, fantasies, and dream analysis – but acts of creativity and, in particular, architecture, were among the most potent. Architecture served to concretize and symbolize psychological conditions and spiritual perspectives in a tangible, material way. The places he created were also thresholds of connection to broader realms of apprehension and understanding. One aspect of Bollingen was its mythological content – it served as a mediator between conscious, earthy existence and the unconscious, archetypal realms of mythology. Mercury appears as an earth spirit, appearing on the wall of the "maternal" tower, a guide for Jung's engagement with his more feminine side.[60] Telesphoros was the god of healing and was known as the "completer." A dark cowl hid his face and the passage to health, the *crypto-portico*, was hidden as well. His appearance at Bollingen reflects Jung's emphasis on the "process" of healing, including stellae as way-finding markers. Each building stage was a process – a practice – an outer manifestation of the inner work of individuation. The transformation of Philemon and Baucis' simple hut into a temple provides an analogy of the house Jung built at Bollingen – a primitive dwelling becomes a sacred place through the guidance of the gods who were once hidden and are now revealed. Jung's recognition of the alignment of the building program with the deaths of his mother and wife, led him to reflect that Bollingen was "connected with death." Jung felt that each of us should "have a myth about death." Not death as "nothingness," but as a portal to another consciousness.

Jung's adaptation of the primitive hut and his adoption of Philemon as a guiding figure provide compelling examples regarding the transformative power of architecture. In alchemy, the transformation of materials symbolized spiritual transformation. Jung argued that one of the "central axioms of alchemy" came from the sayings of Maria Prophetissa, who stated that "One becomes two, two becomes three, and out of the third comes the one as the fourth." The sequence of construction at Bollingen reached a nadir with the quaternary achieved by the courtyard and loggia. The use of geometry, though not explicit, is apparent through the application of the circle and the square and their association with timeless structures – the first tower is a quartered cylinder, the second a pure circular geometry, and the middle buildings, court, and loggia are rectilinear. Sacred architecture has numerous examples of the potent integration of these two pure geometries, most commonly when a dome surmounts a cube, and the reconciliation of geometries can be understood, in part, as representations of the mediating role of architecture.

Jung's simple dwelling on the shores of Lake Zurich provided the setting for deep engagements with the "thingly-real." Here he could play like a child and immerse himself (and others) in the mundane pleasures of existence. It also served as a mediator to a broader, vaster world, where the limitations of time and place were blurred.[61] For Jung, the principal difference between him and others was that the "dividing walls" between the apparent and the hidden were "transparent."[62] For Jung, it was a place that had the ability to join past, present, and future. "In the tower at Bollingen it is as if one lived in many centuries simultaneously. The place will outlive me, and in its location and style it points backward to the things of long ago." There he experienced "life in the round, as something forever coming into being and passing on."[63] "Life in the round" uses formal architectural terminology to describe timeless places and experiences. At Bollingen, similar to the "eternal return" of primitive religious beliefs described by Mircea Eliade, "Thoughts arise to the surface which reach back into the centuries, and accordingly anticipate a remote future."

Jung's presence is still palpable at Bollingen, the spirit of the school of depth psychology he founded expressed through the buildings and carvings executed there as part of his own inner work. For Jung, the media of architecture, painting, and sculpture guided his path to individuation, resulting in his "confession of faith in stone." Here he "carved out rough answers." There is a concave surface on the southern wall of the ground floor of the first tower where Jung painted a symmetrical scene of three male and three female figures, some dark others light, flanked by a bird on the left and a snake the right. Above is a quaternary symbol and above that the sun. Below them a boat-like image floats upon layers of water, each getting progressively darker. It suggests the multiple aspects of the soul, pinned between the forces of earth and heaven, the depths of mystery of the unconscious and the reconciliation of the quaternary. For Jung, the *raison d'être* of his life was "coming to terms with that indefinable Being we call God," and toward the end of his life he wrote: "At Bollingen, I am in the midst of my true life, I am most deeply myself. Here I am, as it were, the 'age old son of the mother.'"

"Philemonis sacrum – Fausti Poenitentia" ("Philemon's Shrine – Faust's Penitence") appears over the doorway of Jung's private tower. One might say that as Jung built Bollingen, he built his life, with all of its complexities and ambiguities. From a symbolic perspective, it represented the world of mystery and mythology in the tradition of symbolic and narrative art. In the context of phenomenology, the material presence and essential nature of the primitive hut accommodated the earthy, messy, and primal aspects of carnal life. It can be understood from a hermeneutical perspective as the means by which Jung reconciled the conflicting individual and collective aspects of his life, and is a place that makes his work and its content accessible and meaningful to us today. Bachelard reflected that the "house is one of the greatest powers of integration for the thoughts, memories and dreams of mankind,"[64] an observation that could logically be applied to Bollingen.

During Jung's lifetime his private tower was kept locked, with the "key with me all the time," a tradition that continues today. The family maintains the sacrality of his private refuge, an acknowledgment, perhaps, that Jung and his discoveries may never be fully understood.[65] Toward the end of his life, Jung admitted that the older he got, the more he could see and accept the mystery of consciousness. The last words of his autobiography state that the "alienation which so long separated me from the world has become transferred to my own inner world, and has revealed to me an unexpected unfamiliarity with myself." In the end, he was reconciled with the paradoxes of life and the richness of experience they revealed. For Jung, "religion becomes inwardly impoverished when it loses or cuts down its paradoxes; but their multiplication enriches because only the paradox comes anywhere near to comprehending the fullness of life."[66] According to Clare Cooper Marcus, Bollingen "was a place where he could reflect upon – and concretize – who he was and would become."[67] The stages of building Bollingen mirrored the stages of his maturation and ultimately individuation or wholeness. It was the medium of architecture that facilitated the connections he was compelled to make and that in the end symbolized his arrival at the center – his spiritual home.

Chapter 6

Earth and Sky

Place and Primordial Architecture

I was conscious of this vanished being and myself as part of an unbroken stream of consciousness . . . With an imaginative effort it is possible to see the eternal present in which all days, all the seasons of the plain, stand in enduring unity.

(Archeologist Jaquetta Hawkes upon discovering a Neanderthal skeleton)[1]

Carl Jung's house in Bollingen illustrates the active role architecture can play in articulating perennial questions and establishing connections to possible resolutions. Jung's process of building can be seen as a means to connect with primal human existence while addressing contemporary ontological issues. In this context, the creation and presence of Bollingen were (and are) both ancient and entirely current – essential and complex. We now turn to ancient examples as a means to unpack the enduring questions they addressed and relationships they established, and suggest the relevance they may hold for the present.

For some, ancient architecture holds little interest – their crude monolithic construction and inscrutable use and significance make them inferior (if not irrelevant) cultural outputs. Others find infinite interest and a multitude of functions, construction methods, and meanings. Inbetween these divergent meanings lie understandings that may more completely explain these enduring artifacts and perhaps exhume meanings that have contemporary relevance. In some ways, the following examples are similar, but on closer examination each reveals particular aspects regarding the in-between realms they described, and the diverse and nuanced symbolism they embodied. In this fashion, they can be understood much like Jaquetta Hawkes viewed a Neanderthal skeleton, as occupying an eternal present and representing a type of unity that transcends time and place.

Spiro Kostof poses the questions, "Where do we start with the history of architecture? Where did architecture begin?" to insist that it was "there from the beginning." In other words, as soon as humans distinguished one area from another by ritual or material means, that was the beginning of architecture. Sacred places, either revealed by the gods, or consecrated in the hope that they would appear, were specific places separated from the surrounding enormity of homogenous profane space (to use Mircea Eliade's terms). In the beginning, simple acts and settings were portentous and established definable and symbolic places. Through the use of existing natural places such as caves, valleys, and ridges, or by transforming natural settings by scraping of the earth or constructing simple enclosures, early humans created places for shelter, refuge, and ritual. As we will discuss in this chapter, the chthonic architecture of caves led to *cave replications* that were further elaborated upon in funerary architecture. *Funerary architecture*, arguably the most symbolically potent and diverse of building types served, in part, to mediate between the living and the dead. *Stone circles*, *earthworks*, and *effigy figures* also served mediating roles, but predominantly between humans and the larger environmental contexts they sought to understand.

The act of building, however simple or primitive, serves to delimit one place from another. Fundamentally, the only place humans have to build is the surface of the earth – a middle ground between the earth and the sky. The earliest shared or civic architecture can be viewed as acts that served to articulate a place in the world and a means to mediate its principal elements. In this context, buildings and other constructions serve, at the very least metaphorically, to bridge both physical and psychic divides. The Dutch Benedictine monk and architect Hans van der Laan researched Stonehenge while developing his contemporary theories of architecture, an endeavor that can be understood as bridging the past and the present. Van der Laan described placemaking as a fundamental act that occupies a liminal space between earth and sky. For van der Laan, architecture occupies the middle ground between the earth and the heavens and mediates between these two realms, and the "mass of the earth below and the space of the air above, which meet at the surface of the earth, is the primary datum" of human habitation and placemaking.

Mircea Eliade referred to archeological finds of animal bones in cave sites in Europe as "documents" with the ability to reveal aspects of the culture that engaged in these deliberate, and we can assume, meaningful acts.[2] Architecture, and in particular sacred architecture, was traditionally a quest for permanence in an impermanent world. The use of monolithic materials is an essential structural type with a lengthy and impressive lineage. Simple stone structures may have been a practical application of available materials and technologies, but they also symbolized incorruptibility. They were subject to the laws of gravity and of decay, but also represented the endurance of the cultural organizations that created them and the religious beliefs they materialized. In this context, they mediated between these two worlds:

The complexity of lithic symbolism and the religious variances of stones and rocks are well known. The rock, the slab, the granite block reveals duration without end, permanence, incorruptibility – and the last analysis a modality of *existing* independently of temporal becoming.[3]

Whereas the interpretation of Jung's house in Bollingen benefited from an extant building and extensive writings by Jung and others, in the analysis of historical architecture, this is a rare condition – one is typically faced with incomplete or corrupted artifacts and limited textual evidence. As Mircea Eliade asserts regarding ancient myths, rituals, and sites, "We are confronted by the poverty and opaqueness of our sources."[4] The case of prehistoric sites presents significant challenges to interpretations of their meaning and use. Here we must rely on archeological findings, restored sites, contemporary scholarship, and, in some cases, ethnographic comparisons to be able to suggest some conclusions. That said, it is a speculative endeavor, which must by necessity mediate between incomplete physical evidence, the absence of any historical records, and a discontinuity of ritual use. Our interpretations, therefore, must rely, in part, on comparative interpretations that utilize other more extant or restored sites, and the architectural manifestations of cultural and religious archetypes. Most importantly, in the context of hermeneutic retrieval, we engage in this study with the recognition of enduring characteristics of the human condition and the hope that ancient sites may inform the placemaking activities of today.

Caves and Cave Imagery

We might consider the first architecture and perhaps shrine to be the cave. It may have been a simple depression under a rock, or a voluminous space, but it was recognized as shelter and taken over as such. Perhaps it was consecrated by fire – light and heat that drove the beasts from its recesses and illuminated its inscrutable shadows. Here was the first place of refuge and safety – but also in its deeper recesses a place of mystery and the setting for the drama of life and death.[5] The town of Escale in Southern France contains the oldest known surviving hearth that dates from over 500,000 years ago, a halfway station in time between now and the first *Homo Sapiens*. All that survives are some charred remains – the dust of fires that burned out long ago, kindled by humans whose bones have long since powdered and been washed or blown away. Other caves have been excavated in the Swiss Alps that contain more eternal remains – the bones of animals carefully arranged presumably as acts of worship.[6]

Caves and cave imagery are perhaps some of the more enduring symbolic images. Hindu temples symbolize the cave and the mountain (see Figure 4.4), sanctuaries for the worship of the late Roman god Mithras resembled caves, and Christian healing sites are often located in grottos (such as Lourdes).[7] Some ancient sanctuaries were carved from living rock, such as the early

6.1

Caves and cave imagery are
perhaps some of the more
enduring symbolic images.
Karli, India, second century
CE, rock-cut Chaitya Hall

Source: Mondadori Electa.

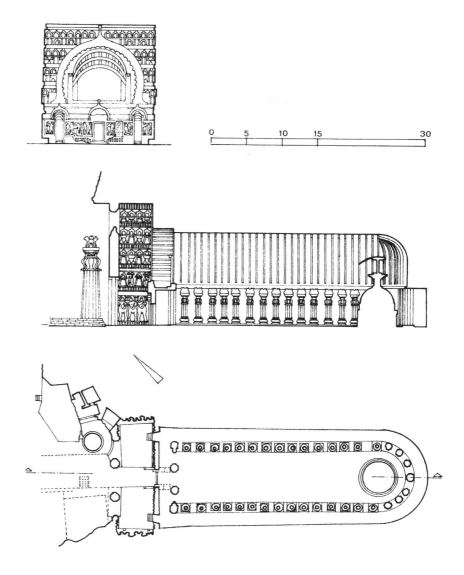

Buddhist monasteries located in the Southern Indian province of Maharesha.
The principal locations at Karli and Ajanta were important monastic centers
and pilgrimage sites where sanctuaries were carved into the sides of rock
escarpments and reached by steep steps. The prayer halls were called Chaitya
Halls, their name derived from the Sanskrit *chita*, which is the mound of ashes
left after cremation. Here, solid rock was transformed into the sanctuaries
and shrines of early Buddhism establishing an archetype replicated throughout
Asia.

At Paleolithic cave sites, a natural setting was appropriated and transformed by art and ritual. Later sites replicated the cave sanctuary, as found
at Ggantija on the island of Gozo, Malta. Here, instead of transforming a natural

place, one was created – a reproduction of the archetype of the cave, but now wholly humanly made. This is important because now the archetype is reproducible, the creation arguably of the first building type.[8] At Ggantija, earth and artifice were balanced, establishing a dichotomy of the natural and the humanly made. It is believed to have been a goddess site where themes of death and resurrection were symbolized by animal sacrifices – ritualized killing to assure the continuity of life. Like many sacred places that followed this earliest of sacred buildings, it comprised an entry sequence of progressively more sacred enclosures, entered by means of paths and thresholds. Similar to Lascaux, a series of constricted passages and linked spaces led to the sacred place. Its form symbolized the fecund goddess, and its articulation the horned beast, an amalgam of the complementary forces that defined the life of the people that constructed this early holy place.[9]

Earthworks, standing stones, ziggurats, pyramids, and the multiple varieties of spires constitute a particular building type in the history of architecture. Though there is a diversity of historical, cultural, religious, and material inflections, there is also a shared agenda of both separating or delimiting a particular place and connecting it to a larger, perhaps unknown, context. Humans found themselves placed in a vast cosmological system they did not create and only partially understood – an existential setting that architecture traditionally was put in service of addressing. According to Spiro Kostof, "To mediate

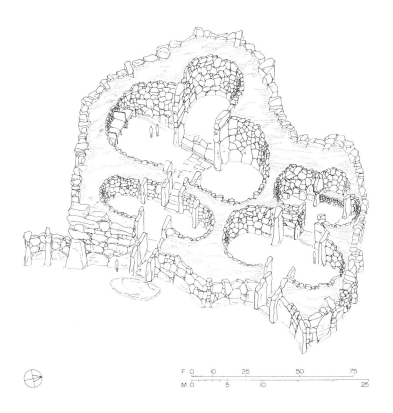

F 0   10   25   50   75
M 0   5   10   25

6.2
At Ggantija, earth and artifice were balanced establishing a dichotomy of the natural and the humanly made. Ggantija, Malta, third millennium BCE, reconstruction

Source: Drawing by Richard Tobias, by permission of Oxford University Press.

between the cosmos and polity, to give shape to fear and exorcize it, to effect a reconciliation of knowledge and the unknowable – that was the charge of ancient architecture."[10]

Funerary Archetypes

Death and place are inextricably bound to the human experience and pose enduring existential questions pertaining to corporality and continuity. It is not surprising, therefore, that some of the oldest surviving architecture are tombs. Placemaking acts established eternal places reserved only for the rituals of the clans, tribes, or cultures that created them, but death, especially of rulers, represented an impermanence that needed to be reconciled. The gods, in all their manifestations, symbolized eternal life and from the earliest building programs, architecture was put into the service of representing their continuity. Deities first appeared as the sun and the earth, living and dying through days and seasons, but ever-present. Early in the history of religion, the god who dies and is reborn appears, and subsequently becomes an enduring type. Rulers – chiefs, pharaohs, kings – became earthly manifestations of deities and when they died, their tombs, with often but not always carefully preserved relics, symbolized transcendence over death and the continuity of their authority.[11] Reliquaries and tombs were important sacred places of power that acted as thresholds between the living and the dead. Funerary architecture had multiple and multivalent roles of mediating between life and death – permanence and decay – humans and their gods.

Architecture, of all the art forms, has proven to be the most effective in commemorating the dead[12] and mortuary architecture is one of the earliest and most enduring of building types. They were built not only to memorialize the dead but as liminal places where contact with the dead was possible. In the case of deified rulers, funerary architecture assumed the role of sustaining the power of rulers beyond the grave and mediating between humans and their god-rulers. This is clearly apparent at the early extensive burial mound-building programs in Japan and Korea. It was in the vast and sophisticated necropolises of Pharaonic Egypt, however, that this type was clearly established. The early funerary complex and step pyramid at the Mortuary Temple of King Zoser were an extensive amalgam of surface and formal symbolizations of political hegemony and environmental setting (see Figure 4.6). The deification of Zoser and his eternal status were made possible through the use of stone and its regular re-vivification through ritual. In the forecourt outside the entrance to Zoser's tomb is a mortuary temple containing the *serdab*, a small room inside of which a statue of Zoser looked out through two small holes.[13] This *serdab* is a cenotaph that complements Zoser's tomb, and communicates most directly the endurance of the ruler and of the political union of Northern and Southern Egypt most closely associated with his reign.

Neolithic Stone Circles, Earthworks, Burial Mounds, and Passage Graves in Europe

By around 7000 BCE, the great sheets of ice that for millennia had covered Northern Europe began to retreat. The recovered landscape and warming climate provided a receptive environment for human habitation. The agrarian culture that developed during the Neolithic Era included farming and animal husbandry, which in many cases resulted in reliable food supplies. It also produced religious and ritual practices that were primarily focused on the dead.[14] Architecture at this early stage of human artistic development was put into the service of Neolithic beliefs and rituals and produced arguably the first sacred architecture. Stone circles, earthworks, and burial mounds constitute the main building type of this time (in addition to dwellings that were built out of much less enduring materials) and are enduring cultural artifacts.

Mircea Eliade argues that megaliths found throughout the world "constitute the unrivaled connection between the living and the dead; they are believed

6.3
Dolmen, Møn, Denmark, Neolithic

to perpetuate the magical virtues of those who constructed them or for whom they were constructed, thus insuring the fertility of men, cattle, and harvests."[15] He identified three principal categories of megalithic architecture – the *menhir* (standing or "long stone"), the *cromlech* (stone circle or "circle place"), and the *dolmen* (trabeated or "table stone" constructions that were graves originally covered by earth mounds). Neolithic people throughout Northern Europe conducted extensive building programs and produced monumental constructions. Some gravesites contained as many as 100 bodies and included paintings, carvings, and sculptures. All of which indicate the existence of beliefs and rituals focused on the dead (and death itself) that were concretized and facilitated through stone architecture.[16]

The island of Møn in present-day Southern Denmark has extensive burial mounds and earthworks. They were built during the Neolithic Age on Møn when hunters following game north after the retreat of the ice sheets crossed land bridges and settled there. Of the numerous ruins found throughout this small island there are a number that deserve our attention because of their extant conditions, and articulation of connections between the living and the dead, and the earth and the sky. Grønjaegers Høj is a 30 × 300-ft earthwork surrounded by 145 standing stones. It is of interest that it was later named for King Grøn, an ancient ruler who was transformed into a mythical figure associated with the terrifying god Odin. Odin was the chief of the Norse gods and was originally an embodiment of the wind who led dead spirits through the skies. The grave's enormous hulk resembles a boat that, though it is moored to the earth, appears to be drifting to another land, and so it is understandable that it came to embody the god Odin.

Nearby is Klekkende Høj, a massive barrow where twin entry passages face the east, the place of the rising sun where each day warmth and light were eternally reborn. (When it was excavated in the eighteenth century, human remains and objects were found that had miraculously avoided being plundered.) Burial mounds found throughout Northern Europe display a remarkable consistency of form and structure. They were the first "civic architecture," commemorating life through memorializing the dead. In their historical setting, they required significant communal efforts that served to bind the community and through artifice symbolize its continuity. These are themes that Christianity, millennia later, would so powerfully appropriate and express.

Kong Asker's Høj is a burial mound that dates from 4000 BCE, and is arguably one of the oldest, extant examples of civic architecture. The tomb of a local chieftain, it anticipates the multitude of funerary architecture that follow. King Asker's Høj is a passage grave that includes a burial chamber – an approximately 6 × 30-ft oblong space enclosed by massive, corbelled, stone construction. It is reached by a narrow passage that faces east and is flanked by two massive stone slabs. This is a place that was built for eternity as if to symbolize that, though the king had died, his people would endure. Its entry, facing the rising sun, connects it with the cosmos as if to say, "though we are here at the center of our world, we are also part of the cosmos."

Aubrey Burl outlines four stages of Neolithic burial rituals and artifacts. In the first stages, the dead were buried in their own houses, then in barrows, which then led to the construction of burial mounds. In the fourth stage of stone circles,

however, bodies were no longer necessary for the commemoration of the dead. Communion with ancestors was an important component of many of these sites and the agenda of many of the Neolithic necropolises was to "transform collective burials into spectacular and indestructible monuments" where "communication with the ancestors is ritually assured."[17] In particular, some megalithic monuments in Western Europe embodied the dead, the enduring stone symbolizing the continuity of the rulers and their people.[18]

West Kennet Long Barrow is located on the highest point of a ridge in the gentle hills of Southwest England. This is one of many important Neolithic works in this area of flat plains and chalk cliffs that include substantive stone circles and earthworks. Its prominent mound was constructed from dirt excavated from two flanking ditches and stretches for over 300 feet along the ridge in an east–west orientation. The east-facing entrance was defined by a transverse row of sarcen stones and led to a series of corbelled chambers that held remains for over a thousand years. Outside, an east-facing forecourt, it is believed, provided the setting for communal rituals.

It is likely that the funerary rites and communal burials that took place at Neolithic barrows were done in phases. First, bodies decomposed on open biers before being disarticulated and placed in the barrows. Sometimes there is evidence that the bones were burned and broken before interment. Because the barrows were periodically cleared out, they appear to have served purposes beyond the simple commemoration of the dead. Rodney Castleden argues that they were not "primarily graves, but cenotaphs. They were not monuments to the dead, but to death itself, and they can be seen as magic gateways through

6.4
Kong Asker's Høj is arguably one of the oldest, extant examples of civic architecture. Kong Asker's Høj, Møn, Denmark, Neolithic, view of east entrance

6.5

The east-facing entrance of the West Kennet Long Barrow was defined by a transverse row of sarcen stones and led to a series of corbelled chambers that held remains for over a thousand years. West Kennet Long Barrow, Wiltshire, United Kingdom, Neolithic

Source: Drawing by Rodney Castleden, courtesy of Routledge.

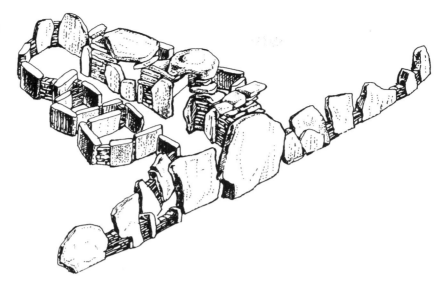

which life could be started anew and where the living and the dead could meet."[19] Others have attributed multiple uses and meanings, even though it is impossible to substantially establish what sites such as West Kennet meant to their creators.

That said, the substantial construction, sustained ritual use, and orientation to the cosmos of Neolithic barrows clearly indicate places of importance. Archeological evidence suggests sustained practices centered on the dead and perhaps death itself. However, there may have been additional displacements as the burial mounds came to serve as environmental and social foci. It is clear they were places that brought people together through the shared condition of death and connected them through ritual to deeper understandings of its meaning. "Remains" is an interesting word, suggesting items left behind as one journeys on to another world – the dead body remains with the living, but the spirit endures much like the sun and the heavens. The architecture both memorialized the continuity of life in a discontinuous world while straddling the two worlds. In this manner the architecture created an enduring material place while simultaneously symbolizing an immaterial threshold that connected the living, the dead, and the cosmos of which they were a part.[20]

The American modern architect Louis Kahn, referencing English history, stated: "I have volumes of it but I never read anything but the first volume. Even at that, I only read the first three or four chapters. My purpose is to read Volume Zero, which has not yet been written."[21] "Volume Zero," as described by Kahn, suggests an absolute beginning point precipitated by a fundamental act, and implies that subsequent acts replicate this archetype. I would argue that the beginnings, or "Volume Zero," of English architecture emerge with the Neolithic barrows, mounds, and stone circles found throughout the British Isles. Here fundamental structures and forms, built in service of placemaking and ritual, remain timeless presences. Ralph Waldo Emerson described Stonehenge as the "simplest of all simple structures – two upright stones and a lintel laid

across – had long outstood all later churches and all history, and were like what is most permanent on the face of the planet."[22]

William Butler Yeats was not as impressed with the Castlerigg stone circle as Emerson was by Stonehenge, describing it as a "dismal cirque of Druid stones, upon a forlorn moor."[23] I would disagree, but also recognize that Yeats' erroneous text illustrates the history of misunderstandings and misappropriations these enduring structures have inspired. Cumbria, the mountainous area in Northwest England, was the location of the earliest Neolithic stone circles in the British Isles and Castlerigg is said to date from approximately 3200 BCE. Its standing stones define an oblong space on a high plateau surrounded by mountains. Two portal stones create an atypical northern entrance and inside, at its eastern side, is an equally unusual rectangular enclosure known as the "sanctuary" (though no religious function for it has been established). Here incorruptible stones were put in service of communal placemaking. Some have suggested that certain stones represent peaks visible from inside the circle and astrological alignments, though none definitively. There is a clear sense of placement, however, and though the standing stones at Castlerigg may have ringed a much smaller circle than at Stonehenge, they appropriated a vast landscape including the mountains surrounding the plateau upon which they

6.6
Even though the standing stones at Castlerigg may have ringed a much smaller circle than at Stonehenge, they appropriated a vast landscape including the mountains surrounding the plateau upon which they were thrust. Castlerigg Stone Circle, Cumbria, United Kingdom, Neolithic

Source: Photo by Andrew Crompton.

were thrust. This environmental perspective is still perceptible today and suggests a particular attribute of places like this – their potential to engender perceptual and emotional responses shared throughout time. Castleden states that stone circles

> incorporate a bewildering matrix of symbols, beliefs and aspirations in their design, showing that they were used in a variety of cere-monial ways to express a holistic view of the universe, a view that saw no real division between man and nature, nor between earth and heaven.[24]

This observation suggests the significance that Castlerigg and other examples of ancient architecture continue to possess today.

CASE STUDY   **Native American Earthworks, Burial Mounds, and Effigy Figures: Cosmological Orientations and Mediations**

The cultural history of North America includes diverse traditions of often highly symbolic architecture. The term "Native American Architecture" broadly (and inadequately) describes a range of building types, environmental settings, historical periods, and cultural artifacts. It includes places where the environment was appropriated and transformed, or where advanced technologies (of their time) were applied to create substantial architecture – all in service of symbolic agendas and ritual use. Because of their cultural and architectural significance, they warrant our scholarship. However, there is an equally important imperative of revealing and reclaiming the beliefs, rituals, and artifacts of cultures that were systematically marginalized, suppressed, or destroyed. American culture is remarkable for its jettisoning of history and subsequent loss of memory.[25] It is a culture that can often abandon the past in pursuit of an idealized future. This takes the form not only of written histories, but physical ones as well, and we have an appalling preservation record when it comes to prehistoric sites.[26] The American palimpsest of history is distinguished by erasure – the physical destruction of the artifacts of the past or an arrogant ignoring of their continued presence. And yet our history runs deep, millennia before the relatively recent dominance of European immigrants. This gap of knowledge, if exhumed, can serve to link us with our predecessors (in the context of the "human family"), and broaden our worldview. In this context a retrieval of meaning can serve to integrate the repressed "material" of past cultures with present understandings.

The chthonic architecture of Anasazi kivas at Pueblo Bonito symbolically connected it with the primordial earth, while their setting in the south-facing courtyard oriented them to the heavens. This earth and sky orientation was anticipated in the "first architecture" of North America found in a vast network of earthworks, burial mounds, and effigy figures from the Great Lakes to the Gulf of Mexico in the Mid-west. These massive earthworks were built of durable materials on a scale that places them alongside the world's significant sacred places, and rivals their antecedents in the British Isles. Vestiges of these cultural outputs are still present, as at the colossal earthworks at what is called Poverty

Point in Louisiana. Poverty Point, named for the crude clay objects uncovered there, entailed the moving of half a million tons of dirt to create six concentric ridges and four radiating passages that enclose an 1,800-ft wide plaza.[27] The use of the great space at Poverty Point is unknown, but most likely it was used for periodic gatherings from settlements in the area for the purpose of kinship, finding mates, and communal rituals.[28] The fluorescence of mound building occurred from 700–1000 CE, reaching its peak in the city of Cahokia, located outside of present-day St. Louis. Here Mississippian religious rituals centered on sun worship and sacred fires found their most complete architectural expression in the trapezoidal, flat-topped mounds that defined this substantial city.[29] The enduring presence of places like these speaks about the ability of architecture to transcend time, and of the value of ruins.

The Spanish explorer Hernando de Soto, who traveled through the region in 1539, first described the native architecture of the North American Southeast. He recorded an extensive network of towns, which included ceremonial town centers and religious structures built on massive mounds. In 1718, the French architect-engineer Antoine le Page du Pratz became the first trained architect to study Native American architecture. His scholarship brought him to the Grand Village of the Natchez (near present-day Natchez, Mississippi), which had first been settled in 1200 CE and remained in use until the 1720s.[30] It wasn't until the mid-nineteenth century, however, that significant surveys and excavations were performed. Ephraim G. Squier, a newspaperman, and Edwin H. Davis, a physician, both of Chillicothe, Ohio, examined or excavated over one hundred sites in southeastern Ohio. Their findings, entitled *Ancient Monuments of the Mississippi Valley*, included detailed illustrations and were published by the Smithsonian in 1848.

The Adena and Hopewell

Squier and Davis documented the artifacts of cultures named by settlers the Adena and Hopewell – as well as some examples from later periods. These titles, which are unrelated to the native peoples they came to describe, actually define rough archeological periods. (Therefore, I will refer to Adena and Hopewell Periods, not to people or cultures.) When nineteenth-century Europeans first saw Adena and Hopewell sites, they attributed them to outside "civilized" cultures that they named the "Moundbuilders."[31] As has often been the case with indigenous Americans, we don't know what the "Hopewell" called themselves. They were named after Captain Mordecai Hopewell, a former Confederate soldier[32] and landowner of what was called the Hopewell Ground, an earthwork complex near Chillicothe in Southeastern Ohio. Naming a people who had a trade network that stretched from the Gulf of Mexico to the Great Lakes, and from the Atlantic seaboard to the Rocky Mountains after an otherwise undistinguished local landowner is a minor example of hubris perhaps, but still remarkable.[33]

Funerary mounds distinguish the Adena Period, which lasted until 200 CE, and earthworks enclosing ceremonial spaces, some of which are still present today. Their dwellings have not survived, but we do know that they were, for the most part, circular wooden structures with a central hearth that, in some cases, held up to forty inhabitants. The Hopewell Period began around the Christian Era (so called), and is known for its geometrically precise and geographically immense earthworks and burial mounds. One Hopewell Period site, located on a prominent ridge above the Little Miami River in Southeastern Ohio, is called Fort Ancient and encloses 100 acres within three and a half miles of earthworks. Its enduring clay walls had sixty-seven openings, some of which may have aligned with the sun and moon. Its cosmological orientation and scale are still an articulate artifact that simultaneously describes the earthbound–skyward-looking orientation of its creators (and, I would argue, their present-day inheritors).

We know little about the people of the Hopewell Period and most likely this will continue to be the case. It has been reliably established that they flourished for 500–750 years during what is known as the Middle Woodland Period; they hunted, fished, gathered edible plants and cultivated crops; and lived in scattered settlements along river valleys near the earthworks that they built. Excavations have revealed the spear and knife points they made and the pottery they fashioned for cooking and storage; and there are still traces of the roads they built to serve their trade network, some of which are contemporary highways. But they are mostly known for their massive earthworks and

6.7

Newark Works, Ohio, showing the circle and octagon of the Moundbuilder's State Memorial in the upper left, Hopewell Period, first century CE

Source: Drawing from Squier and Davis (1848).

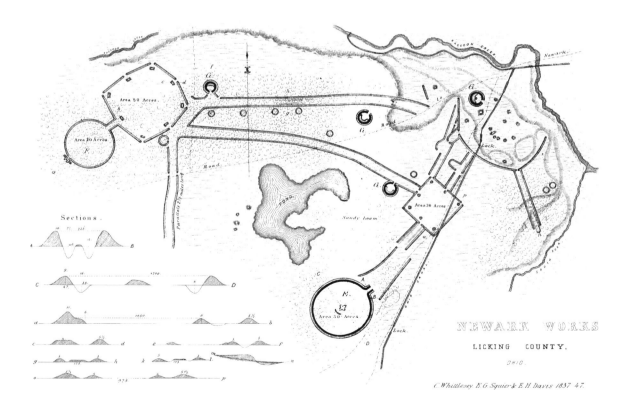

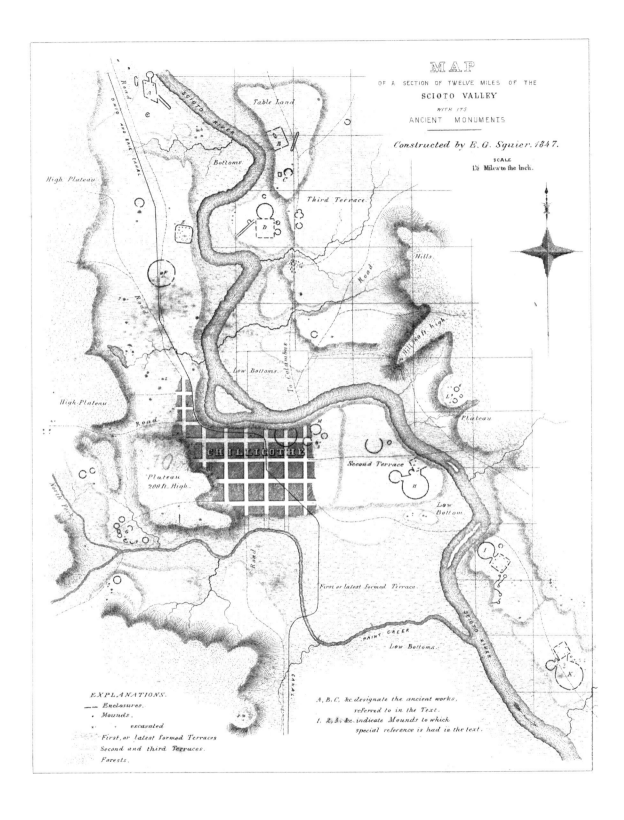

MAP
OF A SECTION OF TWELVE MILES OF THE
SCIOTO VALLEY
WITH ITS
ANCIENT MONUMENTS

Constructed by E. G. Squier. 1847.

SCALE
1½ Miles to the Inch.

EXPLANATIONS.
— — Enclosures.
· Mounds.
⁕ excavated
First, or latest formed Terraces
Second and third Terraces.
Forests.

A, B, C, &c. designate the ancient works,
referred to in the Text.
1, 2, 3, &c. indicate Mounds to which
special reference is had in the text.

6.8 (opposite)

One of the most significant sites from the Hopewell Period is Mound City, located just outside of Chillicothe, Ohio on the banks of the Scioto River and named by Squier and Davis for its concentration of burial mounds within a 13-acre circular earthwork enclosure. Mound City, Chillicothe, Ohio, plan of area

Source: Drawing from Squier and Davis (1848).

burial mounds that, according to one author, should "be ranked among the important prehistoric engineering and artistic accomplishments of mankind,"[34] or, in the words of Squier and Davis, "for many ages will continue to challenge the wonder of men."[35]

Many sites have been lost, not as much through degradation by the elements (they were built to survive these) as by farming, road building, and other impacts dating from the first settlers that reflect the collective neglect of this small patch of the earth's human history. At the Moundbuilders State Memorial site in Newark, Ohio one can walk inside a still-extant circular earthwork that encloses 20 acres. At one time it was connected by an avenue to a great octagonal enclosure of over 50 acres. There were numerous sites in Newark described by Squier and Davis as "so complicated, that it is impossible to give anything like a comprehensible description of them."[36] The sites in Newark were built in a typical location, at the in-between zone between the level glaciated valley and the unglaciated Appalachian Plateau, and at the confluence of a major waterway. There were also many acropolis sites; ridge heights that were modified to create articulated enclosures with gateways, avenues, and openings, some, it has been

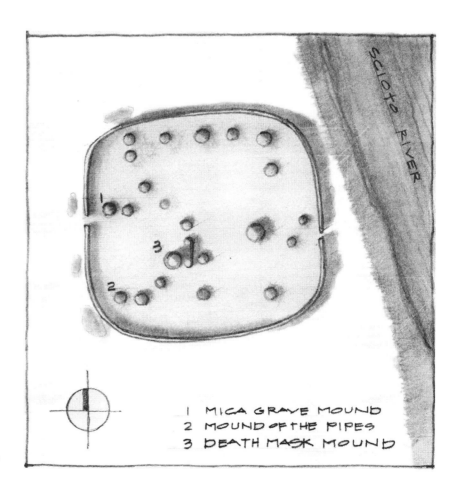

1 MICA GRAVE MOUND
2 MOUND OF THE PIPES
3 DEATH MASK MOUND

6.9
Mound City, Chillicothe, Ohio, plan

Earth and Sky

6.10
Mound City, Chillicothe, Ohio,
view with the Death Mask
Mound in the background

suggested, oriented to the sun and moon. At Fort Hill, walls as high as 15 feet inscribe the profile of a ridge and include thirty-three irregularly placed openings. Like Fort Ancient, Fort Hill was not a fort; its large size and numerous openings made it a very impractical defensive enclosure.[37] Instead, it was a humanly constructed communal ground. The uses of these places, like other sites, is unclear, but most likely they were used for communal rituals related to the clans and perhaps regional trading sites connected to their road network. It has been suggested that some were part of a network of pilgrimage paths and destinations. Perhaps there was a yearly round of rituals signaled by alignments of the cosmos marked by the openings in their earthen *temenos* walls.

One of the most significant sites from the Hopewell Period is Mound City, located just outside of Chillicothe, Ohio, on the banks of the Scioto River and named by Squier and Davis for its concentration of burial mounds within a 13-acre circular earthwork enclosure. Though it is only one of many earthworks in the Scioto River Valley, it is the most well preserved, many having been damaged, lost, or simply unexcavated.[38] Mound City is perhaps the most significant necropolis of the Hopewell Period, with twenty-three mounds within its earthwork enclosure. We do not definitively know the types of funerary rituals performed by the builders of this site, but archeological evidence suggests that only a select number of most likely important individuals were afforded this honor – anointed to play roles in life and in death for the benefit of the community.[39] Mounds usually contained a variety of remains and artifacts, built up

6.11

Shamanic rituals found pan-culturally share themes of the passage from one world (the living) to another world (the dead), and depend on the guidance of one who has the ability to mediate between these worlds. Shaman performing ceremony in a traditional house

Source: From *Mound City Indian Ceremony* by Louis S. Glanzman.

in layers over time. At Hopewell Period mortuary sites, wooden charnel houses, some with multiple rooms, served as repositories for the bodies, bones, and artifacts. At Seip Mound in Ross County, Ohio, for example, the remains of at least 132 bodies have been recorded.

It has been suggested that the wooden charnel houses erected within the over 3-ft-high earthwork that encloses Mound City replicated archetypal houses and were the settings for shamanic rituals performed for the benefit of the dead and the living. Perhaps shamans, dressed as supernatural animals, would perform the rites that mediated between the dead and the living within the dark interior of the house. Archeological evidence suggests that, in some cases, the body was ritually dismembered and its parts cremated in a shallow basin. The remains were then arranged anatomically correctly in a shallow grave inside the charnel house. Once the house was full of the dead, it was often burned before earth was mounded over it. Here impermanent flesh and materials subject to rot and decay were replaced by the permanence of earth, sand, and gravel.

Squier and Davis excavated each mound and cataloged the bones and artifacts they found. The names given to each mound describe their contents, typically effigy figures made from materials brought by their trade network, such as the Mica Grave Mound and the Mound of the Pipes.[40] The largest mound is named the Death Mask Mound because here a "death mask" fashioned from a human skull, and most likely worn by a shaman, was found. Two buildings were constructed here, one replacing the other, and inside the mound were found the remains of thirteen bodies. Each was found in a variety of positions, perhaps reflecting their relative status or roles. The mounds would have looked very different when first built, covered with dark earth or gravel, distinct from their surroundings as befitted their function and symbolic content.[41]

A small figurine found near the Newark earthworks depicts a shaman whose head is covered with a bear mask.[42] Shamanic rituals found pan-culturally share themes of the passage from one world (the living) to another world (the dead), and depend on the guidance of one who has the ability to mediate between these worlds. Though we cannot draw any conclusive findings from ethnographic comparisons concerning Hopewell Period (and, for that matter, Neolithic European) death rituals, they do provide valuable analogs that can enrich our understandings. Mircea Eliade documents the case of a traditional burial of a girl from the Kogi Indians of Columbia that, because it was observed in 1966, provides an accessible glimpse into the belief systems and rituals of this type:

> After choosing the site for the grave, the shaman (*Mama*) performs a series of ritual gestures and declares: "Here is the village of death; here is the ceremonial house of death; here is the womb. I will open the house. The house is shut, and I will open it." After this he announces, "The house is open," and shows the men the place where they are to dig the grave and withdraws.

After the girl's body was laid in the grave, the shaman then announced, "The house is closed," and the excavation filled up.[43] Throughout the ritual, the interrelationship of life (womb), death (house of death), and the house are established. And so in this example, and by extension the Hopewell Period houses of the dead, the house, the place of home, of the warm hearth, of food and family, became a place not to return to, but to depart from. Home, in this context became a vessel, ferrying the dead to the unknown beyond – a place where no roads and no known destinations exist.

The Serpent Mound

Perhaps the most enigmatic but also well-known earthwork site in the Ohio Valley is the Serpent Mound. Like Fort Ancient and Fort Hill, but dating from a later period, it occupies a ridge height, but instead of carefully built earthen walls marking the periphery of the plateau, a 1/4-mile-long colossal earthwork resembling a serpent slithers along its spine. It is clear that this palpably powerful place was designed and built with an eye turned toward eternity. Archeological evidence suggests that it was carefully laid out and then constructed with layers of earth, clay, and rocks, to produce a continuous mound 4–5-ft high with an average width of 20 feet. Its top layer of dark, hard-packed soil would have created a powerful presence – its brooding, precise form writhing across the back of the 100-ft-high plateau. On the ground, its form is difficult to decipher, but viewed from above (now by means of an observation tower), its serpent profile is apparent. At its southern end it turns to the west and winds into a three-ring coil, and along its length there are a series of seven links that end at its "head." The "head" faces the northeast, the direction of

6.12 (opposite)
Perhaps the most enigmatic but also well-known earthwork site in the Ohio Valley is the Serpent Mound, Ohio, Adena Period, first century BCE

Source: Drawing from Squier and Davis (1848).

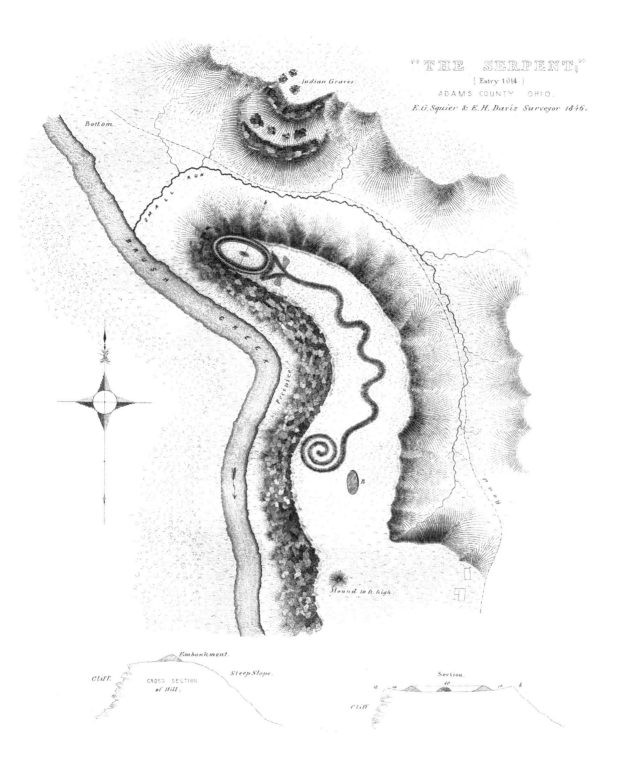

"THE SERPENT."
(Entry 1014)
ADAMS COUNTY OHIO.
E.G.Squier & E.H.Davis Surveyor 1846.

the summer solstice sunset, and its outline suggests an open mouth that is either striking or swallowing an elliptical egg-like form.

Like many sacred sites, this one has been the subject of a plethora of theories and speculations. One thing is certain; it was sited in a prominent and auspicious location. The serpent, an archetypal symbol of the power of the earth favored by the Middle Ohio Valley people,[44] straddles this power spot, binding it along its length. It is clear that this was principally an effigy site – there was no *temenos* enclosure or any burials in the immediate area (though two mounds have been found nearby). Its dynamic form and animated presence, however, speak about the animistic beliefs of a people tied closely to their natural environment. The media of earth, the dark solid material of the ground, the humus to which our molecules return, describes a deep connection to the earth and its media of artistic expression.

The possible uses and meaning of the Serpent Mound have for the most part been lost to the enormity of time. The people who built them left no written records and we have lost much of the perspective of their worldview. In the end, however, perhaps the meanings it held for its creators is not as important as

6.13
The transformation of the earth became the first architecture, and a means for our ancestors to articulate a position in the world and to place themselves in relationship to the cosmos. Serpent Mound, Ohio, Adena Period, first century BCE

Source: Ohio Historical Society.

what they mean to us today. Here, the artifact acts as a mediator between the present and the past and, in some cases, is viewed as a talisman with inscrutable knowledge. The desire to decipher our ancient ancestors by means of their ruins is perhaps more about seeking to understand ourselves, and how we project content onto ancient sites says much about our own culture. Science is invariably put into the service of validating a particular theory; the product of an age that reasons in absolutes and needs definitive, defensible answers.

In the case of Serpent Mound, numerous theories have been advanced, some with the agenda of linking it with lost ancient knowledge – information that presumably could benefit us today. As at other ancient sites, celestial orientation figures prominently, perhaps reflecting a desire to recover lost connections to the earth. Mathematics and geometry are also overlaid, and arguments that Serpent Mound was a highly ordered and sophisticated construction that utilized lost knowledge vociferously made. Dating that places its construction at a much earlier date has also been postulated. In all, the artifact acts as a mediator between who we are now and who we were, with the implicit hope that we will rediscover lost knowledge and thus secure a boon for an age that has been described as "the first atheistic civilization in the history of mankind."[45] I suppose it is good that we no longer consider ancient sites irrelevant – or consider native faiths as the invention of people who did not have the benefit of science to explain the world. We may have a multitude of positions, each reflecting a particular ideology, but implicit in all is the hope that who we are has a greater promise for enlightenment, based on who we were. Even though monuments found in Neolithic Europe and prehistoric America outlive their creators, they continue to retain their communicative efficacy in various forms – which ultimately is the concern of any hermeneutical inquiry.[46]

The first architecture of ancient cave replications, burial mounds, stone circles, earthworks, and effigy figures mediated between an earthbound, corporal existence tied to place and time, and expanded and broadened its context. Thomas Carlyle, Emerson's companion at Stonehenge, as he watched larks soaring overhead in the darkening sky, expressed this interface of time as "the larks were hatched last year, but the wind was hatched many thousand years ago."[47] At many of the ancient sites, time was expanded as life and death were co-joined, and the dead mediated between temporality and the timeless. Place was connected horizontally through alignments of sites and natural features, and vertically to the sun, moon, and stars – a mediation between earth and sky that still resonates today.

The transformation of the earth became the first architecture, and a means for our ancestors to articulate a position in the world and to place themselves in relationship to the cosmos. For some American Indians, the earth symbolized home, the mother, and place to rest, to be healed, to die. As one chief stated:

> The Great Spirit is our Father, but the earth is our Mother. She nourishes us; that which we put into the ground she returns to us, and healing plants she gives us likewise. If we are wounded, we go to our mother and seek to lay the wounded part against her to be healed. Animals too, do thus, they lay their wounds to the earth.[48]

Chief Joseph of the Nez Perces recounts his father's dying words, "My son, my body is returning to mother earth, and my spirit very soon to see the Great Spirit Chief."[49] In these place-bound but timeless settings, the dead returned to the womb of the earth and journeyed on to unknown destinations.

A very thin layer of air, a wisp of life between the earth and the enormity of space, covers our world. We build in an even thinner zone, molding the earth and building upon its surface as a means, perhaps, to symbolically co-join these two worlds. Throughout the history of architecture, the earth has been molded and transformed as a means to articulate the enduring questions of who and where we are. We need to recognize our culturally based prejudices regarding ancient sites to access the plenitude of meaning they still possess. These places, it needs to be said, are not ideals, but can provide perspectives appropriate to today. The enormity of our environmental setting and the mystery of death (and what may lie beyond) are contexts that retain potency. If we ignore, minimize, or objectivize them, we risk truncating our ability to reconcile these perennial conditions and build in ways that may provide contemporary interpretations.

Chapter 7

The Sacred Path and Place

Spatial Sequences and Symbolic Narratives

And that world system Sukhavati, Ananda, emits many fragrant odours, it is rich in a great variety of flowers and fruits, adorned with jewel trees, which are frequented by flocks of various birds with sweet voices, which the Tathagata's miraculous power has conjured up. And these jewel trees, Ananda, have various colours, many colours, many hundreds of thousands of colours. They are variously composed of the seven precious things, in varying combinations, i.e. of gold, silver, beryl, crystal, coral, red pearls, or emerald. Such jewel trees, and clusters of banana trees and rows of palm trees, all made of precious things, grow everywhere in this Buddha-field. On all sides it is surrounded with golden nets, and all round covered with lotus flowers made of all the precious things. Some of the lotus flowers are half a mile in circumference, others up to ten miles. And from each jewel lotus issues thirty-six hundred kotis of rays. And at the end of each ray there issue thirty-six hundred thousand kotis of Buddhas, with golden-colored bodies, who bear the thirty-two marks of the superman, and who, in all the ten directions, go into countless world systems, and there demonstrate the dharma.

(From the *Description of the Happy Land,* first century CE)[1]

Some Neolithic stone circles and earthworks in the British Isles incorporated entry sequences in the form of approach causeways. If we apply Aubrey Burl's four-part sequence of development of Neolithic sites, we might logically call this the "fifth stage." It is well established that Stonehenge included an approach avenue, which began some distance away at the Avon River. At Avebury, there were at least two approach causeways, the best known of which is West Kennet Avenue where opposing pairs of pillar and lozenge-shaped standing stones flanked its path. Though it is not clear what functions West Kennet Avenue and other causewayed enclosures might have accommodated, we can assume that their use went beyond utility and included communal rituals. It is believed that the agrarian Neolithic peoples practiced rituals related to the cycles of the seasons, fertility, and death. Some have suggested that the paired stones of West Kennet Avenue represented male and female entities or attributes. It is possible that it was used as a processional way for seasonal fertility and harvest rites, or for the bearing of the dead – a segmented path sequence flanked by "male" and "female" stones that led to the "sanctuary" of its stone circle and earthwork center.[2]

As illustrated by Avebury, the marking of the center is typically dependent on an articulate means of entry, often elongated to underline its importance. Traversed by the solitary pilgrim, or vivified by the processional retinue, the path served as a mediator between outside and inside – profane and sacred – and underlined the importance of entering the sacred place. Themes related to the approach and entering of sacred architecture, elaborated over time, have an expansive, diverse, and nuanced history. Often the approach to, and passage through, sacred architecture utilized spatial sequences in service of communicating symbolic narratives and accommodating processionals. The symbolism and meaning of the architecture were revealed serially through diverse media, often including communal rituals.

Intersubjective or hermeneutical interpretations depend, in part, on comparative methods.[3] In the case of sacred architecture, identifying repeating organizational patterns, symbolism, and ritual use – often pan-culturally and trans-historically – is crucial to unpacking its critical relationships. Here, the homological emphasis of comparative religion provides a framework for analogous architectural patterns. For example, Mircea Eliade's comparative methods revealed particular themes of sacred places. Regarding path approaches and sequences, he stated that the path to the sacred place is typically a "hard path, sown with obstacles," which "serves the purpose of preserving profane man from the danger to which he would expose himself by entering without . . . having gone through the gestures of approach."[4] For Eliade, the path sequence both underlines the separateness of the sacred place while simultaneously providing a setting for ritual preparations. It is both a path *and* a place. We will develop and expand upon these distinctions in the following examples. Beginning with pilgrimage sites, we will present *the path as a place*, which is both a destination and a journey. Next, we will turn to a brief discussion of *the path as a path*, a symbolic journey to the center comprising spatial sequences and symbolic narratives. Finally, we will present *the place as a path*, illustrated by labyrinths and places of ritual circumambulation. These are important typological distinctions that will form part of the analysis of the Korean Zen Buddhist Monastery of Tongdo that concludes the chapter.

The Path as a Place: Pilgrimage Paths

There is a rich lineage of ritual pilgrimages in ancient and contemporary religion. Even though the reasons for pilgrimage vary according to the religion, and there are inflections within each faith, we can identify certain shared elements. Pilgrims undertake often-lengthy journeys as acts of devotion, for spiritual development, or to fulfill doctrinal expectations or requirements. Typically they involve the departure from everyday life, a journey along a defined route, the arrival at the sacred place, and their return, presumably changed by the experience. Pilgrimage sites can be religious centers identified by scripture, important events, or environmental settings; places where requests for prayers are offered; or locations believed to possess healing powers. Some, of course, can be all of these. Christian pilgrimage to Jerusalem and the Islamic *Hajj* to Mecca are well known, but Judaism, Buddhism, Taoism, Hinduism, and Native faiths also have important pilgrimage sites. In the case of the latter, it has been suggested that Hopewell roads and earthworks served as pilgrimage paths and destinations. In many examples the pilgrimage path can be understood as a discrete symbolic and experiential place. We will discuss the Christian pilgrimage path of the Via Dolorosa in Jerusalem to illustrate *the path as a place*.

The Christian Pilgrimage Path at the Via Dolorosa, Jerusalem

Jerusalem is the ultimate goal of Christian pilgrimage where pilgrims recapitulate Jesus' journey of suffering and apotheosis. A dominant aspect of Christian pilgrimage, encoded during the Middle Ages, was the necessity of suffering and the virtue of self-mortification. Additionally, Christian-inspired literature, from the sixteenth-century Spanish mystic St. John of the Cross' *The Ascent of Mt. Carmel* to the seventeenth-century English writer John Bunyan's *Pilgrim's Progress*, describe the path of trial and redemption. Rituals are often a recapitulation of a mythical event – the Christian Eucharist is predominantly a symbolic re-enactment of the Last Supper. The re-enactment of the spiritual journey of the hero-god is perhaps most significantly expressed through the symbolic ambulation of the Via Dolorosa – the "Way of Sorrows" – in Jerusalem. The journey ends at the Church of the Holy Sepulchre, the sacred site of Jesus' crucifixion, entombment, and resurrection described in the Gospels.

Modern cultures tend to view religious beliefs and rituals as anachronistic vestiges of an earlier time, and its practitioners as revisionists who do not have a mature, modern perspective. A trip to Jerusalem, however, quickly shatters this modernist conceit. There the continuity of religious devotion is explicit and palpable. The Old City of Jerusalem is an unusual place where the past is consistently revivified though contemporary religious practices and rituals, and Christians, Jews, and Muslems consider it to be a sacred city and make pilgrimages to the sites they consider significant. It is the City of David, the symbolic center of the Jewish world, and Jews journey there to pray at its holy sites. At the Western Wall, said to be all that remains of Solomon's Temple, devotees write prayers on pieces of paper and crumple them into its cracks in reverence and supplication – the architectural artifact, in essence, mediating between the petitioner and their god (see Figure 1.3). For Muslems, it is the liminal place where Mohammed ascended to heaven, and they come to pray at the Dome of the Rock that consecrates this holy ground as well as the adjacent El-Aqsa Mosque.

7.1
Jerusalem is the ultimate goal of Christian pilgrimage where pilgrims recapitulate Jesus' journey of suffering and apotheosis. Via Dolorosa, Jerusalem, pilgrims at the Eighth Station of the Cross

Even though most sects admit that the path of Christ's passion along the Via Dolorosa is conjectural and symbolic, its physical presence serves to frame and magnify the ritual. From beginning to end, its spaces are conceived as places where redemption and apotheosis are possible. The path begins at the remains of the Fortress of Antonia, built by Herod in the northeast corner of the quartered Roman city. Here, according to the Gospels, the Roman Procurator Pontius Pilate shouted, "Behold the Man," as he presented Jesus to the gathered crowd, an event marked by remains named the "Ecce Homo Arch." According to scripture, events then followed in succession, marked now by "The Stations of the Cross," and ending with Jesus' crucifixion. The First Station marks the place where he was condemned, the Second Station, the Church of the Flagellation, where he was flogged and forced to carry the cross. Ten stations in all are marked by greater or lesser means along this ancient winding way, a cadence of light and shadow, changing surfaces and sights along streets still lined by shops and full of residents, until the pilgrims reach the Church of the Holy Sepulchre.

After the Emperor Constantine's and subsequently Rome's acceptance of Christianity, pilgrimage to Jerusalem became an important part of the early Christian faith. (Santiago de Compostela and Rome were penultimate destinations.) It was during this time that the Church of the Holy Sepulchre was built – marking the last stages of Jesus' journey of individual and universal redemption and the symbolic center of the Christian world. Inside are the final Stations of the Cross, as well as numerous chapels (one dedicated to St. Helena, the mother of Constantine, credited with founding the first church there). The Tenth Station represents the place where Jesus was stripped of his garments; to its left an exposed stone represents (or, for some, is believed to be) Golgotha, where the cross was planted. Adjacent is a *Stabat Mater* sculpture, a popular subject that depicts Mary, mother of Christ, pierced by a knife, and symbolizing the agony of her (and presumably our collective) loss. Underneath the platform where these scenes unfold, the base of Golgotha is visible, its solid mass revealing a deep crack believed to have appeared at the moment of Christ's death but also, some believe, marking the place where Adam was formed – life and death directly and metaphorically co-joined through the media of stone. Nearby is the Stone of Unction, the Eleventh Station, where it is said Joseph of Arimathea laid the body of Christ. Here devotees kneel before a tomb-sized slab of stone set on the floor, dipping their fingers in its wet surface, anointing their foreheads in supplication and presumably hope.

The sepulchre itself, a small stone box set in the middle of a dark, domed space, is uneasily administered by the Orthodox Armenian, the Orthodox Greek, and the Roman Catholic Churches. A candle-flanked opening marks the entrance to a small outer chamber that leads to the tomb itself – the latter so small that it can hold only one or two people, and so close that one is powerfully confronted by the tomb, which occupies much of the space. It is clear that this most important Christian edifice is not a benign, controlled, or even particularly articulate place. It is instead an affective, dynamic, confrontational place that challenges presumptions about sacrality and belief. Mass is celebrated at intervals throughout the day, but the church also has a constant and (one might say) eternal life – including the cells on the roof occupied by an obscure sect of Ethiopian monks. The path that leads to this sacred center is also challenging,

7.2
Church of the Holy Sepulchre, Jerusalem, Stone of Unction

both physically and emotionally, and mediates the multifarious symbolic content of this complex and, at times, confusing place. The pilgrimage path of the Via Dolorosa leads to the sacred center of the Christian world, but is also a destination itself. It is both an implicit promise that if one follows the "Way of the Lord," then redemption and enlightenment are assured, and an obscured way of the "dark night of the soul."[5] Its power lies in these, and other interpretations, of its content and experiences.

The Path as a Path: Spatial Sequences and Symbolic Narratives

The path in sacred architecture is typically a sequence of gateways and spaces, and leads to a center or destination. The entry, path, and sanctuary of sacred architecture often symbolize the spiritual path and its goal, a dynamic experience where symbolic themes are expressed three-dimensionally and experienced visually, haptically, and emotionally. The symbolism is communicated by the interrelationship of the orientation, plan, surfaces, geometry, form, and spaces of the architecture and the experience of ambulation, devotional acts, and communal rituals – a powerful synthesis of diverse media.[6] The approach, entry, and passage through sacred architecture were typically rich spatial sequences where the narrative aspects of architectural symbolism can be understood as both singular and serial. In other words, each space and its formal and scenographic tableaux can be interpreted in isolation and according to their relationship to the whole.

Sacred architecture can be defined as dynamic spatial organizations vivified through their variety of uses. Articulate paths and places are intrinsic to the symbolism and ritual use of sacred architecture and exhibit the characteristics of clearly articulated entries, spatial sequences, and symbolic narratives. For example, the axial path of the Pylon Temples of Late Kingdom Egypt comprised a choreographed spatial sequence of pylons, courtyards, and hypostyle halls that created a linear, symbolic journey of increasingly more enclosed and sacred spaces until the final goal of the sanctuary was reached. The processional morphology of Pylon Temples was anticipated at the Mortuary Temple of King Zoser where a linear entry hall flanked by forty-two columns led to the inner courtyard. Ottoman mosques, as we will observe later, employed a path aligned with the Mecca axis and was composed of gateways, courtyards, and thresholds that led to the *haram* (worship space) and *qibla* (the wall facing Mecca). The segmented entry path of Japanese Zen Buddhist temples incorporated a variety of path surfaces, spatial sequences, vistas, and imagery and incorporated diverse symbolizations including the journey to the hermit scholar's retreat celebrated in the landscape paintings of the Southern Sung School, as well as the ideals of Zen practice and the path to enlightenment. Even small sub-temples often included elaborate entry sequences.[7]

The Western Medieval Church utilized an articulate path sequence and symbolic narrative, beginning with the tympanum at the western front and ending in the sanctuary, to communicate themes of trial and redemption. At Saint Foy, as discussed earlier, the tympanum initiated a spatial and symbolic journey that culminated in the inner sanctuary of the church where, among other devotional treasures, the statue of the child-saint was enshrined. Saint Foy was particularly compact for a pilgrimage church. French Gothic cathedrals, of course, were much larger with often-elongated paths that culminated in the ambulatory and sanctuary. It is in some examples of English Gothic cathedrals, however, that we find the most significant of enclosed path sequences. Winchester Cathedral, the largest Gothic church in Europe, includes a nave, crossing, choir, and Lady Chapel (dedicated to the Virgin Mary) that stretches 556 feet from the west to the east. The west fronts of English cathedrals, typically massive, broad edifices designed to hold a profusion of statuary, clearly demarcate the beginning of the path and the boundary of the sacred realm within. Unlike the towered westworks of their continental contemporaries, the west fronts of English cathedrals accentuate the horizontal, with Lincoln Cathedral perhaps providing the most distinguished example. Inside, the spaces also emphasize the horizontal, which, along with their length, underline peregrination to the goal at the end of the path. Further demarcations, such as Chancel (or Rood) screens that separate the choir from the nave, elaborate on the predominant theme of journey to the sacred place and the events along the path.

The Place as a Path: Labyrinths and Places of Circumambulation

We now turn to the special case of labyrinths. Pilgrimage, as has often been noted, is perhaps the most substantial of ritual acts related to the trials of the spiritual path and the challenges of attaining the sacred place. What is often not noted is that, once they arrived, pilgrims often undertook a miniaturized pilgrimage path – a replication of the spiritual journey – and performed rituals, all of which further elongated the devotional acts of approaching the sacred. The walking of the labyrinth, similar to ambulation through sacred architecture, was a particularly potent rendering of the interrelationship of setting, form, and ritual. In this context, the path becomes the spiritual place itself.

In Christianity, labyrinths often replicated on a smaller scale the pilgrimage path and there is a long tradition of their use – vestiges of Christianity's appropriation of elements of the native or "pagan" faiths it supplanted. Labyrinths have a distinguished history of symbolism and ritual use. The myth of the Minoan labyrinth and the journey of Theseus to save his fellow Athenians from their annual tribute sacrifice is perhaps the most familiar. Similar to Ariadne's thread, which guided the hero to the center and the Minotaur, labyrinths (in comparison to mazes) are unicursal. Most Roman labyrinths, for example, were round and quartered, with a singular path that systematically traversed each of the quadrants before attaining the center. The earliest Christian example is found at the Basilica of Reparatus in Algeria, which dates from the fourth century CE.[8] Many of the great cathedrals of the Île de France, including Rheims, Sens, and Saint Quentin, had labyrinths in their naves but now the only remaining ones are at Chartres and Amiens. The labyrinth at Chartres is a 42-ft in diameter circle comprising twelve concentric rings. At its center is a rosette, a six-petaled shape

7.3

In Christianity, labyrinths often replicated on a smaller scale the pilgrimage path. Cathedral of Notre Dame, Amiens, France, begun thirteenth century, view of labyrinth

Source: *The Amiens Trilogy, Part II: Revelation*, Columbia University, 1997.

that symbolizes the Virgin Mary, though there is speculation that an image of the Minotaur was once depicted there. The ritual traversing of its over 861-ft length, sometimes performed on hands and knees, was a mimetic act that symbolized a pilgrimage to the sacred center, to the Virgin Mary, and, in some accounts, to Jerusalem.

Amiens Cathedral, built on the flat plains of Picardy in Northern France, features the largest and tallest nave of the French Medieval cathedrals. It was proclaimed by John Ruskin to be the apogee of medieval architecture, and it is known for the unity of its style and the quality of its sculpture. Its nave also features an unusual octagonal labyrinth that resembles a Maltese cross, originally dating from 1288, but accurately re-built in the late nineteenth century. Similar to Chartres, it comprises twelve concentric rings and its 734-ft path meanders back and forth from inner to outer rings, and through all quadrants before attaining the goal of its center. Its many twists and turns, facets and segments, and, most importantly, its vacillating closeness and distance from the sacred center, may be understood as symbolizing the variables of the spiritual path. The first segments lead immediately toward the center, then out, and then back again – followed by segments where only the outer rings are traversed. Then, at the end, the path heads straight for the center, veers out one more time, before suddenly, almost miraculously, reaching the center.[9]

The labyrinth may have only one path but interpretations of its meanings are diverse, even conflicting. On one hand, the placement of the labyrinth in the Christian cathedral and, in some cases, the imagery at its center, suggest that it was not the ultimate goal of the sacred place. Instead it may have simply served to further elongate the entry sequence, offer a didactic (and accessible) message about the spiritual path, and aid in focusing and calming the mind in preparation for the anticipated experiences of the cathedral. However, it also existed as a discrete place with specific expected effects. The labyrinth can be seen as a place that guides the pilgrim from *chronos* time to *kairos* time, from the temporal world to the sacred world. Some insist that labyrinths connect one with eternal patterns that are divine themselves and serve to connect one to this larger context. The agency of personal improvement or transformation often attributed to sacred architecture finds a potent distillation in the labyrinth that retains contemporary potency. According to Lauren Artress: "The labyrinth is truly a tool for transformation. It is a crucible for change, a blueprint for the sacred meeting of psyche and soul, a field of light, a cosmic dance. It is a center for empowering ritual."[10]

The Great Mosque (al-Masjid al-Haram) of Mecca

The physical act of circumambulation, perhaps distilled in labyrinths, is an essential practice in many faiths, where the physical act of circulating around a temple or altar is not only devotional but serves as a metaphor for marking and consecrating the sacred center. Hindus ritually circle temples in a clockwise direction, co-joining movement and prayer, and many are designed to accommodate this ritual act.[11] *The place as a path*, however, finds one of its more potent expressions at the Great Mosque (al-Masjid al-Haram) of Mecca. The *Hajj* is a ritual journey to Mecca, the center of the Islamic world, one of the "Five Pillars of Islam," devotional requirements that all devout Muslims are expected to fulfill. As dictated in *Sura 2, Number 196*, "Make the pilgrimage and visit the Sacred House for His sake." It culminates with the circumambulation of the *Kaaba*, its most sacred shrine, which is located in the courtyard of the mosque.

The *Kaaba* is set in the middle of a voluminous space; its dark gray stone draped in a black cloth upon which are stitched Koranic verses. This sacred covering is renewed every year, an act reminiscent of the dressing of iconic gods in other faiths. However, here the object of devotion is an otherwise plain structure – Islam is an iconoclastic faith that forbids any images of God, the Prophet Mohammed, or other religious figures. (Thus the design and articulation of mosques often express sacredness through more abstract means – geometry, space, and decoration – in the service of their principal role as the setting for prayer.) The spot that the *Kaaba* marks is significant because here it is believed that the Prophet Mohammed received the word of God, as recorded in the

Koran. According to Muslim belief, the significance of this place dates from the beginning of time – it is believed that Adam lived there after his expulsion from paradise, and Abraham dwelt there (as evidenced by what is believed to be his footprint in the courtyard). Inserted in the corner of the *Kaaba* is a dark stone, perhaps a meteorite, which is said to have been received from the Archangel Gabriel. Ishmail, the son of Abraham, is also commemorated within the courtyard with a shrine dedicated to the patriarch of the Islamic branch of the archetypal family tree.

Pilgrims consecrate this holy center by performing *tawaf*, seven counter-clockwise circuits around the *Kaaba*. They wear the proscribed clothes of pilgrims, loose white robes circled with a belt, and special slippers. With their left shoulder exposed, they circle the central axis of the Islamic universe and attempt to kiss its central point. Other ritual journeys follow where pilgrims re-enact mythical and scriptural events. Leading away from the mosque is a wide covered walkway where pilgrims run back and forth seven times, a recapitulation of the desperate search for water that Hagar, the wife of Abraham, made to save her son Ishmail. There are also journeys to cities of Mina and Medina that mark other significant events, and lastly one final circuit around the *Kaaba*.

7.4

The Great Stupa at Sanchi was once part of an extensive early Buddhist monastery. Sanchi, India, reconstruction of the Holy Site, *c.* 250 BCE–100 CE

Source: Mondadori Electa.

The Great Stupa at Sanchi

Ancient Buddhist reliquaries and temples were also settings for devotional circumambulation. The Great Stupa at Sanchi dates from *c.* 250 BCE–100 CE and was once part of an extensive early Buddhist monastery. Three stupas,

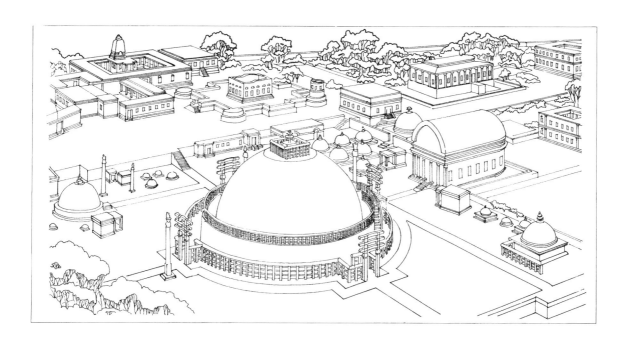

reliquaries for disciples of the Buddha, are all that remain today. The hemispherical form of the Great Stupa, the largest of the three, corresponds to an archetypal burial mound, but also recalls earth mounded over a germinated seed – perhaps paired symbols of the reciprocity of life and death. It rests at a symbolic center, flanked by four stone portals aligned with the cardinal points, which contain intricate carvings, each depicting important Buddhist events. At the East Gate, for example, Ashoka – the powerful king and early promulgator of Buddhism – is shown visiting the Bodhi tree, the place of the Buddha's enlightenment. Pilgrims most likely would have entered through the South Gate, ascended the steps that ring half of its base and then circumambulated around its hemispherical dome in the auspicious clockwise direction. In this manner, the cosmic egg of the stupa was consecrated through the interaction of body, movement, and place, and the path served to create its holy center.

Daitoku-ji Zen Buddhist Monastery, Kyoto, Japan

The Dawn Ceremony is an important ritual at Daitoku-ji Zen Buddhist Monastery in Kyoto, Japan, that is performed in its Buddha Hall at sunrise at the beginning and middle of each month. This great wooden building is one of a number of main temple buildings of this historically significant Rinzai monastery founded in 1319. Originally an extensive monastery complex, today it includes twenty-three sub-temples and some of the most important Zen Buddhist architecture and gardens in Japan. The Buddha Hall is built in the Medieval Zen style, raised above a massive stone platform and distinguished by its complex bracketing system. Inside, a 20-ft-high statue of the Sakyamuni Buddha rests on a central platform and is surrounded by an ambulatory defined by two sets of inner and outer columns. A dragon image is painted on the ceiling above, further consecrating its center.

The Dawn Ceremony, or *Shuto*, is attended by the abbot of the monastery and the abbots of the sub-temples, and has been described as a ritual that re-affirms the communal life of the monks of Daitoku-ji. The abbots arrive in ceremonial robes – brilliant gold, blue, green, and red silks – holding rosaries and ceramic incense holders. The cadence and events of the ceremony, like the architecture, date from Sung Period China. The ceremony begins with the ringing of the monastery bell at dawn and the procession of abbots who enter the dark hall and kneel facing the Buddha at its western wall. Five dirge-like chants honor the emperor and the country, and there are offerings of food and incense. Then, the players in this historic recapitulation circumambulate the altar, its path carefully choreographed by a mandala pattern marked on the dark tile floor. Circling its center, the abbots replicate the mandala's symbolic journey to enlightenment. In this middle ground, they mediate between the Buddha, the *dhamma* (teachings), and the *sangha* (monastic community) – the three refuges of Buddhism, as well as the historical traditions of Buddhism and its contemporary iterations.

Tongdo Zen Buddhist Monastery, Korea: The Path as a Mediator

I now turn to interpretations of the approach, path sequences, and destinations (places) of traditional Korean Zen Buddhist monastic architecture. To do so, I will focus on an ontological interpretation of the organization, path sequences, and symbolic narratives of Korean Zen monasteries in general, before turning to a detailed examination of Tongdo Monastery.

Tongdo-sa was founded in 646 CE as a mountain hermitage by the monk Master Chajang, who is believed to have brought relics of the Buddha from China. Today it is known as the "Pass Into Enlightenment Temple," and dedicated to the Sakyamuni Buddha and his attainment of enlightenment. From its beginnings as a simple mountain hermitage, Tongdo-sa grew to be one of the most important monasteries in Korea. Signs on the One-Pillar Gate proclaim that it is the "main" and "biggest temple in Korea."[12] Today it is an extensive campus of historically significant buildings that support an active community of over 100 monks.[13] Even though at one level, Tongdo-sa is organized according to a hierarchical, axial path sequence – a sequential spatial sequence and symbolic narrative that lead to the sacred center of the main Buddha Hall – a deeper reading reveals a dynamic interrelationship of multiple centers congruent with aspects of esoteric Mahayana Buddhism. In this context, it can be understood as a *path as a place*, a *path as a path*, and even a *place as a path*.

Korean Buddhism

The Buddhism of the Mahayana sect first came to Korea from China in the fourth century CE. Buddhism flourished under the Three Kingdoms Era (57–668 CE) during the late fourth century, and in the Unified Silla Dynasty (668–935 CE). During the Silla Dynasty, Buddhism enjoyed unprecedented state support and through imperial patronage monasteries expanded. It was during this period that Chinese Chan Buddhism (known as Son in Korean, Zen in Japanese), was first introduced.[14] The Koryo Dynasty (935–1392) continued its support of Buddhism, which was seen at the time as essential to the health of the state.[15] During the Joseon (Yi) Dynasty (1392–1910), Neo-Confucianism replaced Buddhism as the state religion, and many monasteries were closed and their holdings confiscated. Even though Buddhism was suppressed for most of this era, warrior monks trained in the martial arts were willing to defend their country against the Japanese invasions of the sixteenth century. Korean Buddhism is defined in part by its syncretic nature, and it incorporated many elements of the indigenous "Shamanistic" faith. It was during the Joseon Dynasty that the folk art that distinguishes Korean Buddhism developed. During this time, monasteries were suppressed, and it was mostly the remote mountain temples that remained. Today most of Korea's major temples are in mountainous areas and reached by long entry paths.[16]

In Mahayana doctrine, the cosmos is both limitless and contains multiple incarnations of the Buddha.[17] The various Buddhas and Bodhisattvas can be understood as representations of this vast and multivalent world.[18] Conse-quently, the self is understood as a constituent part of the whole. The Buddhist doctrine of *anatman,* or "no-self," atomizes the constituent parts of the body, its sensations, and consciousness, to describe a dynamic, ever-changing set of relationships. It does not deny the existence of a discrete self, but insists that "self" can only be fully understood through its relationship to a larger context. Korean monks routinely chant the *Heart Sutra,* a central Mahayana text where the five *skandhas* (the constituent part of each individual: body, perceptions, feelings, mental formations, and consciousness) are described as transitory and "empty:"[19]

> Form is Emptiness, Emptiness is Form: Form does not differ from Emptiness, Emptiness does not differ from Form; whatever is Empty, that is Form; whatever is Form that is Empty. The same is true of feelings, perceptions, impulses and consciousness.[20]

With no "self" to "maintain" or "preserve," one is then naturally led to more articulate relationships with that which is outside of "self." The fluid conditions of the *skandhas* open one to the dynamics of inter-personal and inter-subjective relationships. Robert Buswell recalls a teaching of his teacher Kusan Sunim as follows: "The entire universe is therefore no different from one's own mind."[21] Meditation monks practice individually – not in isolation, however, but as a constituent part of the *sangha,* the community of monks. Spiritual development is viewed as incremental and partial – the often-misunderstood concept of "enlightenment" is actually a relationship between multiple realizations.[22]

Korean Monastic Architecture

The walled compounds of Korean Zen monasteries provide an enclosed sanc-tuary to serve the Buddhist community it physically defines.[23] They comprise consistent layouts, configurations, and building types, with variations and inflections according to their particular emphasis or location. Most monasteries are typically located next to rivers on the south-facing slopes of mountains and employ an elongated path sequence of bridges, gateways, buildings, and courtyards. The location of monasteries on the south-facing slopes of mountains next to rivers with the main temple buildings facing in the auspicious south direction, correspond to the principles of *Pungsu-jiri* ("Wind and Water," or *Feng Shui* in Chinese) that aims to place buildings in harmony with their environmental setting. Entry paths are typically aligned north–south, though there are often shifting segments to avoid inauspicious straight lines, ascending steps up steep slopes and through a series of courtyards.[24] However, there are exceptions and inflections to these general site-planning rules. For example, even though the principal temple buildings of Tongdo-sa face south, its entry path is from east to west.

The overall layouts of the monasteries often correspond to the practice of "substance to the left and function to the right," which indicates the placement of buildings according to their function.[25] The Main Temple building is centered

7.5
Similar to the sacred
architecture of other faiths,
locations, and historical
settings, Korean monasteries
are distinguished by a
choreographed spatial
sequence and articulate
symbolic narrative. Heian
Monastery, Korea, begun
802 CE, Non-duality Gate

on its organizational axis with shrines dedicated to the more practical deities, such as the Bhaisagya (Medicine) Buddha, the Judgment Hall (for funeral services), and the bell pavilion located on the right (as one looks away from the Main Temple's entrance). On the left are temples of a more esoteric nature, such as the Vairocana (Cosmic Energy) and Maitreya (Future) Buddhas. The temple buildings, or image halls of Korean monasteries, serve as symbolic and ritual centers of the monasteries, and the type of Buddha image they hold often represents the emphasis of a particular monastery. Other buildings serve the administrative, scholarly, and religious functions of the monastery, and include shrines to various Buddhas and Shamanistic (indigenous) deities, lecture halls and visitor centers, living and study quarters for the monks, residences for senior monks, and cooking, eating, and washing areas.

Similar to the sacred architecture of other faiths, locations, and historical settings, Korean monasteries are distinguished by a choreographed spatial sequence and articulate symbolic narrative. The gateways, temples, and occasional buildings serve both practical and symbolic functions. The One-Pillar, Four Guardians, and Non-duality Gates mark the thresholds of the ordered entry sequence; the Lecture, Image, and Main Temple buildings provide symbolic centers for communal rituals; and the bell pavilions, stupas, reliquaries, and monks' quarters serve the practical needs of the community of monks. Many monasteries transformed the steep slopes of their mountainside locations to create an elongated entry sequence that traverses a series of gateways and courtyards to attain increasingly sacred spaces until arriving at the main temple buildings. For example, 108 steps ascend to gateways and courtyards at Haein-sa and lead to the main courtyard and temple buildings. Korean monks routinely perform 108 prostrations to symbolize their commitment to overcoming the 108 "defilements," or hindrances that cause suffering. The steps at Haein-sa perform a similar symbolic role.

A long approach path through dense forests and over one or more bridges typically initiates the entry sequence. The bridges provide a physical passage while their evocative names, such as "other shore," "mind washing," "three purities," "traverse the void," or "ultimate bliss," suggest a spiritual passage from one mode of being to another – from delusion to enlightenment. The spiritual theme of "crossing to the other side" is given physical form in the *Dhammapada*:

> Few cross the river. Most are stranded on this side. On the riverbank they run up and down.
>
> But the wise man, following the way, crosses over, beyond the reach of death.

7.6
At Seonam-sa, the graceful stone arch of the Ascending Immortal Bridge, leads across the river to the One-Pillar Gate. Seonam Monastery, Korea, bridge of entrance path

Free from desire, free from possessions, free from the dark places of the heart, free from attachment and appetite, following the seven lights of awakening, and rejoicing greatly in his freedom, in this world the wise person becomes himself a light, pure, shining, free.[26]

At Seonam-sa (located near Songgwang-sa, in Jogyesan Provincial Park in Jeollaman-do province in Southwest Korea), the graceful stone arch of the "Ascending Immortal Bridge," with a stone dragon guardian figure on its underside[27] leads across the river to the One-Pillar Gate. Two bridges cross the river at Songgwang-sa, the latter Uhwagak Pavilion serving as both gateway and bridge. Two massive stairways ascend to the main temple courtyard at Bulguk-sa monastery. These symbolic bridges are named the Blue Cloud and White Cloud Bridges, a reference to the land of sages and immortals described in Taoist myths. According to Hyo Gyun:

> Temple bridges serve a functional purpose while marking the temple precincts as an idealized place. They are symbolic structures that express the desire of the faithful to journey to the Buddha Land. They represent the frontier between the secular world and the Pure Land on the "other shore," and they are a passageway that connects the two realms.[28]

7.7
At Korean monasteries the One-Pillar Gates formally initiate the entry sequence and comprise either two or four aligned wooden columns supporting a massive, overhanging roof. Beomeao Monastery, Korea, One-Pillar Gate

At Korean monasteries the One-Pillar Gates formally initiate the entry sequence and comprise either two or four aligned wooden columns supporting a massive, overhanging roof. Also called the Small Beam Gate, its terms refer to a singularity – which may have multiple interpretations including the unity of the *dhamma* and the "single vehicle" of Buddhism.[29] At Beomeao-sa, the One-Pillar Gateway initiates a path sequence that rises poetically up the steep slope, a path that is inscribed by stone paving, framed by surrounding trees and monastery walls, and marked by a series of gateways. The Four Guardians Gate, a small pavilion with interior spaces on either side of the pathway, is the next threshold marker. Inside, the Four Heavenly Kings, each associated with a cardinal direction, flank the path.[30] The next threshold marker is the Non-duality Gate, its name referencing a central Buddhist concept of the unity of opposites where the "false" boundaries of self and others – individual and universal – are dissolved. The Non-duality Gate creates an in-between space that both separates and joins the outer and inner worlds of the monastery. Implicit is the concept that outside and inside are limited concepts – that divinity can be found everywhere. Each gateway marks thresholds to distinct precincts of the monastery, which are defined by buildings that serve the symbolic agendas and ritual activities of the monastery.

Tongdo Zen Buddhist Monastery

Tongdo-sa is located on the northern banks of a river and the gentle southern slope of Youngchuk Mountain. Its entrance path approaches from the east,[31] where three bridges cross the river and lead to the walled compound that clearly demarcates the sacred ground. The monastery is organized around three courtyards, each distinguished by the temples and buildings that form them.

7.8 (opposite)
The monastery is organized around three courtyards, each distinguished by the temples and buildings that form them. Tongdo Monastery, Korea, founded 646 CE, schematic plan of monastery complex

Source: Drawing by Tim Kiser.

7.9
The path at Tongdo-sa begins at the bridges over the river. Tongdo Monastery, bridges of entrance path

Source: Photo by Shim.

TONGDO-SA

1 Stupa
2 Main Temple
3 Disciples of Buddha
4 Three Holies Shrine
5 Judgment Hall
6 Lecture Hall

7 Mountain Spirit
8 Seminary
9 Monk's Quarters
10 Founders' Shrines
11 Sutra Library
12 Vairocana Buddha

13 Avalokitesvara
14 Maitreya Buddha
15 Non-duality Gate
16 Temple Office
17 Temple Shop
18 Bhalsagya Buddha

19 Sakyamuni Buddha
20 Amitabha Buddha
21 Bell Tower
22 Bath
23 Kitchen
24 Temple Guardian

25 Four Guardians Gate
26 One-Pillar Gate
27 One Vehicle Bridge
28 Shade of Half Moon
   Bridge

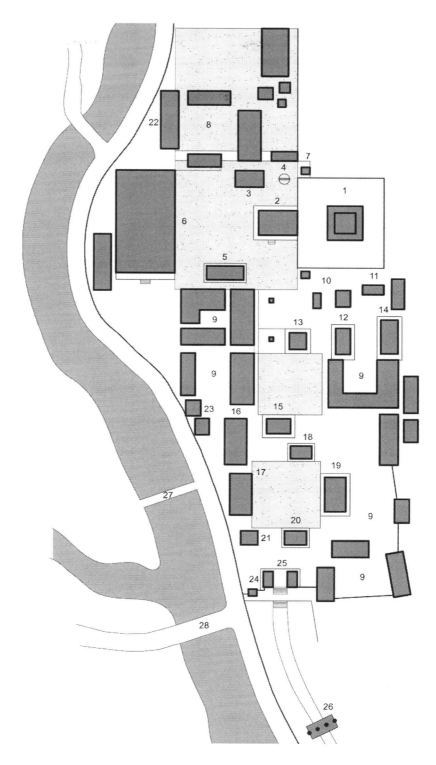

7.10
The two massive round wood columns of the One-Pillar Gate, set on a raised stone platform and supporting a large overhanging roof, provide a clear threshold to the beginning of the path. Tongdo Monastery, One-Pillar Gate

Source: Photo by Shim.

The first courtyard includes temples dedicated to the Bhalsagya (Medicine), Sakyamuni, and Amitabha (Pure Land) Buddhas and provides places for the prayers and supplications of lay worshippers. (A fourth building was originally a lecture hall and now serves as a gift shop.) The next courtyard serves the monks and comprises buildings that house the four levels of the Buddhist college. Adjacent buildings include temples to the Maitreya (Future) and Vairocana (Cosmic Energy) Buddhas, a shrine to Avalokitesvara (Bodhisaava of Compassion), a sutra library, and shrines dedicated to the founders of the monastery. The third and largest courtyard is dedicated to the Buddha and features the Main Temple (the Deaewungjeon or Hero Hall), as well as a temple dedicated to the Disciples of the Buddha, a Judgment Hall and a large Lecture Hall.

7.11 (opposite)
Tongdo Monastery, Four Guardians Gate

7.12
Inside the Four Guardians
Gate, the flanking figures of
the "Four Devas" dominate
the enclosed space. Tongdo
Monastery, Four Guardians
Gate showing the devas

Source: Photo by Shim.

7.13
Tongdo Monastery, view
through the Four Guardians
Gate

Tongdo-sa evidences articulate spatial compositions that sequentially deliver a range of symbolism and embody meanings for the lay and monastic communities. The path begins at the bridges over the river – the first called "Half Moon and Three Stars," the second "Shade of Half Moon." The first two bridges lead to the One-Pillar Gate, where plaques on each column contain admonitions regarding harmonious monastic life.[32] (The third bridge, located closest to the monks' area, leads to hermitages and is called the "One Vehicle Bridge.") Two massive round wood columns on a raised stone platform support a large overhanging roof to provide a clear threshold to the beginning of the path.

After passing through the One-Pillar Gate, the path shifts to the right and approaches the main entrance to the monastery, clearly established by its size, scale, depth, and flanking monastery walls. Wide stone steps lead up to the broad platform of the Four Guardians Gate, where inside the flanking figures of the "Four Devas" dominate the enclosed space. This shadowed space leads to a small forecourt defined by a two-story Bell Tower on its southern side.[33] Passing by this open, wooden, trabeated structure, one ascends a single step into the first courtyard. This lowest courtyard is defined by shrines to serve human desires – health, well-being, and future wishes (represented by the Bhalsagya, Sakyamuni, and Amitabha shrines). At its western edge, a step leads to another forecourt and the Non-duality Gate.

The Non-duality Gate, entered by a set of steps, leads to the second courtyard and marks the threshold from the realm of human desires to one defined by the community of monks committed to overcoming them. The three-bay building, enclosed on three sides with a central entrance opening on its eastern side but open to the west, frames a view of the main temple. Passing the Avalokitesvara Hall on the right, one enters a forecourt to the main temple and ascends steps to the third courtyard. This is the court of the Buddha, the enlightened one, fronted by the south-facing Hero Hall. To the north of the

7.15 (opposite)
The Non-duality Gate leads
to the second courtyard and
marks the threshold from the
realm of human desires to
one defined by the community
of monks committed to
overcoming them. Tongdo
Monastery, Non-duality Gate

7.16 (opposite)
Tongdo Monastery, view of
main temple

Source: Photo by Shim.

Hero Hall is the stupa and to the west of the courtyard is the seminary for meditation monks.

Symbolism, Meaning, and Ritual Use

Clearly demarcated boundaries and spaces, choreographed spatial sequences calibrated by proportion and geometry, and an extensive symbolic narrative, create the articulate sacred space of the *sachel* – the monastery realm. Its boundaries are clearly demarcated by walls and buildings, and entered and traversed by a sequence of gates and courtyards. However, there are multiple aspects regarding its use, symbolism, and meaning. For example, lay worshippers may understand the path sequence as a hierarchy of spaces leading from lower to higher realms. Furthermore, even though the monastery is a symbolic fortress protected by the guardian deities of the Four Devas and the Mountain Spirit, it also comprises multiple centers, an organization of discrete places serving specific functions and symbolizing discrete worldviews. Its multivalent scales and meanings comprise a dynamic hierarchy that is both created and mediated by the path sequence.

In its broadest context, the monastery occupies five centers or realms: (1) the realm of humans (and human desires) of the lower courtyard; (2) the realm of Bodhisattvas (the Sangha or community of monks) of the middle courtyard; (3) the realm of the Buddha of the third courtyard; (4) the realm of Ahrats (the seminary of meditation monks); and (5) the mountain itself to the west. Youngchuk Mountain (also known as Vulture Peak), is named for a mountain in India where the Buddha is believed to have delivered the *Lotus Sutra* and its incorporation into the spatial composition of the monastery symbolizes the possibility of enlightenment for all that this sutra describes.

The organization of multiple realms surrounding a center suggests a mandala pattern. Mandala, which translates as "circle," is a two-dimensional and in some examples three-dimensional diagram utilized by Mahayana Buddhism as models of Buddhist cosmologies and as meditative mediums. The mandala has its origins in India and is most closely associated with Tibetan Buddhism. However, other esoteric schools of Buddhism, such as Tendai, also have an extensive tradition of mandala art. Three-dimensional mandalas, though less common, are also found in Tibetan Buddhism, but are not limited to Mahayana Buddhism. Borobudur, located on the island of Java, is a massive architectural mandala where concentric passages lined with serial narrative carvings are traversed by pilgrims.[34]

"Palace Architecture" mandalas typically feature a Buddha figure at the center of a "palace" that includes symbolic gateways aligned with the cardinal points, and is ringed by lotus flowers, Bodhisattvas and guardians, as well as enclosures and gateways.[35] Mandalas replicate the unified cosmic model of multiple Buddhas from the three realms of past, present, and future described in the *Lotus Sutra* of Mahayana Buddhism.[36] In Mahayana Buddhism, mandalas are meditative mediums where a symbolic path that leads to the sacred center circumambulates through a sequence of realms. In this context, we may consider Tongdo-sa a symbolic *place as a path* where, as in other examples, the path

defines the place (albeit conceptually). The *Lotus Sutra* includes descriptions of multiple worlds, each created and maintained by Bodhisattvas. Mandalas of the Eight Bodhisattvas, favored by Pure Land Buddhism, symbolized these worlds and featured eight Bodhisattvas surrounding a seated Buddha. According to Denise Patry Leidy, they were manifestations of a "specific divinity in the cosmos and *as* the cosmos" (italics in original).[37] The eight principal temples at Tongdo-sa[38] surrounding the main temple and stupa can be viewed as a replication of this prevalent mandala pattern.

7.17
Mandala of Saravid Vairocana, Tibetan, sixteenth century

Source: Photograph © 2009
Museum of Fine Arts, Boston.

Monasteries that correspond to these patterns are hierarchical organizations with the main temple at the center, surrounded by lesser shrines and temples, and reached through a series of gateways. The axially symmetrical main temple precinct of Bulguk-sa corresponds to this organization with the main temple building located at the center of a raised platform surrounded by colonnades and reached by its famous stone "bridge" stairs. At Beopju-sa, a five-story pagoda, a place of ritual circumambulation, is located at the center of its axial plan. At Tongdo-sa, the Hero Hall and stupa form twin centers of the mandala pattern of the five realms of the *sachel*.[39] The multiple tiers, thresholds, and passages of the mandala symbolize the spiritual journey, a central element of Buddhism. The journey from the outer to inner realms of the monastery also symbolizes the path to the mountain hermitage of the enlightened Zen master. Tongdo-sa, like many Korean Zen Buddhist monasteries, was founded as a simple hermitage. Zen landscape paintings from the Chinese Southern Sung period idealized the prototypical hermit scholar's retreat. The first Chinese Zen monasteries are believed to have begun as mountainside retreats founded by Zen masters who then attracted students who built their own huts nearby. The journey of the religious aspirant at Tongdo-sa, across bridges and ascending a series of spaces towards a sacred mountain, replicates the archetypal pilgrimage to the sacred place of an enlightened being celebrated in Zen Buddhism. The individual quest to the solitary teacher symbolizes the individual effort stressed in Zen Buddhist practices.[40]

The multiple scales of the paths, buildings, spaces, and environmental setting of the monastery articulate the dynamic relationships of its multi-centered composition and reinforce its individual and collective symbolism. The bridges, gates, path surfaces, steps, scales, hierarchies, and framed vistas reinforce the individual nature of the spiritual path of Buddhism. However, singular, humanly scaled gateways and courtyards are also integral elements of the cosmic scale of the *sachel*. Additionally, collective symbols of proportion and geometry unify the complex and create hierarchies of spaces and buildings. Gateways, for example, are typically three-part compositions comprising three symbolic entrances that represent the triad of the Buddha, the *dhamma*, and the *sangha*. Their placement marks the path sequence and they include surface decoration that reinforces their symbolic function. The Korean "Kan" system of modular design of buildings governs the plans of the halls and temples, with most comprising either 2 × 3 or 3 × 3 bays. The first two courtyards are approximately the same size and proportion and lead to the third which is approximately twice their size, and is dominated by the 3 × 5-bay Hero Hall.

The articulate relationships within and between the realms of the monastery were created over time to serve multiple functions and constituents. The cosmic scale of its mandala pattern symbolizes aspects of Mahayana Buddhism; the collective scale of the individual courtyards accommodates the lay and monastic communities; and the individual scale of the shrines and hermitages serves the individual penitents and practitioners. The symbolism and significance of the hierarchies of scale reinforce the multi-centered organization. The monastery complex, in accordance with the collective beliefs of the earth energies of *Pungsu-jiri*, is aligned with its cosmic context. Its location on the southern slopes of a sacred mountain and in the bend of the river corresponds to the auspicious siting in the "belly of the dragon." The southern orientation of the temple buildings and the subtle shifts of buildings along the main axis, correspond to geomantic principles. The monastery's alignment with the quaternary of the four cardinal points is made explicit by the four devas guarding its entrance – each associated with a direction. The ritual ringing of the four instruments of the Bell Tower, each calling a realm of the material world, also has cosmic implications, and paintings of the beings of the four realms – the air, land, water, and hell realms – are found throughout the temple buildings.

The dynamic path sequence, reinforced by inflections of its surfaces and building orientation, negotiates and unifies the realms of the monastery. The result is a multivalent hierarchy comprising a linear spatial sequence that leads from the lower realms to the sacred center but with each realm creating its own center and purpose. The function and symbolism of each courtyard are discrete, and suggest both the levels of enlightenment of Buddhism and the hierarchy of Korean culture,[41] while simultaneously the "asymmetry of their experiential space" suggests a larger context. Throughout, the Buddhist concept

7.18
Tongdo Monastery, main temple and stupa

7.19
The main Hero Hall at Tongdo-sa is unusual because it does not contain any statue of the Buddha. Instead, a large, horizontal opening at its north wall frames a vista of the stupa – the temple is both a center and a threshold to a larger realm. Tongdo Monastery, main temple interior, view toward stupa

Source: Photo by Shim.

of *anatman*, or "no self," and its conceptualization of multiple relationships, find articulate expression in the monastery's organization.

As it evolved, Buddhism became a highly systematic religion; hence Buddhist texts include both specific spiritual practices and themes that address the immensity of cosmic realms and an individual's place within it. Korean Buddhist monastic life, as symbolized and accommodated by the architecture, is also explicitly structured. Within its formal and hierarchical structure, however, each monk has freedom to find their own path. Monks tend to move from monastery to monastery, especially early in their careers, and time limits are not imposed on their training. Within the systematic organization of the monastery – both implicit (the architecture) and explicit (the structure and rules of the monastery) – there are multiple paths.[42]

The main Hero Hall at Tongdo-sa is unusual because it does not contain any statue of the Buddha. Instead, a large, horizontal opening at its north wall frames a vista of the stupa – the temple is both a center and a threshold to a larger realm. Even though Buddha figures are absent, the Sakyamuni Buddha's presence is manifest in the relics contained in the stupa and the symbolic imagery of the hall. Symbols of the Wheel of the Dhamma are carved on the stone steps that lead to the temple platform, and lotus flowers decorate its stone base. On the wooden ceiling panels, intricate multicolored paintings of lotus flowers are shown. The lotus is the most common Buddhist symbol and a decorative motif found in many Hero Halls. Originally an indigenous Indian and Hindu symbol of purity, it became a Buddhist symbol of the perfection of the Buddha and the *dhamma*. Buddha statues are typically seated on a lotus flower in *padmasana*, or "lotus pose." Buddhist texts state that when the Buddha gave

7.20

Tongdo Monastery, stupa

Source: Photo by Shim.

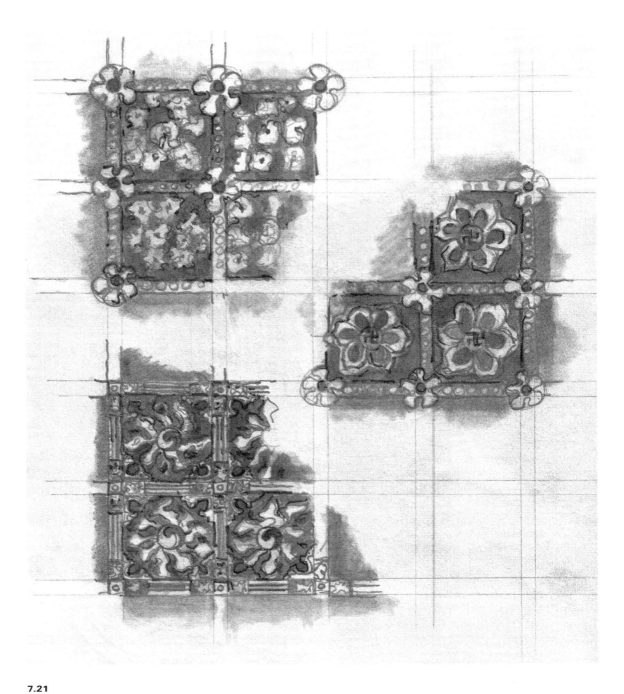

7.21
The imagery of the Buddha hall symbolizes a theme common to many religions, of the "first place," an eternal realm where the gods were present and still are. Tongdo Monastery, main temple ceiling

his first sermon after reaching enlightenment, the heavens rained flowers. The imagery of the Buddha hall symbolizes a theme common to many religions, of the "first place," an eternal realm where the gods were present and still are. The monastery and its ritual uses symbolize the continuity of belief and time.

Active monasteries such as Tongdo-sa perform roles as mediators between past and present where the past is animated by the architecture, its use, and their interplay. Tongdo-sa is a cultural artifact from which we can, in part, understand its historic and religious settings, perhaps more effectively than scripture or historical sources. It also occupies the present. Lay worshippers pray at its shrines, the Judgment Hall serves funerary functions, tourists visit its historically significant artifacts and monks train in the college and seminary.[43] Multiple mediations are at play here: the triangulation of participant, place, and larger contexts are multiplied through the different levels of symbolic content, which are calibrated and encoded for the lay and monastic participants. For example, scenographic elements represent accessible Buddhist symbols and scripture. The main Buddha Halls are typically referred to as "dragon ships," or "wisdom dragon ships,"[44] vehicles for conveying the Buddhist practitioner from delusion to enlightenment. On the rear wall of the Amitabha Buddha Hall at Tongdo-sa, a boat in the form of a dragon is depicted ferrying souls to salvation. This is appropriate as the Amitabha is the Buddha of the Western Paradise, but dragons are also depicted in the Main Buddha Hall. The beneficent dragon figure is both a guardian and a guide – protecting the Buddhist Sangha and leading the devout to enlightenment. Meanwhile, the complex relationships of the monastery's organization delineate Buddhist philosophy. Overall, similar to communal rituals, the hierarchies of symbolism include a full range of those who choose to "play along."

Korean Zen Buddhism is distinguished by its adherence to traditions that are said to date from the time of the Buddha. These patterns of practice, organization, and ritual constitute the "eternal return" to the original time of the Buddha. In the sacred setting of the monastery monks perform a mimesis of the deeds of the Buddha, spiritual practices transmitted by the *dhamma*, the goal of which is enlightenment (in all its forms). This primordial orientation is not only temporal, but spatial as well. The Sakyamuni Buddha is often shown at the center of mandalas, occupying the symbolic center of the world, sometimes referred to as the world mountain.[45] Tongdo-sa recreates this *imago dei*, transforming a sacred mountain into a symbolic center of the cosmos.

The multiple hierarchies of Tongdo-sa include an interrelationship of multiple centers where Bodhisattvas occupy distinct realms, and protect and grant blessings to the faithful. All are mediated by the dynamics and time sequence of the path, a reciprocity of space and form that both separates and joins each realm. At the center of the *sachel* realm is the Buddha Hall and stupa where the boundaries of time and space collapse and relationships between self and other – mind and cosmos – are blurred. The mandala as a transformative medium is created in space and time, and the possibility of "crossing over" to realms of enlightenment is made material.

Chapter 8

Ordering the World

Means and Meanings of Proportion and Geometry

> Man has to construct the universe, just as he had to build his houses,
> in order to make it intelligible for himself.
>
> (Richard Padovan)[1]

We have observed the variety of ways that sacred architecture serves to disclose, explain, and explicate otherwise hidden information or meanings, and how it was often believed to be a place where, through revelation, the divine was rendered more accessible (though sometimes only to the priesthood). The organization and morphology of paths and destinations, as illustrated by the previous chapter, were one means by which relationships could be articulated in service of delivering symbolism and structuring meaning. Any articulate architecture must first *articulate* the relationships of its parts to the whole and the whole to its constituent parts. Geometry and proportion have often been put in service of creating the critical relationships essential to coherent and efficacious sacred architecture.

Most cultures with mature building traditions have employed methods of geometry and proportion, typically in service of cultural and religious agendas. Historically, there were a variety of methods and applications, but a limited number of imperatives for doing so. For the purposes of this study, I have identified five imperatives of proportioning that are most related to the mediating roles of sacred architecture. In the first, sacred architecture serves as a *replication of the cosmos*, of the divine orders of nature and therefore, by extension, embodies those sacred qualities. In the second, the proportioning of a temple is at the specific (and often detailed) *directive of the divine* – either directly by god or through an intermediary. The third are examples of *archetypal authority* in which exemplars from the past are replicated and historical continuity is achieved, in part through proportion, as a means to validate the veracity of the sacred place.[2] In the fourth, *sacred practices* of geometry and proportion (often in guilds or societies sworn to secrecy) are believed to be sacred activities. In the fifth type, the architecture is a *manifestation of understanding* – it does not reflect the cosmos, but represents our understanding of it (however imperfect).

Replication of the Cosmos

The first type is perhaps the most common and diverse, and descriptions of a divinely ordered universe are often found in world mythology and scripture. Creation myths describe the primordial cosmos as a *tabula rasa*, an enormity of homogenous space subsequently (and often sequentially) ordered by god. The universe, created by god, was a reflection of god's perfection. The Sumerian myth of *Enuma elish* describes how the first couple Apsu and Tiamat created the earth and heavens from vast undifferentiated waters.[3] The Japanese primordial gods Izanagi and Izanami, brother and sister and husband and wife, create the world from an aquatic abyss. Typically the world is created by a series of subdivisions and additions – the fundamentals of geometry and proportion. The Book of Genesis describes the earth as "without form." However, God is present "over the face of the waters," and what follows are a series of divisions: light from dark, sky from water, and water from land.[4] The principal subdivision of earth and sky was also symbolized by the gods – Geb and Nut in Egyptian mythology; Ouranos and Gaia in Greek. For the Greeks, Ouranos and Gaia represented the formative cosmos of heaven and earth – the additive process of their progeny created the cosmos – two begetting many. The Garden of Eden is divided between good and evil and then quartered by four rivers that flow from its center – the Pishon, Gihon, Tigris, and Euphrates.

Architecture as a cosmic model is a predominant theme in the history of architecture. At the Emperor Hadrian's Pantheon to the gods in Rome the symbolic agenda of representing a cosmogonic microcosm of the known world was achieved, in part, through the application of pure spatial geometry. Ottoman architecture and, in particular, the Ottoman mosque, applied geometry in plan, section, and elevation as a means of representing a divine paradise through non-iconographic means. In India, one of the world's oldest continuous building traditions, the divine origins of the ordering of temples and cities were represented by the geometric form of the mandala.[5] The *vastu-purusha* mandala is a subdivided square found in the *vastu-vidya*, a Vedic branch of occult knowledge that focused on architecture and included extensive practices of geometry and proportion. Brahma, the "one and the infinite,"[6] was believed to have created the *vastu-purusha* by pairing the geometry of the square with the primordial figure of Purusha.[7] It symbolized the divine orders of the universe and provided the means to replicate them.[8] According to one manual of architecture, the *vastu-purusha* mandala can be drawn 32 ways through equal subdivisions of 4, 9, 16, 25, 36, 49, 64, 81 . . . squares, all the way up to 1024.[9] It was applied as a model to govern the layout of all parts of the building, from wall thickness to the sizes of spaces. The temple plan was systematically sited, laid out, and proportioned according to the precise proportional system of the mandala. According to George Michell, "This arrangement of central squares with others

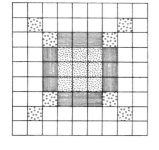

8.1

The *vastu-purusha* mandala is a subdivided square found in the *vastu-vidya*, a Vedic branch of occult knowledge that focused on architecture and included extensive practices of geometry and proportion

Source: Courtesy of George Michell.

that surround it is taken to be a microscopic image of the universe with its concentrically organized structure."[10] Temples are commonly named *vamana* (well-proportioned), and the temple's ability to attract the deity to dwell there depends on the success of its proportioning. Therefore, "Every part of the temple, . . . is rigorously controlled by a proportional system of measurement and interrelated by the use of a fundamental unit."[11]

Directive of the Divine

Examples of divine directives for the creation of sacred architecture may be less common, but comprise an important aspect of its conception. In one of the

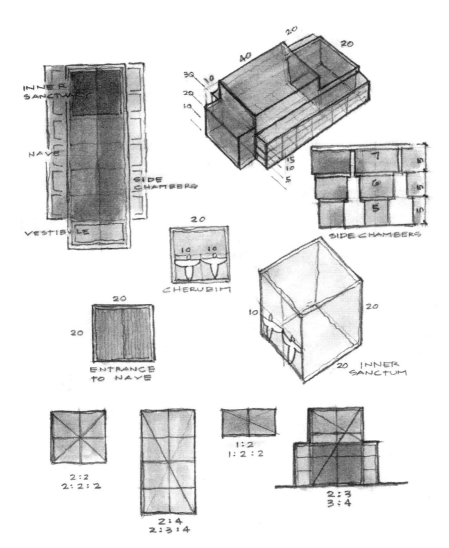

8.2
Solomon, to whom the God of the people of Israel gave "wisdom and understanding beyond measure," built the "house of the Lord" according to precise proportions. Solomon's temple reconstruction showing proportions

earliest examples, a statue of King Gudea of Lugash, a third millennium BCE Sumerian ruler, holds in his lap a plan revealed by god for a temple. In the Hebrew tradition, God is conceptualized as the builder of the world and often the words he speaks in scripture are architecturally specific. In the Book of Isaiah, it is God who "stretches out the heavens like a curtain, and spreads them like a tent to dwell in."[12]

Solomon, to whom the God of the people of Israel gave "wisdom and understanding beyond measure," built the "house of the Lord" according to precise proportions:

> The house which King Solomon built for the Lord was sixty cubits long, twenty cubits wide, and thirty cubits high. The vestibule in front of the nave of the house was twenty cubits long, equal to the width of the house, and ten cubits deep in front of the house.[13]

The wishes of the deity, in this case through the intermediary of Solomon, were manifested in the Temple of Jerusalem. God tells Solomon, "Concerning this house which you are building, if you walk in my statutes and obey my ordinances and keep all my commandments and walk in them, then I will establish my word with you."[14] The structure and organization of the temple symbolize the order of God's statutes, which can be understood as reciprocal. Throughout the "house for the Lord" specific dimensions govern every aspect of its organization – precise calibrations required by the divine. Similar to the Hindu temple, this was necessary for God to dwell in "his house." The result was a series of proportional relationships derived from a base measure of 5 cubits, and spatial modules of 20 cubits (on each side).

The space of the inner sanctum, reserved for the Arc of the Covenant, was a 20-cubit cube:

> He built twenty cubits of the rear of the house with boards of cedar from the floor to the rafters, and he built this within as an inner sanctuary, as the most holy place . . . the inner sanctuary was twenty cubits long, twenty cubits wide and twenty cubits high.[15]

Winged cherubim, made from olive wood, were placed at the entrance to the inner sanctum,

> each ten cubits high. Five cubits was the length of one wing of the cherub, and five cubits the length of the other wing of the cherub; it was ten cubits from the tip of one wing to the tip of the other.[16]

The nave was a space 20 cubits wide, 30 cubits high and 40 cubits long – and was entered through a pair of doors set within a 20-cubit square. Three levels of side chambers, each 5 cubits high, flanked the nave and are also described precisely. "The lowest story was five cubits broad, the middle one was six cubits broad, and third was seven cubits broad."[17] Eventually the entire interior was covered in gold and gold chains stretched across the threshold of the inner sanctum. And, because the Temple of Jerusalem was built in accordance with the wishes of the deity, he promises to "dwell" there. As Solomon states, "The Lord has set the sun in the heavens, but has said that he would dwell in thick darkness. I have built thee an exalted house, a place for thee to dwell in for ever."[18]

Archetypal Authority

The replication of historical archetypes depends on the reproduction, in detail, of previously accepted norms and symbols of the sacred. As we observed in Chapter 4, codified building traditions and symbolic languages were typically put into the service of reproducing an established type and its broadly accessible symbols of authority. What I have termed archetypal authority is perhaps best illustrated by the periodic rebuilding of certain Japanese Shinto shrines. The indigenous Shinto faith shares many aspects of other animistic belief systems; its gods, associated with celestial bodies and elements of the natural world, grew out of its agrarian roots.[19] Like similar faiths, reverence for the dead and historical continuity were important elements. In Shinto, ritual purity associated with funerary rites significantly influenced its sacred architecture, and the practice of the periodic re-building of prototypical temples. Ise Jingu, the most significant of Shinto sites, is distinguished by the periodic construction of the Naiku or "Inner Shrine." The Naiku's fenced enclosure contains the Main Hall and the East and West Treasuries. These buildings, stylized replications of vernacular structures, are fastidiously re-built every twenty years. Their highly ritualized re-construction is in service of a recapitulation of an ancient archetype. Precise geometry and standards of construction and materials govern the process – all in service of the historical continuity (and thus sacred authority) the buildings symbolize.

The Practice of Geometry

As humans came to understand the procession of the heavens and their predictable, repetitive patterns, they developed beliefs regarding a divinely ordered cosmos.[20] The practice of geometry, as a means to articulate these divine orders, was often considered to be a divinely sanctioned activity. The authority over these practices was often held by the priesthood (such as the Brahmin caste in India) or secret societies (such as Medieval Masonic guilds). Geometry is a word that comes from the Greek *geometria*, which translates as *geo* (earth) and *metria* (measuring), and the practice of geometry was often the result of a culture's environmental setting. For example, the yearly flooding of the River Nile necessitated that the land be surveyed each year to re-establish farming plots. Egyptian surveying was essentially based on triangulation through the use of a rope-stretcher's triangle. A rope was knotted, for example, to create twelve equal subdivisions, and then stretched on the ground to form a 3-4-5 right triangle. These basic units of measure (which are also golden sectional ratios), would be used to subdivide the land recently emerged from the deluge of the Nile. Order was re-established annually through a system that was to guide Egyptian building for millennia. "The laying of squares upon the earth had, for the Egyptians, a metaphysical as well as physical and social dimension."[21] Through the agency of geometric practices humans, in essence, became the demiurge.

Manifestations of Understanding

Richard Padovan cites three principal systems of proportion – systems that primarily utilize the square root of 5 and the Golden Section; Renaissance applications of geometric and harmonic relationships; and the proportioning system developed by the Dutch Benedictine monk and architect Hans van der Laan. Padovan states that architecture provides for "the satisfaction of a higher existential need: to perceive and to know the world and make it our own by giving it measure."[22] He inverts the conventional understanding of proportion as a reflection of the inherent order of the world by suggesting that instead the order we perceive is the order of our minds applied to the perceivable world.[23] It is through *empathy* that we know the world as part of us and it is by means of *abstraction* that we interpret our understanding through constructions of our own making.[24] For Padovan, van der Laan's "plastic number" (which will be discussed later in this chapter), is a concise mediation between empathy and abstraction. Architecture, in this context, is an abstraction imposed on nature as a means of understanding it more.[25] "The plastic number does not belong, therefore, to a Platonic world of pure mathematics, but constitutes a bridge between the abstracting mind and the world of concrete phenomena."[26]

Van der Laan was explicit in insisting that we learn about the world and our place in it through the act of making architecture, a progressive sequence of knowledge building. Consequently, the work itself becomes a source of knowledge, and so we find in van der Laan's theory aspects of a hermeneutical dialog between the object, its making, and our experience of it. For van der Laan, the measuring of the world through the application of proportion in architecture is, in essence, an imitation (however imperfect), of God's measuring of the world. Therefore, the architecture is the result of a system, not the expression of an individual, and thus more universal in its capacity to entice and engage us. In van der Laan's words, "the more developed his skill, the more universal the work will be."[27]

Proportioning Systems

Padovan suggests that our understanding of the world comprises what we experience and our understandings of these experiences – it is both *sensible* and *intelligible*. Heraclitus' statement that "nature loves to hide" illustrates the dynamic and unknowable qualities of the world we perceive and seek to understand through its intelligible ordering. Vitruvius introduces *Book III* of the *Ten Books of Architecture* by observing the limits of the intellect to transmit knowledge. If we were not required to translate and interpret the finding of others "by untrustworthy powers of judgment," then a "singular and lasting influence would thus be lent to the learned and the wise." From this position,

Vitruvius then proceeds to describe the immutable dimensions of the human body as an illustration of symmetry and proportion and by implication applications appropriate for conveying "singular and lasting" knowledge central to the design of "temples of the immortal gods:"

> The design of a temple depends on symmetry, the principles of which must be most carefully observed by the architect. They are due to proportion, in Greek *analogia*. Proportion is a correspondence among the measures of the members of an entire work, and of the whole to a certain part selected as a standard. From this result the principles of symmetry. Without symmetry and proportion there can be no principles in the design of any temple; that is, if there can be no precise relation between its members, as in the case of those of a well-designed man.[28]

The Vitruvian Man, illustrated during the Renaissance by Leonardo da Vinci, superimposes the geometry of the circle and the square.[29] There are no further subdivisions, as in the *vastu-purusha* mandala, but instead a static representation of the immutable orders of nature. Vitruvius, referencing Plato, does cite proportions and numbers derived from the measure of the human body and by implication their applicability to the proportioning of architecture. According to Vitruvius:

> If it is agreed that number was found out from the human fingers, and that there is a symmetrical correspondence between the members separately and the entire form of the body, in accordance with a certain part selected as a standard, we can have nothing but respect for those who, in constructing temples of the immortal gods, have so arranged the members of the world that both separate parts and the whole design may harmonize in their proportions and symmetry.[30]

Vitruvius' treatise can be seen as essentially Platonic in its predisposition to describe an ideal, ordered, and immutable world perceivable through the intellect.[31] Unlike Vitruvius, however, Plato's philosophy is essentially religious and seeks means to part the veil of the sensible world to reveal the eternal divine. For Plato, the ephemeral nature of the sensible world is rendered comprehensible through transcendental, archetypal "Forms." In *Timaeus and Critias*, the ordering of "an ideal state and its citizens"[32] is equated with the agency of god. Its creation is attributed to the divine, referred to as the "father, goddess, maker or craftsman." In one passage, Critias[33] states,

> You see what great attention our law devotes from the beginning to learning, deriving from the divine principles of cosmology everything needed for human life down to divination and medicine for our health, and acquiring all other related branches of knowledge. The goddess founded this whole order and system when she framed your society.[34]

In Book VI of *The Republic*, Plato represents the human condition in the "Allegory of the Cave," where men are described as living their lives chained together in a cave in such a manner that they can only look at the wall in front of them. Shadows cast on the wall from figures and objects passing in front of a fire burning behind them are the only reality these men have ever known:

> "And so you see," I said, "men passing along the wall carrying all sorts of vessels, and statues and figures of animals made of wood and stone and various materials, which appear over the wall? Some of them talking, others silent." "You have shown me a strange image, and they are strange prisoners." "Like ourselves," I replied; "and they see only their shadows or the shadows of one another, which the fire throws on the opposite wall of the cave?" "True," he said, "how could they see anything but the shadows if they were never allowed to move their heads?"[35]

Plato's point is clear – the perceptual world that we consider to be reality is mere shadows. He goes on to describe that when one confronts the truth, it is seen as strange and even dangerous. "Being and Becoming" is the Platonic dichotomy that describes the human condition illustrated by the men in the cave. "Becoming" is the partial and incomplete world perceived by the senses – "Being" the world of immutable Forms. How does one turn toward the light and perceive the world outside of the dark cave of ignorance described in Plato's allegory? Plato argues that empirical observation is inferior to intellectual under-standing. It is mathematics that represent the "order and system" of god, and it is through mathematics that one may intellectually understand it.

Plato's cosmology comprises the four essential (and separate) elements of fire and air, and their complements water and earth. The relationship of these primary elements constitutes the foundation of Platonic geometry, which is made articulate through one element mediating between the others. Plato describes these relationships as two extremes that are joined by a *mean*. It is through the agency of mediation that the world is constructed, integrated, and made whole.[36] Plato describes this "binding together" as follows:

> So god, when he began to put together the body of the universe, made it of fire and earth. But it is not possible to combine two things properly without a third to act as a bond to hold them together. And the best bond is one that affects the closest unity between itself and the terms it is combining; and this is best done by a continued geometrical proportion. For whenever you have three cube or square numbers with a middle term such that the first term is to it as it is to the third term, and conversely that the third term is to the *mean*, the mean is to the first term, then since the middle becomes first and last and similarly the first and last become middle, it will follow necessarily that all can stand in the same relation to each other, and in so doing achieve unity together.[37]

The mean, as described by Plato, forms the basis of the conceptual and practical aspects of proportion that has resonated throughout the history of western architecture. A geometric *mean* is an interrelationship of three members such that the middle number is to the lower as the higher is to the middle, and can be written by the formula A:B = B:C (where A is the lowest and C the highest). It is through the relative position of the mean that any articulate relationships and consequently unity are possible. For Greek philosophers such as Pythagoras (a Pre-Socratic philosopher), Plato, and Aristotle (Plato's student and successor), mathematics were revelatory of the divine and served to mediate between the sensible and the intelligible. "Let no one unacquainted with geometry enter here," was inscribed above the doorway to Plato's Academy.

It has been suggested that, especially in *Timaeus and Critias*, Plato was an interpreter of Pythagoras, the fifth-century BCE Greek philosopher who founded a school of philosophy at Croton (in Southern Italy), that included spiritual practices, initiation rites, levels of development, strict vows, vegetarianism, and communal living. Pythagorean philosophy focused on relationships – most importantly on dichotomies, or the division of the world into paired opposites – and the interrelationship of intellectual, ethical, and spiritual ideals. Imbued with the secrecy of the mystery religions with which it was aligned, Pythagoreans remain mysterious. However, we do know that mathematics and musical harmonies were central to practices that aspired to a union with the "world soul." According to Pythagoras, "All is arranged according to number," establishing the primacy of measure and relationships to his philosophy. Even though he did not leave any philosophical texts, his school had significant influence on Greek (and subsequent Western) thought, through the writings of Plato.

Before we turn to specific examples of Gothic and Renaissance proportioning systems (as a means of introducing the case study of van der Laan's plastic number), it is useful to review the principal methods of proportion and their essential characteristics. In this way, we can understand the fundamental relationships established by proportion and how, through a series of mediations, an interrelated whole is created (or believed to be). "Analogia" is a concept that describes the proportional interrelationships within a whole – otherwise known as symmetry. Symmetry to the Greeks was not an axial subdivision resulting in identical halves but, as described by Vitruvius, "consonance between every part and the whole." Sacred geometry is a term often used to describe the perfection of the universe as revealed by the measure of, and relationships between, its elements. It is interesting to note that the most enduring element of sacred geometry, the Golden Section, is formed by a simple act of subdivision, and its discovery is attributed to Pythagoras.

The mathematical systems applied in the creation of proportioning systems are complementary methods believed to render the hidden world intelligible. From a hermeneutic perspective, it is through the recognition of the focus and limitations of each, in relationship to all, that more complete understandings of their significance can be achieved. There may be a limited number of proportioning systems related to the articulation of architectural relationships – but there are numerous ways of representing, explaining, and applying them. It is not my purpose to comprehensively address the variety of formulations, or to champion a particular one, but instead to illustrate that through the mediation of proportion a more comprehensible set of relationships within the architecture and between the architecture and its context (local and cosmic) are manifest.

We also need to be cognizant of the fact that, in Rudolf Wittkower's words regarding proportional analysis, "almost anything under the sun can be proved." The "answer" may not lie in unitary conclusions, but paradoxically in multiple interpretations. Conversely, applying one proportioning system to analyze a particular work can often serve to unpack the architecture in some depth (though incompletely) while illustrating that it is only one of multiple approaches. Ultimately, the unifying question is *why* proportion has proven to be an enduring concern of humans, not necessarily *how* we may (or may not) produce (or understand) proportioned architecture. Fundamentally proportion is intrinsic to the human quest for order – it is a means of disclosure.

The primary methods of proportion and geometry are *arithmetic*, *geometric*, and *harmonic* – each one a specific triangulation of relationships established by a mean. According to Robert Lawlor, the "cornerstone of ancient philosophical mathematics [is] the science of mediations,"[38] and that a mediating proportion can be defined as "a group of three unequal numbers such that two of their differences are to each other in the same relationship as one of these numbers is to itself or to one of the other numbers."[39] An *arithmetic mean* establishes a relationship between numbers such that the middle number is equal to the difference between the lower and higher numbers. It can be written as the formula where the mean number $B = (A + C)/2$. The mathematical operations of addition and subtraction govern arithmetic systems. The *geometric mean*, as we have observed, does not string together numbers arithmetically, but instead reconciles them through multiplication and division. In other words, the formula $A:B = B:C$ can also be written as $B/A = C/B$. The *harmonic mean* is a combination of the first two where the middle number exceeds the lower number and is exceeded by the higher number, by the same ratio. To do so, the mean divides both the sum and the difference of the other two numbers into two equal parts and can be written as $B = AC/A + C/2$ or, as simplified $B = 2AC/(A + C)$.

Arithmetic, geometric, and harmonic proportions produce interwoven sets of numerical relationships where each subsequent mean mediates between lesser and greater numbers. The Golden Section is principally a divisional relationship that is created by bisecting a unit of measure so that the first part is to the second part what the second is to the whole. In its formula of $A:B = B:(A + B)$ it is clear that "B" mediates between the lesser unit "A" and the greater number ("A" + "B"). From this, a Golden Sectional summation series can be generated. This arithmetic system, attributed to a twelfth-century mystic mathematician Leonardo of Pisa, is a summation series where each number is the sum of the proceeding two numbers such as $3 + 5 = 8$, $5 + 8 = 13$, $8 + 13 = 21$ . . . – the ratios of the numbers – 3, 5, 8, 13, 21, 34, 55, 89 . . . – are approximately equal to Golden Sectional ratios, or .618. Additionally, in a Golden Sectional rectangle, the ratio of the larger to the smaller side is approximately 0.618. If you plot each of the numbers of a Fibonacci series according to the progression of rectangles the numbers describe, the result is an elegant spiral.[40]

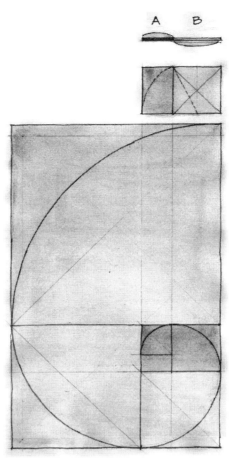

Gothic and Renaissance Proportioning Systems

It is well known that Western European cathedrals were designed and constructed by means of arithmetic number series and applied geometry. The master masons utilized the "secret" knowledge of geometry and proportion to generate plans, sections, and elevations, as well as the dimensions of piers, window tracery, and details. The occult (and fiercely guarded) knowledge of the masons was actually Greek philosophical mathematics, geometry, and philosophy rediscovered in the Islamic Middle East during the Crusades of the Middle Ages.[41] All of which was set in the context of Scholasticism where, in the twelfth century, the previously lost knowledge was re-vivified at the cathedral school at Chartres.

According to Erwin Panofsky, the Gothic system of measure, geometry, and proportion, analogous to the totality of Christian philosophy, theology, and canon law, aimed at a synthetic totality. It comprised a uniform and consistent system of proportional subdivisions that utilized squares, circles, and triangles to produce profiles, plans, and details:[42]

Like the High Scholastic *Summa*, the High Gothic cathedral aimed, first of all, at "totality" and therefore tended to approximate, by synthesis as well as elimination, one perfect and final solution; we may therefore speak of *the* High Gothic plan or *the* High Gothic system with much more confidence than would be possible in any other period. In its imagery, the High Gothic cathedral sought to embody the whole of Christian knowledge, theological, moral, natural, and historical, with everything in its place and that which no longer found its place, suppressed. In structural design, it similarly sought to synthesize all major motifs handed down by separate channels and finally achieved an unparalleled balance between the basilica and the central plan type, suppressing all elements that might endanger this balance, such as the crypt, the galleries, and towers other than the two in front.[43]

Even though the word "geometrie" appears in medieval writings, and versions of Plato's *Timaeus and Critias* and Euclid's *Elements* were available, the Medieval mason's knowledge was not theoretical but practical. The geometric and proportional systems were generative and typically utilized constructive geometry and arithmetic number series to produce a set of interrelated proportions. Its constructive geometry was principally based on the square (*ad quadratum*), or the triangle (*ad triangulum*). Subdivided or progressive squares created by striking arcs produced the repeating dimensions of the square root of 2 or of the Golden Section. In this case, the use of irrational numbers does not mean that they were arrived at or understood mathematically. Instead, they were simply the result of the practice of geometry, a practice that generated dimensions and interrelated proportions. Geometry and proportion revealed the divine orders symbolized by the cathedral – an occult media that was kept secret and must have seemed magical.

At Ely Cathedral in England, the ground floor plan comprises a set of overlapping squares, modular dimensions derived from the base measure of the choir. The section of Milan Cathedral, the subject of much debate in its time as to whether it should be *ad quadratum*, or *ad triangulum*, in the end was based on a series of equilateral triangles.[44] The plan of the choir of Beauvais Cathedral corresponds to two paired equilateral triangles with additional dimensions created by striking arcs to form the *vesica piscis* (the almond-shaped form that typically framed Christ in "mandorla").[45]

Cistercian architecture is distinguished by its emphasis on geometry and proportion and a unity of planning and form, adjusted only slightly by regional variations. This was the result of the strict dictates of St. Bernard of Clairvaux that required that monasteries be built in remote locations near sources of water, devoid of sculpture, stained glass, and any other non-essential decoration, and without imposing towers and westworks.[46] The iconoclastic St. Bernard asserted that in Cistercian monastic architecture "There must be no decoration, only proportion." Relieved from the task of embellishing the architecture with ornament, the master builders could concentrate on the formal, structural, and spatial components of the abbey church and monastic buildings.[47] The result was a reciprocity of belief, practice, and architectural expression.

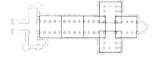

8.4

At Ely Cathedral in England, the ground floor plan comprises a set of overlapping squares, modular dimensions derived from the base measure of the choir. Ely Cathedral, United Kingdom, twelfth century, square module diagram

Source: British Museum Press.

The Cistercians, founded in the twelfth century as a reform movement to the Benedictines, were committed to restoring the essentials of St. Benedict's credo of "poverty, chastity, and obedience," which they deemed lost at the rich and ostentatious Cluny. St. Bernard's reforms were not only philosophical but architectural as well, as when he wrote:

> O vanities of vanities, but more vain than foolish! The walls of the church are ablaze with riches, while the poor go hungry; its stones are covered in gold and its children go naked; the money for feeding the poor is spent on embellishments to charm the eyes of the rich.[48]

The architecture of the Cistercians expressed and symbolized their iconoclastic and ascetic beliefs and, in the absence of decoration, emphasized structure and proportion.[49]

St. Bernard posed the question, "What is God?" which he then answered as "He is length, width, height and depth."[50] St. Augustine argued that music and geometry were effective meditative devices and that architecture should correspond to musical ratios. These proportional ratios, part of the re-discovered knowledge of Greek mathematics, were easily generated from the square and included 1:1; 1:2 (the octave); 2:3 (the fifth); and 3:4 (the fourth).[51] Both men would have been familiar with the description of Solomon's Temple where, as we observed, repeating squares in plan and section produce all three of these ratios. The thirteenth-century sketchbook of Villard de Honnecourt shows the plan of a square-ended Cistercian church and illustrates the application of musical consonances in its layout. The base measure is the square of the crossing comprising four square modules and a ratio of 1:1. The ratio of the width of the transept to the length of the church is 2:3; of width of aisle to nave and width to length of the transepts 1:2; and the width to depth of the choir 3:4.[52] The Cistercians were a silent order who spent their days occupied in labor, prayer, and music, and the interiors of their churches, devoid of most decoration including stained glass, were proportioned in such a way that they functioned as colossal sounding boards that reverberated the cadence of the sung mass.[53] The Cistercian day was a mathematical structure that precisely determined the monk's devotional lives, including services sung in the church seven times a day.[54] The result, according to St. Bernard, was "Geometry at the service of prayer."

Consistent with Platonic Forms, the geometry and proportion of the Medieval church were believed to disclose the otherwise hidden order of the world. According to William Swaan, the church and cathedral were an "earthly embodiment of the Divine Jerusalem," and represented the *splendor veritas* or "divine truth." This had its roots in Plato's *Timaeus and Critias*, where the universe and its elements of earth, air, fire, and water were defined by geometry and, in particular, the triangle and the square. "The four most perfect bodies which, though unlike each other, are some of them capable of transformation into each other on resolution."[55] And so the origin of the ordering of the universe becomes the basis for the ordering of its amalgam in Christian architecture to create a *civitas dei*. All of which was seen as "anagogical," able to lead the mind from the

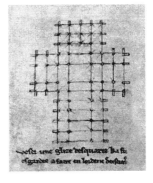

8.5
The thirteenth-century sketchbook of Villard de Honnecourt shows the plan of a square-ended Cistercian church and illustrates the application of musical consonances in its layout

Source: Cistercian plan by Villard de Honnecourt

8.6 (opposite)
The Tempietto at the Monastery of S. Pietro in Montorio, Rome, Donato Bramante, 1504

Source: Vanni/Art Resource, New York.

mundane to the divine,[56] a transformation akin to healing and alchemical transubstantiation, a power and presence revealed though the medium of geometry and proportion.

The "Middle Ages" served to mediate between the ancient Greek world and its revivification in the Renaissance. Whereas the Medieval church and its geometry symbolized a hidden, omnipotent god or represented the orthodox hegemony, in Renaissance Italy, the scale of the sacred place relates to an empowered human being. Leonardo da Vinci's "Vitruvian Man" of 1490 encapsulates this new orientation where the circle and the square no longer hold God but man. The Renaissance humanist orientation, in many ways a radical break from the Medieval and Byzantine positions, was often cogently expressed in its architecture. This was the first time in Europe that theories of architecture had been systematically formalized. Writers such as Sebastiano Serlio (1475–1554), Leon Battista Alberti (1404–1472), Andrea Palladio (1508–1580), and Giacomo Barozzi da Vignola (1507–1573), wrote books pertaining to the design of buildings, including their proportioning. The latter's *Regole delle cinque ordini* of 1562 outlined a modular interpretation of the classical Vitruvian orders, and remained a popular text for many years.

The use of the square in Medieval architecture is well established (as we observed earlier), and this simple geometry has proven to be a reliable proportioning device (and means of analysis). Even though the Renaissance can be legitimately viewed as a break from the Medieval, there was also continuity in

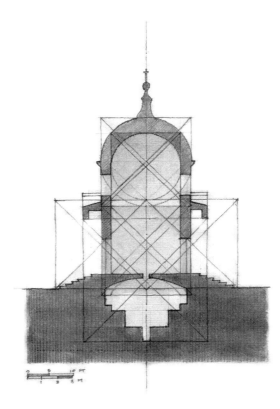

8.7
The Tempietto at the Monastery of S. Pietro in Montorio, Rome, section showing square proportions

proportioning techniques, most clearly in the use of the square. According to Wittkower, the square was of "exceptional importance during the Middle Ages and the Renaissance," but was applied differently and in ways that illustrate the respective agendas of these periods. During the Middle Ages, square geometry was used constructively and was often rotated and subdivided, yielding sets of irrational numbers. The acceptance and application of irrational numbers are consistent with the medieval interest in the anagogical capacity of proportion and architecture. During the Renaissance, however, the square was applied much more rationally, primarily as a module and proportioning device. "It was during the Renaissance that artists became aware of the simple numerical ratios on the sides of a square, and in the ratio 1:1 (unison in music) a Renaissance mind found beauty and perfect harmony."[57]

Bramante was one of the leading High Renaissance architects in Rome. His Tempietto, or "little temple," a small martyrium dedicated to St. Peter, is located in the courtyard of the church of S. Pietro, Montorio in Rome. Completed in 1502, it marks the place where St. Peter is believed to have been crucified, and its size and scale relate to that of a single human being. The Renaissance may have inherited the use of the subdivision and repetition of the square from the Medieval masons, but applied them for very different agendas. At the Tempietto, proportions are utilized not to facilitate the sequence of spaces leading to the sanctuary, or interrelated volumes tuned to the sung mass, but to create the self-contained, sculptural form of a classical temple. This small,

8.8
S. Maria Novella, Florence, 1460–1467, view of façade by Leon Battista Alberti

centralized, symmetrical building reconciles the circle and the square through a series of interrelated proportions. In plan, it is actually a series of concentric circles – an outer ring of steps, a single story colonnade, and the cylindrical enclosure of the temple itself.

We do not know exactly how Bramante proportioned this austere martyrium, but it appears that its formal composition of base, colonnade, upper arcade, and dome are interrelated by means of the square. For example, two vertical squares correspond to the interior space (above the crypt) and two horizontal squares the colonnade level (including the steps). Even the lowest level of the crypt, the bottom of the shaft that symbolizes where St. Peter's cross was planted, appears to align with square geometry. The three-part organization of crypt, colonnade, and dome, connected by a vertical axis, establish an in-between realm that straddles the below and the above.[58] Consequently, an iteration of a traditional means of proportion resulted in a unique formal composition that, in turn, materialized an archetypal condition.

Alberti completed the rebuilding of the western façade of the original basilican church of S. Maria Novella in Florence in 1470. It is clear that he did not align the new façade with the formal profile of the original basilican church, so that it could be proportioned without the constraints of the original building. Once again, the square governs the outline of the main façade. A horizontal line bisects this square and establishes the line between the first and second stories. Above this line is a smaller square flanked by two half squares, and on the bottom

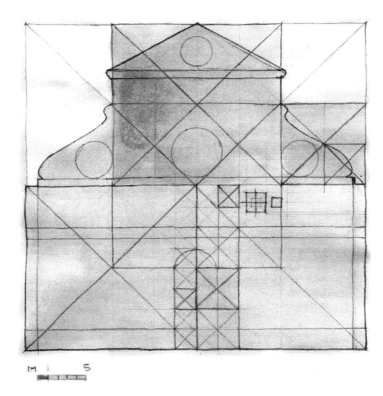

8.9
S. Maria Novella, Florence, façade proportioning diagram after Rudolf Wittkower and others

two squares. Further subdivisions of these smaller squares reconcile the old and the new and yield lines for other important parts of the façade to produce harmonious relationships between all parts of the building. The Romanesque basilica was visually transformed, its irrational components superseded by the rational overlay of Renaissance proportions in a manner that was both formal and ideological. This was a fulfillment of the Renaissance ideal of *concinnitas universarum parbium*, derived from their interpretation of Vitruvius and the buildings of antiquity.[59]

According to Vitruvius, the fundamental principles of architecture included: *order*, or the elements of composition; *arrangement*, the placement of these elements; *eurythmy*, the dimensions of the elements; *symmetry*, the harmony of the whole; *propriety*, the appropriate use of orders; and *economy*, the use of materials, the site, and other practical considerations. According to Vitruvius, "Order gives due measure to the members of a work considered separately, and symmetrical agreement to the proportions of the whole."[60] Proportions in the form of harmonic ratios were employed by Renaissance architects, and mediated between the parts and the whole. Renaissance architecture was a science[61] that demanded all parts be interrelated through mathematical ratios. Rationally applied proportions were utilized as the medium to create an architecture that reflected the divine world and man's place within it. At S. Maria Novella a series of subdivisions achieve a composition of interrelated parts (columns, entablature, pediment, attic, scrolls), and create harmonic ratios of 1:2, 1:3, and 2:3.

Over the course of his career Andrea Palladio systematically developed a comprehensive harmonic proportioning system. Though he built a range of works, including a number of chapels and churches, it was in his villas where his theories found their most complete expression.[62] According to Rudolf Wittkower, Palladio's villa plans developed from subdivisions of the square, but also included three-dimensional harmonic proportions. It is important to recognize that for Palladio the model for the villa is the centralized temple, now translated into a private home. His best-known work is the Villa Capra (or Rotunda), located on a prominent hill in the countryside near Vicenza. Four temple fronts define the exterior elevations, each aligned with a cardinal direction. The result is a self-contained sculptural object that subverts religious motifs to create a monument to temporal man, and appropriates the surrounding countryside as part of its purview. The dominant element is its central space, a square surmounted by a dome. Now instead of the immensity of a domed space for God as conceptualized by the Medieval Church, we have a humanly scaled space built to the glory of man.[63]

All of the proportioning systems that I have introduced served to establish sets of both sensible and intelligible relationships. In this way, analogous to any proportioning system, relationships between participants and the sacred place – and the sacred place and its temporal and ecclesiastical contexts were clearly established. In some traditions, as in the Hindu temple, these exact alignments were a prerequisite for any possible theoretical or sensible connection with the divine. Similar to the mean of arithmetic, geometric, and harmonic proportioning systems, the sacred architecture's ability to mediate between humans and their gods was dependent on the correct and concise applications of proportions. It was also elucidative – by means of structuring a part of the world of their own making, humans, by extension, structured their understanding of its larger contexts, including the divine. And, as in any progressive number series, these contexts were limitless.

Saint Benedict's Abbey, Vaals, Holland, by Dom Hans van der Laan: Designing a Middle Ground

I now turn to the work of the Benedictine monk and architect Hans van der Laan and the proportioning system he developed to materialize his architectural theories. Van der Laan built very few buildings, but over the span of his ecclesiastical and professional life he developed what he claimed was a comprehensive theory of proportion that expressed and reconciled fundamental ontological conditions of human existence. Born in 1904 to a family of architects, he studied architecture at Delft. He did not complete his studies, however, but entered the Benedictine community in 1926 where he was ordained in 1934. He never abandoned architecture, however, but designed, tested, and built his ideas throughout his career. His most extensive work was Saint Benedict's Abbey at Vaals, but he also designed the Convent at Waasmunster, Belgium, and the Naalden House in Best (all located in Holland). He also lectured on architectural theory at a program directed by his brother Nico, with whom he collaborated on all his commissions. He died and was buried at Vaals in 1991.

The Plastic Number and Placemaking

In 1960, van der Laan published a short book entitled *The Plastic Number*, which outlined a proportioning system of the same name. This was followed in 1977 by the more ambitious *Architectonic Space: Fifteen Lessons on the Disposition of the Human Habitat*, which further refined his ideas and their applications through proportion. For van der Laan, the proportions of what he called the plastic number are not mystical or sacred, but objective responses to the fundamentals of perception, essentials of placemaking, and elements of structure. He was very aware of Roman, Gothic, and Renaissance theories and practices of proportion, and claimed that his theory and system resolved the geometric, arithmetic, and harmonic systems that preceded it. However, van der Laan was careful to point out that the plastic number (and by implication the architecture) was not created to reveal the order of the world – for van der Laan the immensity of creation was beyond human understanding. Instead, all methods of proportion are applied to the world, through the medium of architecture, as a means to structure our (inadequate) understanding of it. It is not derived from, but imposed on, nature.[64] The result is not idealized Platonic "Forms" but practical applications of measures that mediate between our perceptual predispositions and the space and material of architecture.[65]

Since he was a child van der Laan had been interested in direct observation of the world as a means to understand the order that it represents. He described it as follows:

> This . . . was something that has fascinated me ever since my child-hood: to find in the subdivision of a thing the aspect of the whole. Thus I remember my discovery, as a schoolboy with a passion for nature, that the profile of the tree is reflected in the form of its leaves . . . That rediscovery of the whole in its parts and the analogous relationships that arise from it, became the *leitmotiv* of all my studies in the liturgical, architectonic and philosophical fields.[66]

His interest in fundamental relationships led him to consider placemaking as a fundamental act. For van der Laan, architecture mediates between the earth and sky, a liminal space that is the "datum of architecture." The vertical wall complements the horizontal earth and forms the first division between nature and man. But it is the space between two walls that clearly delimits the homogeneity of nature and creates architecture. Walls and the spaces between them comprise the essentials of architectural form and volume, and thus a careful delineation of their relationship through proportion is necessary. Architecture has larger goals, however, related to its role of mediating between humans and nature. In van der Laan's theory, "art" (architecture) mediates between the "limited created intelligence" (humans) and the "unlimited creating intelligence" (nature/the divine). "In this sense art can be said to imitate nature: the things made by art are related to the limited created intelligence, created nature to the unlimited creating intelligence."[67] And so, according to van der Laan, we have a threefold relationship of humans, art (architecture), and the divine:

> Thus architecture reveals itself as an art to the power of three: we work against the background of nature and complete it by the intelligent work of our hands, and this process itself contains twice over a background and a completion.[68]

An intriguing aspect of van der Laan's work that, perhaps more than any other, aligns it with the continuum of sacred architecture, is the range of scales he incorporates and articulates. Here cosmological perspectives are suggested consistent with the inspiration he found in nature, and symbolize how humans might establish a position within the enormity of the cosmos. Throughout his writings he refers to three-part relationships. First of all, there are three levels of human existence: *experience*, *perception*, and *knowledge*. Related to this is the fundamental ways humans measure and understand the environment. In van der Laan's theory, humans intuitively measure the physical environment and structure their understanding of it through size and type relationships. The "how-manyness of things" becomes a coherent pattern through three scales – *margin*, a large grouping of similar objects; *type*, groups of size; and *order*, the range of size. Lastly, and most directly architectural, are the three scales of *domain*, *court*, and *cell* – three progressive scales that range from the overall complex, to its constituent parts which comprise a single module.

His proportioning system builds upon Vitruvius' theory of "symmetry" – the interrelationship of a standard, a series of measures, and the whole. It is likely that he also applied Palladio's harmonic proportioning system for the three-

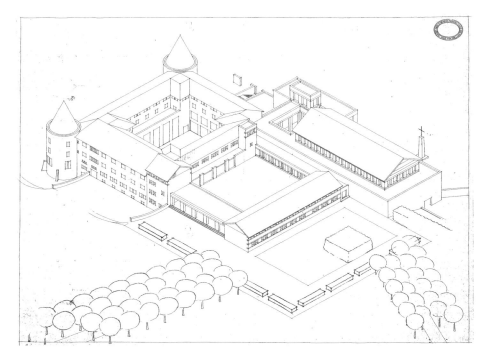

8.10
Saint Benedict's Abbey, Vaals, Holland, Dom Hans van der Laan, axonometric view of entire complex showing original buildings by Dominikus Bohm, 1921–1923, and additions by Hans van der Laan, 1956–1968

Source: Courtesy of Saint Benedict's Abbey, Vaals.

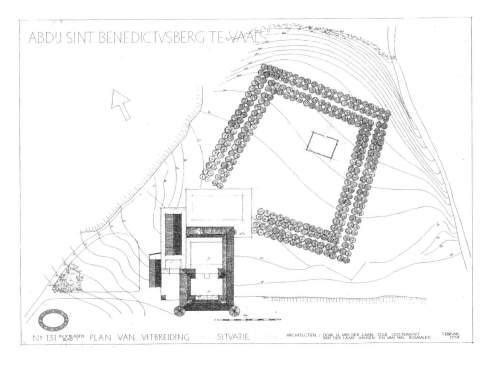

8.11
Saint Benedict's Abbey, Vaals, site plan

Source: Courtesy of Saint Benedict's Abbey, Vaals.

8.12
Saint Benedict's Abbey, Vaals,
view of entrance façade

dimensional disposition of rooms (the calibrating of harmonic means between the widths and lengths of rooms to determine their heights). Similar to Palladio, van der Laan utilizes a three-part system in which there is a correspondence of each measure to the other, the units are multiples of a standard module, and each are also subdivisions of the whole or largest dimension. His system is divisional, additive, and proportional, which he claimed resolved geometric, arithmetic, and harmonic systems. Padovan states:

> As a geometric progression of types of size the plastic number generates a chain-like relationship between the parts of the design, based on the ground ratio. At the same time, it sets up an order of size in which every measure is both a multiple of the unit and a subdivision of the whole.[69]

Similar to a musical scale, his system is limited to lower and higher ends, but also has a series of scales, from the thickness of a wall to the entire complex, all of which served to create an interrelated, volumetric whole.[70]

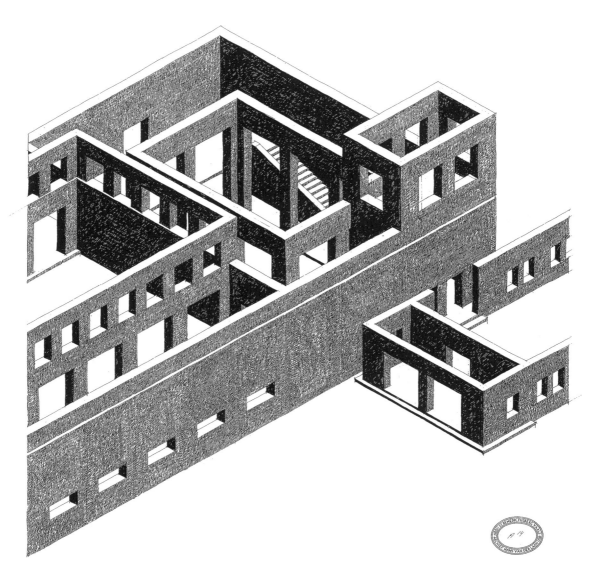

8.13
Saint Benedict's Abbey, Vaals, axonometric view of the entrance

Source: Courtesy of Saint Benedict's Abbey, Vaals.

Saint Benedict's Abbey, Vaals

Van der Laan's Benedictine monastery is set in a remote area near Maastricht, Holland, and is distinguished by its architecture: the original energetic brick and concrete buildings designed by the German Expressionist Dominikus Bohm were built in 1921–1923; and the austere and ordered abbey church and associated buildings by van der Laan. In 1956, van der Laan began work on the abbey church. In 1962, the lower church was completed and in 1968, the upper church. The other monastery buildings designed by van der Laan include a guesthouse, the cloisters, library, and sacristies for both the upper and lower churches. He also renovated the refectory and other parts of the original buildings, and designed most of the furnishings and liturgical objects. Surrounding the abbey are grounds also designed by van der Laan, including the cemetery where he is buried.

  The monastery is sited on the side of a hill and approached by a steep drive. It is of interest that Bohm's original plan for the monastery showed a typical east-oriented church. It is not clear why van der Laan departed from Bohm's plan, but one result is that the western façade of the north-facing church reinforces the enclosure of the monastery, clearly demarking the sacred realm. Its siting also sets up the elongated entry sequence that culminates in the sanctuary of the church. One enters by means of a single-story separate wing that contains a vestibule and a series of visiting rooms where the monks may meet with the outside world – a "mean" between the secular and the sacred. From the vestibule another set of doors leads under the bell tower to a two-story

open courtyard called the "atrium." From here one can enter the lower church (now known as the crypt), the residential portions of the monastery or, by means of a set of stairs, the upper church. Throughout, essential relationships unfold: wall and enclosure; inside and outside; vertical and horizontal; *domain, court,* and *cell*; – all, according to the architect, brought into alignment by his proportioning system.

The principal building material is brick with flush mortar joints covered by a thin layer of lime cement, which has the effect of emphasizing the modular dimensions of the piers and openings. It also allowed for variations in the wall surfaces that express the workmanship of the masons and reflect the flexibility of van der Laan's system. Apparently he even encouraged the workmen to drink "a few glasses" of red wine during lunch to encourage their personal

8.16
Saint Benedict's Abbey, Vaals,
atrium from upper level

8.17
Saint Benedict's Abbey, Vaals,
Abbey Church, view toward
altar

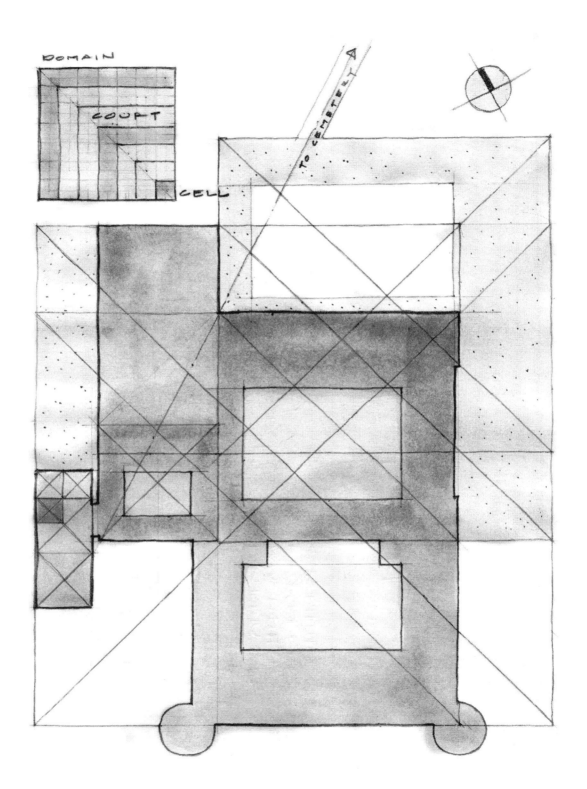

DOMAIN

COURT

CELL

TO CEMETERY

8.18 (opposite)
One way to understand
van der Laan's system, the
monastery he designed, and
its significance is to examine
it according to his three-part
scale system of domain, court,
and cell. Saint Benedict's
Abbey, Vaals, site
proportioning diagram

expression in brick. Other materials include concrete floors; wood ceilings, walls (in some cases), railings, and furniture; and red tile roofs. Overall, he utilizes a spare, modernist palette of materials, but employs an expansive range of expression.

Van der Laan did not document the proportioning of the monastery. His writings primarily address the theoretical and ontological foundations of his system and offer generalized applications. Consequently, the key to understanding his work is not through numbers and their generation, but by unpacking the position and goals of his theory. Even though his working sketches for the abbey include voluminous numerical notations – numbers generated by his system – they were in service of larger goals. For van der Laan, his system was a means, not an end, of making architecture, and he argued that "discrete number has nothing to do with architectonic expression as such; it must be regarded simply as a sort of work-method used in the practice as a craft."[71]

8.19
Saint Benedict's
Abbey, Vaals,
church level plan

Source: Courtesy of
Saint Benedict's Abbey,
Vaals.

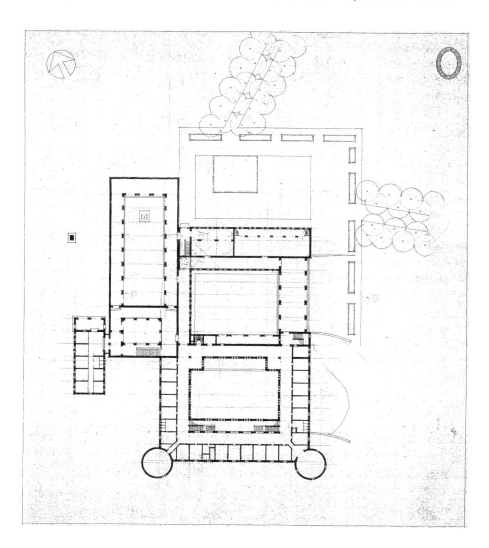

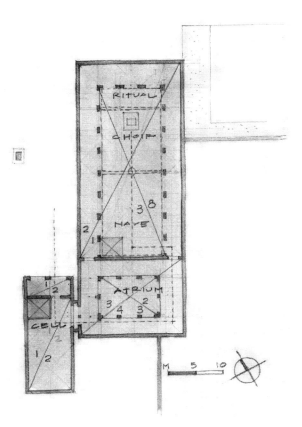

8.20
Saint Benedict's Abbey, Vaals,
plan of Abbey Church and
entry showing proportionally
interrelated spaces

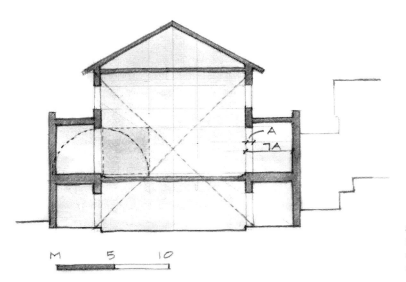

8.21
Saint Benedict's Abbey, Vaals,
section of Abbey Church
showing proportional module

In this context, there may be range of ways to interpret Vaals and van der Laan's proportioning system, a system that remains idiosyncratic in that it has not been explicated or expanded through applications by others. Its significance lies in its foundations, which position architecture (and its proportioning) as a means to understand the world and materialize its scales of interrelationships. Therefore, it may be understood, at least in part, in the context of fundamental proportional relationships.

One way to understand van der Laan's system, the monastery he designed, and its significance is to examine it according to his three-part scale system of *domain*, *court*, and *cell*. To do so, we can utilize an overlay of squares as a means to reveal levels of order (a method, it turns out, that van der Laan utilized in his analysis of Stonehenge). Beginning with the largest scale, van der Laan's additions appear to incorporate the existing buildings resulting in an interrelated whole. Overall, an arithmetic progression of seven equal measures aligns with the outer perimeter of buildings and grounds (at the largest scale) and the single module of a cell in the entrance wing (at the smallest scale) and a range of measures in between. At the next smaller scale, a sequence of proportionally interrelated spaces defines the entry sequence and abbey church. Beginning with the single module of the cell of the visitors' wing, in plan, the entry porch and visiting spaces are each 1:2, the inner atrium space 2:3, the outer atrium space 3:4, and the overall dimensions of the church 1:2. The

8.22
Saint Benedict's Abbey, Vaals, Abbey Church, view toward entrance

smallest scale order is the cell, introduced at the entry porch, reinforced by the visitors' cells, and revealed in the nave of the church, which in plan comprises a series of modules creating the overall proportions of 3:8. The 55mm-thick brick piers of the arcade are the lowest in a scale of interrelated measures. For example, the width of the aisles is 385mm (measured from the centerlines of the piers), which is 7× this module.

In accordance with Vatican II, the church space is open and without the explicit spatial hierarchy of the orthodox church. This is reinforced by minimalist materials and decoration, which recall the language of Modernism. And, reminiscent of Cistercian architecture, it is the proportioning that is the predominant design element. The church can be understood as comprising interrelated spaces, each proportioned for its specific functions – all contributing to its overall unity. The monks' choir and altar space are a three-bay square (with a 1 × 3-bay space located at its rear so that ceremonies can be performed facing the

8.23
Saint Benedict's Abbey, Vaals,
Abbey Church, altar

congregation). The congregational space is a 3 × 4-bay space and, in section, the volumes of the church are inscribed by proportions of 1:2 and 2:3.

One of the most outstanding elements of the interior of the nave is the relationship between the arcade and the clerestory where the openings of the lower level arcade and the upper level clerestory windows do not align, but appear to follow their own sets of dimensions. Here, the interwoven proportions create relationships that are both independent and interdependent. The dimensions that determine the size and locations of the piers and the windows above them appear at first to be unrelated – there are five bays over three, and fourteen bays over eight, and the windows are not centered on the column bays, but march to their own cadence. At the center of each of the arcades of the nave, however, they align, and each subsequent shift indicates the interrelated proportions that determine and reconcile each. At Vaals, all the interwoven proportions are not explicit, but its overall order is apprehensible. This is consistent with van der Laan's insistence that we principally perceive spaces and their proportions intuitively and unconsciously. The end result is not an explicit expression of measure, but an implicit communication of order. The quiet austerity of the

8.25
One of the most outstanding elements of the interior of the nave is the relationship between the arcade and the clerestory where interwoven proportions create relationships that are both independent and interdependent. Saint Benedict's Abbey, Vaals, Abbey Church, arcade

monastery expresses van der Laan's feeling that in the quiet of the complex but reconciled geometry, "a great peacefulness goes out from it."

Materializing Proportion

Van der Laan's compelling architecture occupies a middle ground between tradition and innovation – vernacular and contemporary. It embodies Vitruvian and Renaissance theories of proportion, transforms archetypal forms of gable-roofed structures, and applies rational, modernist materials and methods of planning and construction. It has been described as having "the ability to evoke the past and the present simultaneously"[72] and as "neither looking forward or backward in time (but occupying) that still point in the turning world where we begin to catch glimpses of the eternal."[73] The Benedictines are a conservative order that maintain a liturgy and ecclesiastical orders that date from the sixth century. Van der Laan stated that the five bells of the bell tower he designed were tuned to the "Pythagorean system, on which the Gregorian chant is based."[74] The ordering of the architecture at Vaals, through the application of van der Laan's proportioning system, reinforces the essential austerity of the Benedictine monastic life. However, it is not a static hierarchy (though spatial hierarchies do exist in the entry sequence) but a dynamic set of relationships that invite the individual to participate in their reconciliation. According to Alberto Ferlenga:

> This particular number is called the plastic number because, at one and the same time, it refers to the continuous size typical of spaces and masses and the discontinuous size of the abstract number; which alone permits our intelligence to count.[75]

In this context, spaces of communal worship are also places where the solitary contemplation of their multivalent orders leads to considerations of broader contexts.

It is the rules of architectural organization that perform a double-mediating role of establishing relationships of building components to each other and the building itself to its participants. In this way, the architecture engages us, and in these intimate connections leads us to the broader relationships of which it is a part.[76] Analogous to the goal of religious practice, individual entities are bound to a larger whole and it is those strands and weaves of connection that are preeminent at Vaals. According to van der Laan, we build to materialize proportions,[77] and it is through proportion and the media of architecture that the world is rendered more intelligible. The result is both epistemological and ontological – the architecture makes connections to philosophical mathematics through the empathetic connection of the individual. Multiple relationships are established: part to whole – earth and sky – universal and particular – past and present – sensible and intelligible. It is both empirical and ephemeral:

> For van der Laan, whose thought is steeped in that of the ancient Greeks, the plastic number functions as a bridge; its purpose is to bring about "the meeting together of the continuous quantity of concrete size and the discrete quantity of abstract number."[78]

For the architect, the participatory nature of the architecture included its making. He stated that it was by building that we learn to build,[79] and "in this way the cycle of spirit and matter is completed: the intellect is itself moulded by the things it makes."[80] The individual is similarly joined with the community through the architecture, which is of "utmost importance for the mutual bond between people. To dwell together with others in a domain, court, or a cell signifies and confirms the varying bond between people at an individual and social level."[81] And, finally, the architecture is an act of reconciliation between humans and the larger contexts of which they are a part – rendering nature "both habitable and intelligible."[82] Even this relationship is reciprocal where through the agency of architecture there is a "mutual completion of art and nature."[83] In the words of van der Laan, "it is as if nature awaited the work of our hands to be wholly complete."[84] Throughout, the fundamental relationships upon which our lives are framed are mediated by the architecture.

The ordering and cadence of the structure and spaces at Vaals reflect the structured life of the monastery. According to the Rule of St. Benedict, the day is subdivided into discrete apportionments of prayer, communal services, work, study, and free time. The monks at Vaals sing the Latin Mass seven times a day, an ordered progression that results in all 150 Psalms being sung each week. This is in accordance to the dictates of Psalm 119, which states "Seven times a day I praise thee for thy righteous ordinances."[85] At Vaals, van der Laan served as sacristan; his liturgical role was to prepare the priests and altar for services. It was traditionally the sacristan who regulated the hours of the monastic community and rang the bells calling the brothers to the church. He set the "order" of the community, a word, like "ordinance," that comes from the Latin *ordinare*, which means "to put in order." Referring to Vitruvius, van der Laan stated that any "architectural disposition must be completed by ordinance,"[86] and at Vaals, the sacristan not only determined the order and cadence of the monastic hours, but also the order and cadence of the architecture with the goal of achieving a unified, interrelated whole.

Chapter 9

Perfected Worlds

Cosmograms and Connections

Heaven is my throne and the earth is my footstool; what is the house which you would build for me?

(Isaiah 66.1)

We have observed through a variety of examples how sacred architecture often served as a replication of the divine cosmos. One significant aspect of the symbolism of Tongdo-sa was that, at one level, it represented a microcosmic model of the multiple worlds of Mahayana Buddhism. Korean temples such as Tongdo-sa appropriated textual and visual sources and translated them into built form and spatial sequences. Similarly, certain Hindu temples relied on the myth of Brahma and the primordial man (the *vastu-purusha*) and its translation into the mandala to validate the ordering of a place that both reflected and incorporated the divinity. Analogously, the high Gothic cathedral symbolized the perfected celestial city of God (*civitas dei*), and for the devout was anagogical in establishing connections with the divine. It was through the replication or representation of the perfected world of (and by) God, that this realm could now be entered and thus contact made portentous (and possible).

Once again, Mircea Eliade provides a cogent description of the perennial human impetus to create, what he termed, the *imago mundi* or image of the world. Eliade offers a concise summary of the predominant imperatives of religion and sacred architecture when he argues that they were the means for humans to articulate their place in the world and to create an orientation for their existence. As an antidote to disorientation (the most uncomfortable condition for humans), religion and the architecture built to serve it, represented the sacred center. According to Eliade, the sacred place was created either through revelation or provocation – the divine appeared in a particular place or was evoked (usually through ritual):

It is clear to what degree the discovery – that is, the revelation – of the sacred place possesses existential value for religious man; for nothing can begin, nothing can be done, without a previous orientation – and any orientation implies a fixed point. It is for this reason that religious man has always sought to fix his abode at the "center of the world."[1]

As valuable as Eliade's model is, it neglects the more dynamic qualities of spatial sequences and conflicted aspects of political and social agendas. In this context his useful typology offers us a departure, not an arrival point, for understandings of the sacred place as a powerful, perfected world where contact with the divine (or through mediums) was believed to be possible.[2] The sacred place rarely presents a static scene but nearly always a series of dynamic tableaux, as we observed in the spatial sequencing, symbolic narratives, and ritual uses of previous examples. In the primordial architecture of North America, burial mounds eternalized and vivified the dead, but also served to lay claim to territorial boundaries. At Tongdo-sa, the path mediates between multiple (and often conflicting or complementary) representations of Buddhist realms – its religious content is calibrated to the needs and level of understanding of the participants, but there is also indigenous, historical, social, and political content. Even in the rational and impassive order of van der Laan's monastery there emerges not-so-hidden (and conflicting) aspects of the diverse intellectual engagement it requires and an orthodox suppression of ambiguity.

To reiterate – the primary goal of religion is to establish an ontological position in the world – an orientation for one's temporal existence. Its essential task is articulating where one is (and is not), and in which direction one is to go. Sacred architecture is a means to construct one's place in the world – to make it concrete and palpable. In essence, it re-presents the figural content of religion by providing the places and serial spaces required to symbolize and deliver its symbolic content. And, because it often represents the perfection of the divine (as the divine typically is), the architecture itself symbolizes this perfection. It is an "architectural cosmogram" of the perfected world required if the divine is to dwell there.[3] Furthermore, we can broaden our definitions of the sacred place as a perfected (or perfect) world, by distinguishing four particular types, as follows.

First, we can understand the cosmic symbolism of sacred architecture as a reproduction of the *Celestial City* – the place where God is (or the gods are) present. It also provides *Representations of the Divine* – the order and immensity of the divine or divine knowledge, symbolized through the scale, order, content, and organization of the architecture, and a *Place of Purity and Perfection* – a rarified place that is purified for the divine (and where one may be purified). And lastly, we can understand it as a *Place of Devotion* – the setting for prayer and communal rituals.

To further develop the argument and types outlined above we now turn to three buildings that quite possibly are among the most significant works of architecture. I suggest that they are because of their inventive applications of structure and materials, their calibrations of light, and, what I term, their "packed agendas" of ecclesiastical and political symbolism. First I will discuss the Emperor

Hadrian's Pantheon in Rome, then the Byzantine Hagia Sophia in Istanbul, and will conclude with the works of the Ottoman architect Sinan. That all are domed buildings is worth noting in the context of the symbolic ascendancy the domed space came to achieve in the history of architecture. E. Baldwin Smith offers an intriguing proposition when he suggests that the earliest of domestic structures were circular in plan and covered by expediency by curved roofs of whatever light and flexible materials were available:

> Therefore, in many parts of the ancient world the domical shape became habitually associated in men's memories with a central type of structure which was venerated as a tribal and ancestral shelter, a cosmic symbol, a house of appearances and a ritualistic abode.[4]

"Dome" or *domus* (in Latin) means "house" or "roof," and though it began as a practical means to cover space, its subsequent iterations were subservient to the "idea" or symbolism of its form. In other words, the masonry dome that came to distinguish particular strains of Roman, Christian, and Islamic architecture was developed more for symbolic than structural reasons.[5] The dome in all of these cases, albeit with multiple iterations and meanings, was put in service of depictions of cosmogonic models and perfected worlds.

The Pantheon

The Pantheon in Rome, built by the Emperor Hadrian[6] has rightfully been described as the most significant and enduring building of antiquity.[7] Within its central space (and it is primarily an interior space), there is a packed agenda of symbolic, mythological, religious, and political content. The Pantheon is arguably the greatest building of the Roman Empire, and it was through the application of sophisticated structural and material means that the Romans realized this potent and complicated place.[8] Here the sophisticated application of material technology in the form of concrete and structural technology by means of the dome, created one of the most enduring, enigmatic, and compelling spaces in the history of architecture.

Roman architecture is distinguished by the inventive ways they appropriated and applied architectural orders, motifs, and building technologies. However, unlike their Greek predecessors, their architecture is not only formal but, more importantly, spatial. They created significant interior volumes by developing the known systems of the arch, vault, dome, and timber tied-truss roof construction, and perfecting cast-in-place concrete.[9] The extensive Baths of Caracalla, which date from the third century CE, included the 115-ft in diameter domed space of the caldarium. All that remains today of its expansive interior spaces are some of the concrete walls that formed the superstructure – the fine stonework, decorations, and furnishings are all gone. The Baths of Caracalla are ruins in which the spaces are barely discernible, but the Pantheon is mostly extant, due in part to it becoming the Christian Santa Maria Rotunda in 609 CE. The forecourt that originally fronted its southern entry portico, an entry that was axially aligned with the cardinal points and was the terminus of

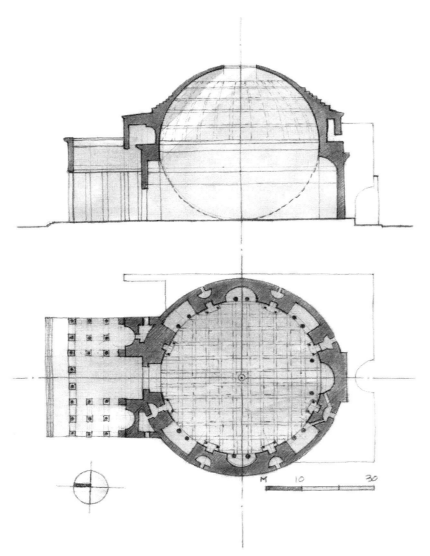

the Via Flaminia, is gone, as are the deep blue paint and bronze stars that once covered the coffers of its dome. But passing through the columned space of the portico and the entry doors, one enters the largest dome of antiquity that looks very much like it did when it was completed in 126 CE.[10]

At the Pantheon the greatest dome of antiquity rises to 150 feet above the floor. At its top a 30-ft in diameter oculus is open to the sky creating an "eye" to the heavens.[11] This was a dome that was not surpassed until Brunelleschi solved the riddle of the dome of Florence Cathedral nearly 1,300 years later. Great architecture has always elicited feelings of surprise and wonder. When one enters the Pantheon today one is "amazed," by this bewildering, mysterious

9.2

At the Pantheon, the greatest dome of antiquity rises to 150 feet above the floor. At its top a 30-ft in diameter oculus is open to the sky creating an "eye" to the heavens. The Pantheon, Rome, view of dome

Source: Photo by Julio Bermudez.

place. The dome appears to lightly soar above the drum, an illusion accomplished by the clever hiding of its massive structure behind the veneer of the upper drum. The five rings of coffers pixilate the huge drum, fracturing it into myriad surfaces, all of which are uniquely aligned to the viewer on the floor. There are twenty-eight coffers in each row, a number that does not align with the eight niches of the drum, thus reinforcing the dome's dynamic effects. But it is the light, streaming through the oculus above that animates the space, vivifying the polychromed materials while simultaneously de-materializing them.

The Pantheon served a number of complementary symbolic agendas – it was a temple dedicated to "all gods," a representation of Roman cultural hegemony and a place of secular, political power. The synthesis of the sacred and the secular was possible because by this time the power of the old cults had waned, creating the opportunity for their appropriation by Hadrian in service of more hybrid political agendas. Inside the Pantheon's great space statues of the planetary deities – the Sun, the Moon, Mars, Mercury, Venus, and Saturn – occupied the seven exedrae. The dome and its oculus represented Jupiter, the omniscient and supreme god of the cosmos (though other groupings of gods have been suggested).[12] Here we have perhaps the most convincing symbolization of the *axis mundi*, the vertical connection between humans and their gods. The sun tracking its course throughout the day and the seasons, dynamic and ever changing, suggests lunar and astrological points of confluence. The geometric and spatial order of the Pantheon may have reflected the omnipotence and power of Imperial Rome, but it was the oculus, and the light it admitted, that mediated between the earth and the cosmos.

For the Romans, it was not only a sacred place that housed their gods, but also a place built in service to the state religion of Romanism – the belief in the eternal and all-encompassing power of the Roman world. At the time it was built, Imperial Rome controlled all of the "known world" (or perhaps in the Roman mind all of the world worth knowing), and its geometry and spatial ordering symbolized the center of this world. It incorporated materials from significant Roman conquests – Egyptian granite, colored African marble, and white Aegean marble – to express the collective nature of Romanism.[13] Its structural sophistication spoke of Roman technical hegemony and its self-contained form and space the endurance of the Roman Empire. The conjunction of the cosmos represented by the planetary deities and the dynamics of the movement of the sun can be understood as a representation of the eternal mechanisms of the Roman state. Even the repetitive circles of the drum and dome suggest the completeness of the Roman world.[14] According to John Stamper,

> Universality and unity were expressed throughout in the Pantheon, thus strengthening the cult of the Emperor. It brought together all of the gods in a space built to symbolize the community of the heavens under its prodigious and daring dome.[15]

It was also an imperial audience hall and a place of political power. As one biographer noted, Hadrian "transacted with the aid of the Senate all the important and urgent business and held court with the assistance of the foremost men, in the Forum or the Pantheon or various other places, always seated on a tribunal."[16] Hadrian had a sincere interest in religion, including the Mysteries, but was also skillful in applying religion for political advantage.[17] Hadrian's tribunal, flanked by the gods, occupied the symbolic center of the Roman political and sacred world. The sun charting its course through the sky streamed in through the oculus, and cast its light upon the gods in their niches – connecting man, emperor, and gods with the cosmos. It was a synthesis: a co-joining of inside and outside, ruler and god, populace and gods. However, as William MacDonald reminds us:

> The Pantheon captured and described the underlying culture and texture of the High Empire. It is as extraordinary a document in this sense as it is a masterpiece of Roman engineering, but its more immanent qualities are harder to pin down.[18]

And that: "the ultimate meaning of the Pantheon remains in all its complexity, enigmatic."[19] The symbolic power of the Pantheon lay in its spatial composition, which was made possible by the technological developments of the Romans. An interior sacred place was created, habitable by both humans and their gods and connected to the sun and the passage of time – themes that Christianity would capitalize on and transform, validating the lasting legacy of Roman architecture.

The Hagia Sophia

Geometry and proportion were instrumental in creating the cosmogonic image of the Pantheon. The practice of geometry, facilitated, in part, the transmission

9.3
Over the doorway in the south vestibule of the Hagia Sophia, a tenth-century mosaic depicts the Virgin Mary flanked by the Byzantine Emperor Justinian holding a model of the church and the Roman Emperor Constantine holding one of Constantinople. The Hagia Sophia, Istanbul (Constantinople), Turkey, 532–537 CE

Source: Werner Forman/Art Resource, New York.

of architectural knowledge and the replication of sacred exemplars. In Christian art, figures are often depicted holding a model of a church: a Gothic painting from the Bible of St. Louis depicts God as the architect of the universe, holding a mason's compass,[20] another the City of God being revealed to St. Augustine; and a fifteenth-century painting shows St. Jerome holding a model of the Temple of Jerusalem. At the Byzantine church of the Hagia Sophia in Istanbul, a mosaic over the doorway of the south vestibule shows the Virgin Mary flanked by the Byzantine Emperor Justinian holding a model of the church and the Roman Emperor Constantine holding one of Constantinople. All suggest that sacred architecture is discovered and not created – its divine proportions revealed through the intervention of the divine.

Byzantine domed spaces were heir to Roman precedents and the traditions of domed construction in the Middle East. Through plan typology and measure, proportional scale shifts were made possible – larger and larger spaces evolving from early experiments. The Hagia Sophia, the cathedral of the Eastern Church built by Justinian in Constantinople (532–537 CE), extended this structural and spatial lineage.[21] Subsequently, the structural, spatial, and geometric prowess of the church served as a precedent and perhaps model for Ottoman Turkish architecture. In particular, the life work of the greatest Ottoman architect Mimar ("architect") Sinan, was informed by Byzantine precedents and, according to some, dedicated to developing and surpassing them. It wasn't until the end of his life when he completed the magnificent Selimiye mosque at Edirne that Sinan surpassed the size of the dome of the Hagia Sophia.

The spatial organization of the Hagia Sophia is a domed basilica. Its central dome is flanked on the east and west by half-domes, which creates a voluminous interior space without allowing the vertical dimension to dominate, and extenuates the horizontal direction in service of liturgical processions. Its spatial and linear composition recalls the earlier church of St. Irene, which is located close by.[22] St. Irene, as well as Justinian's other major work, San Vitale in Ravenna, elongates the horizontal axis by means of an exterior atrium and narthex. Similarly, at the Hagia Sophia, a large colonnaded atrium led to two narthexes before attaining the central space. The central domed space predominated, however, defined by four massive columns set at the corners of a 100-ft Byzantine square and crowned by a dome. To the east the processional way culminated in the ambo, altar, and stepped synthronon. Aisles and galleries, most likely assigned to the laity, flanked the central space on its northern, western, and southern sides. The dome, pierced by forty windows, appeared to mysteriously float on the pendentives and sail vaults that supported it.

The architectural archetype of the cube surmounted by the dome is appropriated on a colossal scale at the Hagia Sophia. This is a very different place than the first Christian house churches, converted structures for a devoted few. In the early church the place of worship was where the converted connected with God through communal prayer and the celebration of the Eucharist. Now the architecture is the place of God, not of humans – revealed by God and on a scale that symbolizes the enormity of the deity's presence. The church, dedicated to the "Christ of Holy Wisdom," was described by Justinian's court historian as an amalgam of the perfection of God. "Whenever one enters this church to pray, he understands at once that it is not by any human power or skill, but by the

9.4 (opposite)
Just as the mysteries of the eucharist were revealed by the clergy within the rarified space of the chancel, the mysteries of the cosmos were revealed within the atmospheric and evocative space of the church itself. The Hagia Sophia, Istanbul (Constantinople), interior, view toward altar

Source: Erich Lessing/Art Resource, New York.

Perfected Worlds

influence of God, that this work has been so finely tuned."[23] In the Byzantine church, the dome surmounting a cube represented the universe, and typically Christ Pantocrator was depicted at its apex.[24] Through pure geometry, the terrestrial square plan and the heavenly circle of the dome were reconciled. As in Solomon's Temple, this was a place where God would "dwell," a liminal place connecting the devout with the divine.

Eliade presents the Byzantine church as "imitating the Heavenly Jerusalem" while "it also reproduces Paradise or the celestial world." The church, for Eliade, was primarily (or exclusively) a representation of the cosmos, its elements marking the cardinal points and its dome delimiting the heavens: "as a 'Copy of the Cosmos' the Byzantine church incarnates and at the same time sanctifies the world."[25] As an "earthly analogue to heaven"[26] the space of the Byzantine church aimed to create a place where the mysteries of God could (or, appear to) be revealed. Just as the mysteries of the Eucharist were revealed by the clergy within the rarified space of the chancel, the mysteries of the cosmos were revealed within the atmospheric and evocative space of the church itself. A court official of the time described the space as resembling the "encircling heavens."[27] This revelatory aspect of the architecture is consistent with traditions of the early Eastern Church that viewed the church as a "mystic temple, a replica of the comprehensible universe," as realized by domed central spaces.[28] E.B. Smith recalls a Syrian "hymn" which describes a domed church as a heavenly abode:

> Small though it is, says the poet, it resembles the universe. Its vault expands like the heavens and shines with mosaics as the firmament with stars. Its soaring dome compares with the Heaven of Heavens, where God resides, and its four arches represent the four directions of the world, with their variegated colours like a rainbow. Its piers are like the mountains of the earth; its marble walls shine like the light of the image not man-made, the Godhead; three windows in the apse symbolize the Trinity, the nine steps leading to the chancel represent the nine choirs of the angels. In short, the poet concludes, the building represents heaven and earth, the apostles, the prophets, the martyrs, and, indeed, the Godhead.[29]

However, as many have pointed out, the Hagia Sophia did not exist solely as a representation of a "Heaven of Heavens," but also communicated a more direct ecclesiastical and political content. Justinian inherited a shrinking empire and assumed the task of restoring its cultural and political borders to the days of Hadrian. Like Hadrian, he was recognized as the supreme ruler and worshipped as a god. A mosaic of Justinian at the Baptistery of Ravenna shows him as both a Roman emperor and a Christian saint,[30] and, as we observed earlier, the mosaic at the southern vestibule of the Hagia Sophia shows him in the company of both gods and rulers. It was through the enactment of rituals within the space of the church that these relationships were more fully established. In the sixth century the hierarchy of the clergy was believed to represent the nine levels of the angels, with the patriarch (or *hierarch*) at its apex. In the "play" of the rituals, the emperor was assigned a role on the divine "side of the house." (He was considered, hierarchically, to be on the same level as the apostles, and even at

9.5

The Hagia Sophia, Istanbul (Constantinople), east end showing location of the *omphalos*

Source: After Rowland Mainstone.

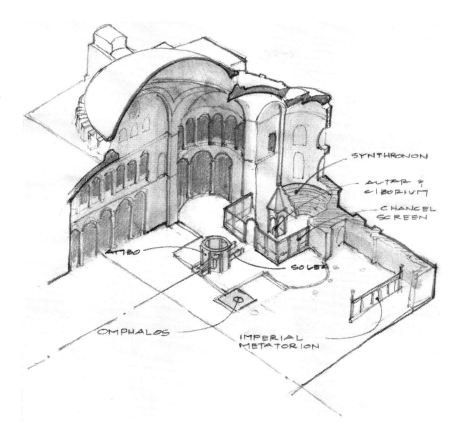

times, played the role of Christ.) The celebration of the mass on holy days included both the clergy and the emperor. It is likely that the nave was reserved for the "actors" with the aisles and galleries assigned to the faithful (separated by gender). The mysteries of the Eucharist were hidden inside the chancel, with the clergy and the emperor only periodically emerging – providing epiphanies for the laity.

The Hagia Sophia, as we have observed at other sacred sites, was a complex and nuanced place that cannot be easily summarized. In the middle of its multitudinous symbolism, revealed through surface, space, and ritual, lie some understandings regarding the significance it held in its time, and what it (and other places) can offer us today. We can safely state that, in a variety of ways, it symbolized an earthly heaven and created an ecclesiastical and political center for the eastern Christian Church. At the right side of the ambo there is an *omphalos* (navel) stone set in the paving, demarcating the center of the Byzantine world. It was here that the Byzantine Emperors were crowned – a co-joining of earthy and heavenly power and wisdom. Through ritual, the clergy and the emperor served to maintain the empire and reveal God's mysteries. The rituals, either of liturgy or coronation, were enacted at the center of this world – strategically and symbolically underneath the dome of the cosmos. The devout observed all this in the shadows of the aisles and galleries and, in this fashion, participated in rituals that, in essence, performed a double mediation – co-joining the emperor and the clergy, and through them the devout with God.

The Late Works of the Ottoman Architect Sinan: Multitudinous Contexts, Packed Agendas, and Diverse Interpretations

Many have noted the unrivaled influence that the Hagia Sophia exerted on Ottoman architecture and, in particular, the Ottoman mosque. As a potent symbol of an admired, but deemed inferior culture, the Hagia Sophia became both a model and an incentive for Ottoman architects.[31] In particular, the works of the court architect Mimar Sinan, who was responsible for the extensive building programs of three sultans at the height of the Ottoman Empire, have been characterized as dedicated to surpassing this Byzantine exemplar. Even though Sinan acknowledged the goal of exceeding the dome of the Hagia Sophia, there were clearly other agendas at work in a career that spanned over fifty years and produced some of the most important buildings of its time (and arguably, in the history of architecture). From a contemporary perspective, it is necessary to recognize the architectural lineage that informed Sinan's work, while also examining it on its own merits and in its specific contexts. There is a recognizable continuity from the Byzantine to the Ottoman, but clear distinctions as well. For example, whereas structural and spatial clarity are clearly sub-servient to the symbolic agendas of the Byzantine church, they are much more refined and integrated in the Ottoman mosque. The interior of the Byzantine church aspired to create a dematerialized place of mystery, the Ottoman mosque one of elucidative and symbolic clarity. The exterior of the Hagia Sophia, modified over time to overcome its structural deficiencies, is decidedly inferior to the more sophisticated and balanced compositions of the Ottoman. According to Hillenbrand, "Where the Byzantine Church suggests, its Ottoman successors display."[32]

Sinan: Historical, Socio-political, and Architectural Contexts

I will focus on two of Sinan's last, and perhaps most significant works, The Ismihan Sultan and Sokollu Mehmed Pasa complex in Kadirga, Istanbul, and the Selimiye complex in Edirne, as a means to illustrate the symbolism of the Ottoman mosque and the symbolic agendas of its patrons and creators. However, before turning to interpretations of these important works, it is necessary to briefly establish their historical, socio-political, and architectural contexts. Understanding these contexts is a challenge for a number of reasons: the reluctance of Ottoman culture to record histories and biographies untainted by political and religious ideologies;[33] the misrepresentation of Ottoman culture and its artifacts in Western (and most egregiously Orientalist) histories; and the dearth of architectural scholarship on the long and distinguished career of Sinan.

Sinan has been called the "Turkish Michelangelo"[34] but we know much more about the latter than the former. Even though the quality, inventiveness, and breadth of his work were commensurate with his Renaissance contemporaries, it is still little known in the West and has not benefited from the substantial scholarship afforded his Renaissance peers. Even though some recent studies have ameliorated some of the deficiencies of scholarship on Sinan, if compared to Renaissance architects (some of whom wrote prodigiously about architectural theory and subsequently have been extensively analyzed), there is a dearth of information on the career and working methods of this important architect. Moreover, modernist interpretations of his work have predominantly focused on its formal, typological, spatial, and structural aspects. While these are effective means of analysis (which I utilize), the symbolism of his *külliye* (mosque complexes) has not been adequately addressed in relationship to Islamic beliefs, rituals, and socio-political contexts.

The exact date of Sinan's birth is not known but assumed to be around the end of the fifteenth century. It is known that in 1513 he was conscripted into the Janissaries, a branch of the sultan's army for non-Muslims.[35] His early career in the Janissaries allowed him to travel throughout the empire, as part of the major military campaigns of his time, and he saw many examples of Christian and Muslim architecture in Southeast Europe and the Middle East. He eventually became a military engineer whose responsibilities included the construction of bridges, siege works, and harbors. It was Suleyman the Great who recognized his talents and eventually appointed him Court Architect in April 1536. This was a time of great prosperity and territorial expansion, served by a rigid, centralized, and highly organized political and social hierarchy.[36] During his first twelve years as court architect, his projects included a range of relatively anonymous works such as bridges, baths, aqueducts, soup kitchens, and caravaransari throughout the Balkans and Anatolia. His first important mosque was the Sehzade in Istanbul, and from there an astounding output of religious buildings and a remarkable record of experimentation and development distinguish his career. Almost 500 building projects were either directly or indirectly under his control during the twenty-five years he spent directing the office of the court architect.

Sinan's work arguably defined the Classical Period of Ottoman architecture[37] and can be understood, in part, in the context of three distinct, but interrelated, building traditions: the Roman domed space, the Byzantine dome on a cube, and the Islamic dome-on-squinches.[38] In his late works, Sinan coalesced and incorporated many of his early formal, spatial, epigraphic, and symbolic motifs and strategies. Of these, site, form, structure, spatial composition, geometry, and ornament found their most potent expression. Even though Sinan worked within a highly circumscribed conservative political, religious, and artistic setting, his works are consistently distinguished by their inventiveness within the established norms of their time. One means of understanding his work is to trace the lineage of sequential experimentation and development throughout his *œuvre*. In particular, his late works can be viewed as a culmination of his previous experimentation, which achieved a maturity of formal, structural, symbolic, and religious expression that both reflected and transcended their cultural setting.

9.6
Mimar Sinan, comparative plans showing square baldachin system

1. Şehzade Mehmed, Istanbul (1543–48)
2. Mihrümah Sultan, Üsküdar (1543/44–1548)
3. Süleymaniye, Istanbul (1548–59)
4. Mihrümah Sultan, Edirnekapı (c. 1563–70)
5. Shahsultan and Zal Mahmud Pasha, Eyüp (1577–90)

Source: Drawing by Arben Arapi, courtesy of Gülru Necipoğlu.

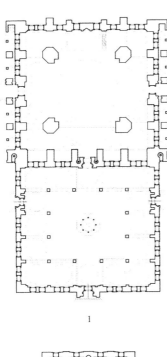

1

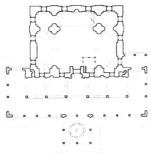

2

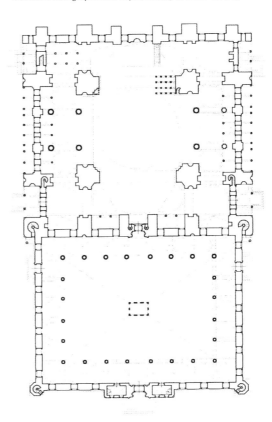

3

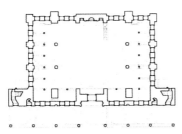

4

5

0   5   10 m

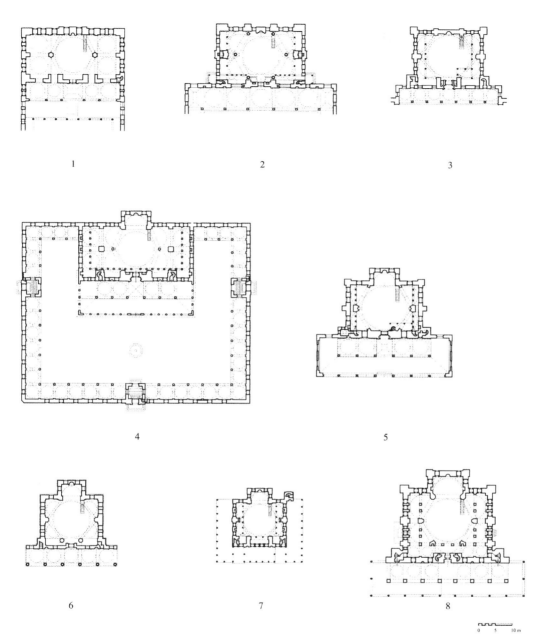

9.7
Mimar Sinan, comparative plans showing hexagonal baldachin system

1. Sinan Pasha, Beşiktaş (1554–1555/56)
2. Kara Ahmed Pasha, Topkapı (1555, 1565–71/72)
3. Ismihan Sultan and Sokollu Mehmed Pasha,
   Kadırgalimanı (c. 1567/68–71/72)

4. Nurbanu Sultan, Üsküdar (1571–86)
5. Semiz Ali Pasha, Babaeski (c. 1569–75, 1585–86)
6. Molla Çelebi, Fındıklı (1570–84)
7. Kazasker Ivaz Efendi, Eğirikapı (1586)
8. Cerrah Mehmed Pasha, Avratpazarı (1593–94)

Source: Drawing by Arben Arapi, courtesy of Gülru Necipoğlu.

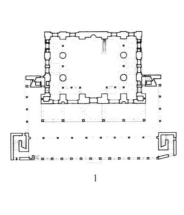

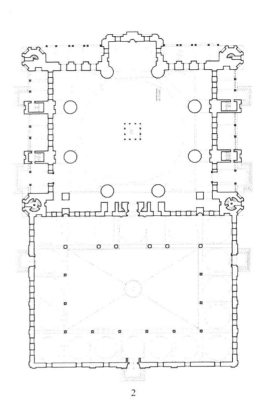

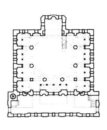

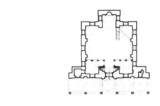

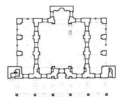

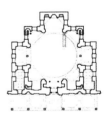

0   5   10 m

1

2

3

4

5

6

9.8
Mimar Sinan, comparative plans showing octagonal baldachin system

1. Rüstem Pasha, Tahtakale (c. 1561–63)
2. Selimiye, Edirne (1568–74)
3. Sokollu Mehmed Pasha, Azapkapı (c. 1573–1577/78)

4. Mehmed Agha, Çarşamba (1584–85)
5. Mesih Mehmed Pasha, Yenibahçe (1584–1585/86)
6. Nişancı Mehmed Pasha, Karagümrük (1584/85–1588/89)

Source: Drawing by Arben Arapi, courtesy of Gülru Necipoğlu.

Sinan's long career is distinguished, in part, by a systematic inquiry of formal, spatial, and structural compositions. Three distinct spatial and structural types define his mosque architecture – the square, hexagonal, and octagonal baldachin supporting a centralized dome.[39] However, these typologies only provide an *entreé* to a multifaceted examination of his work. For it to be substantially understood, it is necessary to include the broader contexts of site planning, formal relationships, building elements, materials, scale, spatial sequences, and geometry, some of which are directly related to the socio-political culture negotiated by Sinan. The Age of Suleyman, who came to be called "The Lawgiver,"[40] was one in which social stratification was made explicit through visual and formal means. Precise codes of dress were proscribed according to one's trade, role, and status. As the highly organized and imperial Ottoman Empire sought the means to communicate order and hierarchy, its rulers turned to architecture as a potent means to do so. Houses were subject to the same "dress codes" applied to the Sultan's subjects, but it was the mosques where architectural language was specifically encoded. Sultanic mosques, for example, were clearly distinguished from those commissioned by lesser patrons. This was accomplished by an extensive architectural language including: being built on prominent hills and on a monumental scale; utilizing large, centralized domed plans flanked by four minarets (with multiple galleries), and employing arcaded, marble-paved courtyards.[41] Sinan's mosques, it has been argued, supported and expressed the social hierarchies and political hegemony of their time. According to Gülru Necipoğlu, "The hierarchical conceptions of empire found its counterpart in the nuanced gradation of mosque types codified by Sinan, who brought architecture in line with the rank-conscious mentality of the classical age."[42]

Additionally, the decorative and epigraphic language of imperial mosques communicated socio-religious themes. Passages from the Koran and Hadith, typically rendered in colossal Arabic script, provided exhortative, inspirational, and didactic content. The path to the righteous life was explicitly outlined and

9.9
The Sehzade complex in Istanbul, built for Sultan Suleyman and dedicated to his son and heir Sehzade, is one of Sinan's most important early works. Sehzade complex, Istanbul, Turkey, Mimar Sinan, mid-sixteenth century, aerial view

Source: Photo by Aras Neftçi.

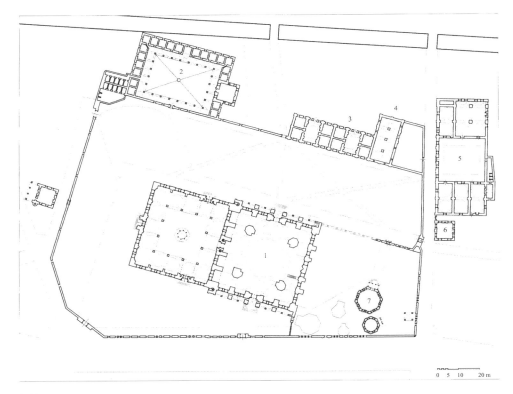

9.10

Two adjacent squares define a marble-paved courtyard and the prayer hall of the Sehzade Mehmed Mosque – their interface marked by two double-galleried minarets. Sehzade complex, Istanbul, plan of complex

1. Mosque
2. Madrasa
3. Guest Rooms
4. Caravansaray
5. Hospice
6. School
7. Mausoleum of Sehzade

Source: Drawing by Arben Arapi, courtesy of Gülru Necipoğlu.

9.11

The central space of the Sehzade Mehmed Mosque includes distinct horizontal zones marked by moldings, indicating a vertical hierarchy that culminates in the apex of the dome. Sehzade complex, Istanbul, interior

Source: Photo by Aras Neftçi.

integrated with the larger symbolic agendas of the mosque. Naturalistic decorative motifs, set within the geometrically ordered space of the *haram* (worship hall), symbolized the eternal garden of paradise promised to those who follow (and submit to) the will of God so explicitly summarized by the calligraphy.

Necipoğlu points out that it was during the time of Suleyman that the centralized domed mosque became the preferred type[43] and outlines three major periods of its development by Sinan. The Sehzade Mehmed complex in Istanbul marked the end of the Formative Period, the Suleymaniye complex (also in Istanbul), concluded the mature Classical Period, and the Selimiye complex in Edirne was the culmination of the post-Classical Period. The Sehzade complex in Istanbul, built for Sultan Suleyman and dedicated to his son and heir Sehzade, is one of Sinan's most important early works. Overall, two adjacent squares define a marble-paved courtyard and the prayer hall – their interface marked by two double-galleried minarets. The bi-axially symmetrical plan of the mosque[44] employs a central dome on a square base surrounded by four half-domes with four smaller domes at its corners. The central space includes distinct horizontal zones marked by moldings, indicating a vertical hierarchy that culminates in the apex of the dome. The mosque is sited at an oblique angle to the street, affording dynamic views that reveal its sequence of domes, half-domes, and weight towers producing the pyramidal form that distinguished Sinan's work of this time. Prince Sehzade's tomb is located in a garden outside the *qibla* wall (the wall on the Mecca side of the mosque), and employs diverse imagery and

9.12

The Suleymaniye complex, completed in 1559, is situated on one of the highest hills of Istanbul. It dominated the Ottoman skyline then and still does today. Suleymaniye complex, Istanbul, Turkey, 1548–1559, aerial view showing mosque

Source: Photo by Aras Neftçi.

calligraphy to describe the paradise garden promised to the devout in the Koran. Inside the mosque, similar imagery is incorporated, and the verticality of the space, supported by the symmetrical half-domes and capped by the window-ringed central dome, represents the paradise garden more explicitly symbolized in the Prince's mausoleum, but which would find full expression in Sinan's later works.

The Suleymaniye complex, completed in 1559, was the culminating work of Sinan's Classical Period. Situated on one of the highest hills of Istanbul, it dominated the Ottoman skyline, as it still does today. Its extensive building program included a voluminous mosque with mausolea on its *qibla* side and a marble-paved courtyard at its entry (opposite) side. Additionally, schools, a hospital, a hospice, a guesthouse, and baths are inserted into a topographically

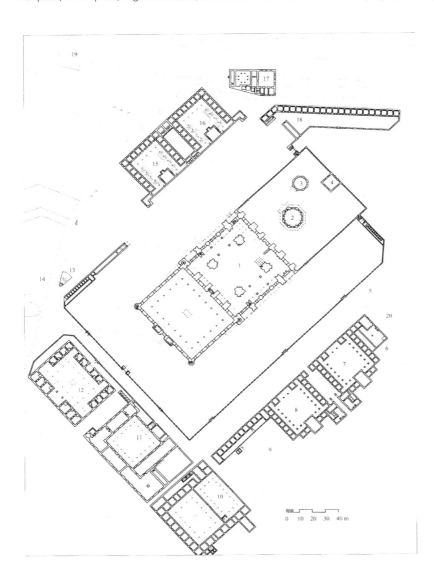

9.13
Suleymaniye complex, Istanbul, site plan

1. Mosque
2. Mausoleum of Suleyman
3. Mausoleum of Hurrem
4. Hall of the Mausoleum Keepers
5. Public Fountain
6. School
7. First Madrasa
8. Second Madrasa
9. Medical School
10. Hospital
11. Hospice
12. Guest House
13. Sinan's Tomb
14. Janissary Agha's Residence
15. Third Madrasa
16. Fourth Madrasa
17. Bathhouse
18. Hadith College

Source: Drawing by Arben Arapi, courtesy of Gülru Necipoğlu.

9.14

The spatial configuration of the Suleymaniye Mosque is the accentuation of its axial orientation toward Mecca. Suleymaniye complex, Istanbul, view toward entrance

Source: Photo by Aras Neftçi.

complex hilltop site in a dense urban neighborhood. Four minarets, a pair of three-tiered ones flanking the mosque side of the courtyard, another pair of two-tiered ones flanking the other corners of the courtyard, further establish the visual prominence of the site. Throughout the complex Sinan skillfully responds to the slope to suppress the visual impact of the supporting structures and maximize the prominence of the mosque.

At the Suleymaniye mosque Sinan continued to develop the unified centralized prayer hall that defines his work. Similar to Sehzade, it includes a central dome on a square base, flanked by half-domes on the *mihrab* axis. Unlike Sehzade, however, (but similar to the Hagia Sophia), half-domes are not employed at the adjacent sides of the dome. Instead a series of smaller domes are used, along with slender columns utilized to support the arcade. The result is a central space that opens dramatically to the *mihrab*, but does not achieve the degree of cross-axial openness of Sehzade. Sinan had to wait for future projects to further his development of a fully unified central space, and for the Selimiye mosque to fully realize it. One effect of the spatial configuration of the mosque is the accentuation of its axial orientation toward Mecca. The axial entry path passes through a number of courtyards and gateways before culminating in the *mihrab*. Aligned with the axis is Suleyman's tomb, followed by a small religious hall (known as the Koran Recitation Hall, or Hall of Mausoleum Keepers).[45] According to Necipoğlu, "the white marble *mihrab*, with its *muqarnas* hood evoking a gate, invites the congregation to enter into the promised eternal garden represented by the actual garden containing the mausolea of Suleyman and [his wife] Hurrem."[46]

The Ismihan Sultan and Sokollu Complex in Kadirga, Istanbul

Sinan developed the centralized dome on a hexagonal base in three late works, all located in Istanbul: the Kara Ahmet Pasa Mosque in Topkapi, the Murbanu Sultan (Eski Valide) Mosque in Uskudar, and the Ismihan Sultan and Sokollu complex in Kadirga. It's safe to say that the Sokollu Kadirga Mosque (as it is commonly referred to), was a culmination of the development of the dome on the hexagonal base (as the Suleymaniye was of the dome on a square base). The Kara Ahmet Pasa Mosque was completed in 1561 and is an example of Sinan's early experimentation with the hexagonal baldachin. The small rectangular mosque is fronted by a large courtyard that includes the cells and classroom of its *madrasa* (school). The central dome rests on a hexagonal base which transitions to the supporting walls by means of half-domes at the four corners of the space. Columns engaged with the massive rectangular piers somewhat awkwardly support the dome base at its east and west sides. The construction

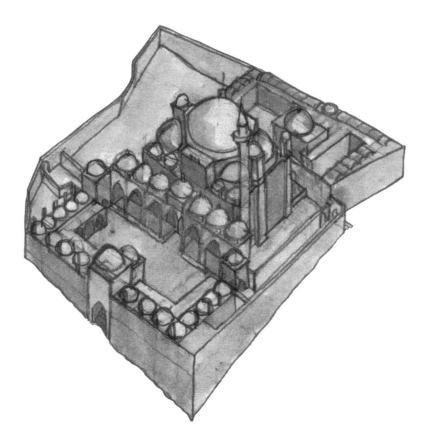

9.15
The complex resolves the steep slope of the site in a manner that displays the skills of Sinan and his office. The Sokollu complex in Kadirga, Istanbul, Turkey, Mimar Sinan, 1572, axonometric view of the complex on its steeply sloped site

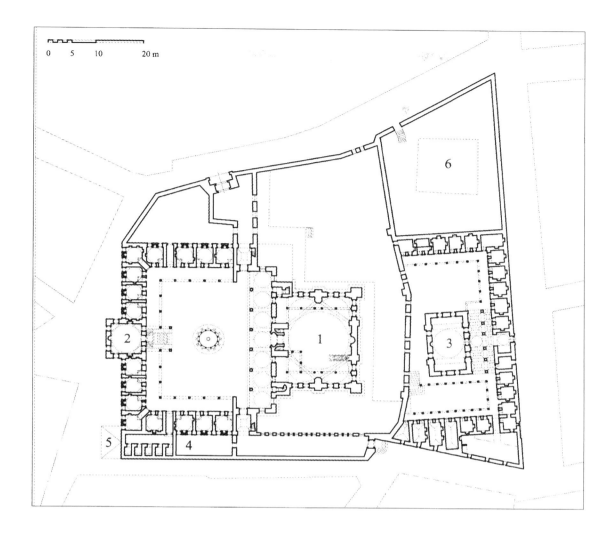

9.16

The Sokollu Kadirga complex, Istanbul, site plan

1. Mosque
2. Madrasa
3. Tekke
4. Latrines
5. Reservoir with street fountains
6. Site of former mosque

Source: Drawing by Arben Arapi, courtesy of Gülru Necipoğlu.

of the Murbanu Sultan complex was begun in 1571, just as the Sokollu Kadirga was near completion, but it is difficult to ascertain which design preceded the other.[47] The Murbanu Sultan Mosque, which was expanded in 1577, employs the hexagonal baldachin, but its east and west supports are delicately engaged slender columns, resulting in a more spatially unified interior space than at Kara Ahmet Pasa. Also, unlike the Kara Ahmet and Sokollu Kadirga, it includes a half-domed apse in the *qibla* wall that further diminishes its cross-axial orientation.

The Sokollu Kadirga was one of Sinan's last works, completed in 1572 just as the Selimiye Mosque in Edirne was nearing completion. It was built for Ismihan Sultan, a daughter of Selim II who was married to the Grand Vizier Sokollu Mehmed Pasha (to whom it is often attributed). It was located near his palace on the steep slope of the hill that descends from the Roman Hippodrome to the old fishing port of Kadirga. The complex resolves the steep slope of the site in a manner that displays the skills of Sinan and his office. According to one

9.17 (opposite)
At the Sokollu Kadirga complex a set of steep stairs passes under the raised, domed space of the classroom and enters a marble-paved courtyard. The Sokollu Kadirga complex, Istanbul, main entrance

Source: Photo by Aras Neftçi.

historian, "It is rare in the history of architecture to find a building that expresses so well the relation of its site to its constitution, its plan and its elevation."[48] Similar to the Sulemaniye complex, Sinan leveled the site for the mosque and *madrasa* in a manner that cleverly reconciles its high and low points. In contrast to the extensive grounds and prominent dome of the Sulemaniye, however, the site of the Sokollu Kadirga complex is small and irregular and its mosque diminutive. The mosque and courtyard plan at the Kadirga complex are very similar to the earlier Kara Ahmet Topkapi, but was adapted to fit its steeply-sloped site. One enters through a gateway on the northwest side that, because of the slope of the land, originally included ground-level shops below the cells of the *madrasa*.[49] A set of steep stairs passes under the raised, domed space of the classroom and enters a marble-paved courtyard (which was unusual for a non-Sultanic mosque). The entire complex is organized along a central axis that is aligned with the direction of Mecca. Along this axis are located the street-level entrance, *sardivan* (ablution fountain), the *son cemaat mahalli* (the portico used as an overflow prayer space), entry porch, *pishtaq* (main entrance), the *haram* (prayer hall), *mihrab* (prayer niche in the *qibla* wall), and lastly the *tekke* (which originally was a school and accommodations for students and dervishes of the Medlavi sect). There are two other secondary entrances to the courtyard from the southwest and northeast that pass through gateways under towers, which on their second levels originally provided accommodations for, respectively, the caretaker and the *muezzin* (the man who performs the call to prayer).[50]

9.18
The Sokollu Kadirga complex, Istanbul, courtyard from above

Source: Photo by Aras Neftçi.

9.19
The Sokollu Kadirga complex,
Istanbul, courtyard showing
sardivan on right

In Ottoman architecture the organization of the exterior elevations was important but secondary to its formal compositions. In contrast to the studied arrangement of the openings, orders, and decorative elements of Renaissance elevations, Ottoman architects focused on the interrelationship of geometry, scale, mass, and form.[51] The section through the courtyard, mosque, and *tekke* at the Sokollu Kadirga reveals a composition of domes of varying sizes and

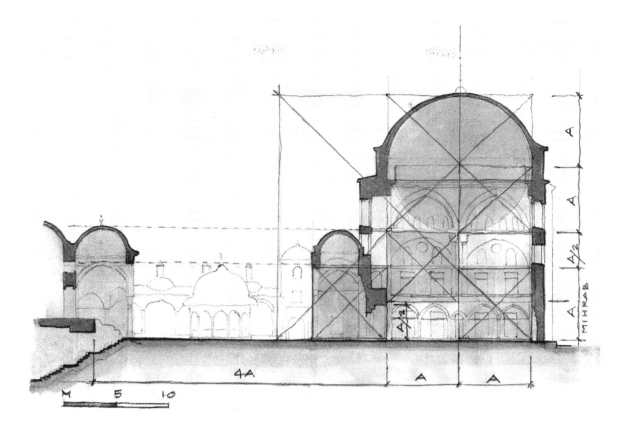

9.20
The Sokollu Kadirga complex, Istanbul, site section proportions

scales that visually and spatially culminate in the central dome of the mosque. The entrance dome steps down to a smaller one that is flanked by the still smaller domes of the *madrasa*. The muezzin and caretaker towers step up to the porch, followed by the rising half-domes and dome of the mosque itself. The exterior materials also transition along the entry path – the *madrasa* employs bands of stone and brick, the north portico features white marble columns, and the mosque utilizes grey ashlar. The effect is a stunning austere amalgam of repetitive arcades and chimneys, gray ashlar walls, green copper-covered domes, light and shadow. Blue and white tile-work above the windows and doors of the porch, and polychromed decoration on the inside of its domes, add another weave to the warp of its scale relationships.

Inside, the mosque comprises a single space, capped by a central dome, and surrounded on three sides by a diminutive mezzanine gallery. This is a non-hierarchical, unified space delicately rendered in load-bearing masonry. The dome rises from a hexagonal baldachin but, unlike the other examples cited where freestanding columns were employed, here Sinan utilized engaged faceted columns at the two sidewalls. At the corners he employed shallow pilasters from which rise the four half-domes and above them the 13-meter diameter central dome. There is no need for buttressing – the dome rests confidently on its hexagonal base, flanked by the graceful half-domes. Exterior

weight towers are located on top of the six load-bearing columns, but most likely only as part of the composition of masses as they are hollow.

Similarities have been established between Turkish and Cistercian arcaded and domed architecture. Stierlin suggests that caravanserais' dating from the early thirteenth century were built by Armenian craftsmen who applied the constructive and spatial techniques of Cistercian churches to these secular

9.22
The Sokollu Kadirga complex,
Istanbul, dome

Source: Photo by Aras Neftçi.

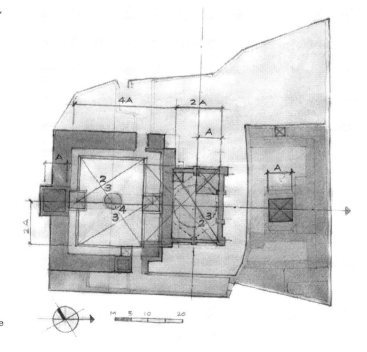

9.23
At the Sokollu Kadirga
complex, geometry is
employed as
a means to integrate the
various formal and spatial
components and calibrate the
entry sequence. The Sokollu
Kadirga complex, Istanbul, site
plan proportions

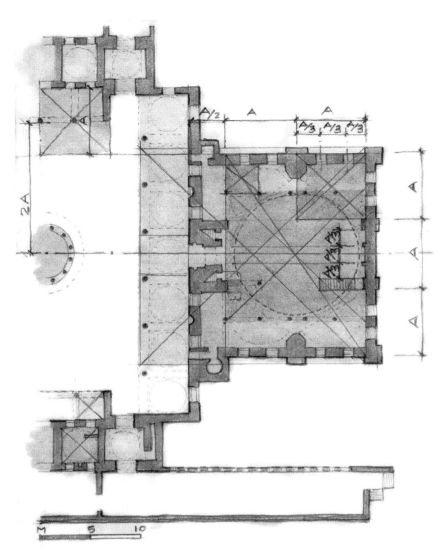

9.24
The Sokollu Mehmed Pasa
Mosque and *madrasa* in
Kadirga, Istanbul, Turkey,
Mimar Sinan, 1572, plan
proportions of mosque

buildings. The use of the square to proportion Cistercian churches was previously noted, and therefore it is intriguing to discover its appearance in Sinan's
work. Even though Sinan did not document his design methods, it is clear that
his mature works were developed according to geometry and proportion.[52] At
the Sokollu Kadirga, geometry is employed as a means to integrate the various
formal and spatial components and calibrate the entry sequence. The square is
a dominant proportioning element, which establishes the outline of the central
space under the dome (framed by the *qibla* wall, the entrance piers, and the
mezzanine galleries), the outside dimensions of the mosque and porch, and
the proportions of the interior space. Six units of a repeating standard module
determine the plan of the *haram* and establish a space of a 2 to 3 proportion.

The same dimensions and proportions are applied to the courtyard, which in plan is twice as large as the prayer hall. Along the main axis there are also a number of repeating squares. In particular, the square module determines a number of dimensions of the court and is repeated at the classroom of the *madrasa* and the rooms of the *tekke*.

At the Sokollu Kadirga, the entry sequence is a cadence of light and shadow. The entrance stair passes through a cool dark space to enter a bright, light courtyard. At its center is the octagonal fountain, its deep pool an oasis cooled by the shadow of its roof overhang. The porch is a shadowed intermediary that leads to the dim light of the mosque itself. The gray ashlar walls provide a calm backdrop to the brilliant colors of the tiles, carpet, and, originally, the dome. Eighteen windows ring the dome, and at its center an excerpt from Sura 35/41 states, "It is God who keeps the heavens and the earth from falling. Should they fall, none could hold them back but Him. Gracious is God, and forgiving."[53]

9.25

The Selimiye, completed in 1574, is arguably Sinan's most extensive and accomplished work. The Selimiye complex, Edirne, Turkey, Mimar Sinan, 1567–1574, view of complex

Source: Photo by Aras Neftçi.

The Selimiye Complex in Edirne

Just as Sinan's structural experimentation of square and hexagonal bases resulted in mature works, earlier experimentation with domes on octagonal bases anticipated its culmination in the Selimiye Mosque. The Edirnekapi Mihrimah Sultan, Rustem Pasa, and Azakapi Sokollu Mosques, all of which are located in

Istanbul, suggested the spatial and symbolic possibilities of this structural-spatial type. In all, consistent with Sinan's methods of experimentation, a limited palette of structural elements is employed in different configurations, resulting in a variety of spatial relationships and exterior expressions.

The Selimiye, completed in 1573, is arguably Sinan's most extensive and accomplished work. After Suleyman died in 1566 on the Hungarian front, his wife Roxelena's son Selim succeeded him as sultan. He spent the first year of his reign in his favored city of Edirne, and in 1568 instructed Sinan to begin work on a complex there. Work was begun on Selim's mosque in 1567 and the building inaugurated in 1574. Similar to the Suleymaniye complex, the Selimiye complex occupies a prominent hilltop that defines the city's skyline. The flat Thracian plain that surrounds the city makes the mosque visible from miles away. The site was not as steep or irregular as either the Suleymaniye or the Sokollu Kadirga, but once again offered Sinan and his office the opportunity to apply their site planning talents.

The mosque complex is symmetrically arranged around an axis that is aligned with the direction of Mecca, and surrounded by a *temenos* wall with gateways on all four sides. One begins the primary entry sequence from the

9.26
The mosque complex is symmetrically arranged around an axis that is aligned with the direction of Mecca, and surrounded by a *temenos* wall with gateways on all four sides. The Selimiye complex, Edirne, site plan

1. Mosque
2. Madrasa
3. Madrasa
4. School
5. Bazaar

Source: Drawing by Arben Arapi, courtesy of Gülru Necipoğlu.

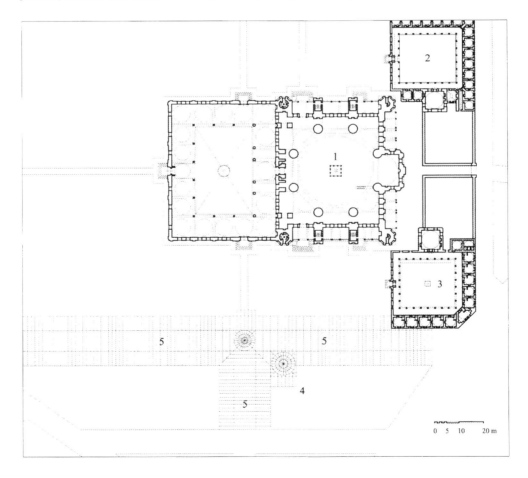

9.27
One begins the primary entry sequence from the western gateway, passes through the gardens, and then ascends steps to the courtyard gateway. The Selimiye complex, Edirne, west gate

9.28
The Selimiye complex, Edirne, entry and porch

9.29 (opposite)

The Selimiye complex, Edirne, interior toward *mihrab*

Source: Photo by Aras Neftçi.

9.30 (opposite)

The muezzin's lodge at the Selimiye stands at the center of a simultaneously expanding and contracting universe, its geometry both fracturing and coalescing – a potent image of infinity. The Selimiye complex, Edirne, *muezzin mahfeli* (muezzin's lodge) from above

Source: Photo by Aras Neftçi.

western gateway, passes through the gardens, and then ascends steps to the courtyard gateway. Once inside the courtyard the roofless *sardivan* is a physical but not visual barrier to the main entrance (*pishtaq*) that leads to the prayer hall (*haram*). The *haram* is bi-axially symmetrical, with only the projecting apse of the *mihrab* deviating from this composition. This spatial and visual element establishes directionality to an otherwise centralized space capped by its magnificent dome. The centralized composition is reinforced by the *muezzin mahfeli* (muezzin's lodge), unusually located at its center. Eight columns that support the dome and the surrounding galleries further establish the centrality of the space. The sultan's lodge and *minbar* (pulpit), located on opposite sides of the space, are asymmetrical but balanced elements.

Geometry is a primary organizing and symbolic element at the Selimiye Mosque, as we have observed in the Islamic mosque in general, and Sinan's work in particular. Once again, its proportioning can be understood according to the geometry of the square. For example, the site plan corresponds to proportionally interrelated squares. As at the Sokollu Kadirga, the plan can be analyzed according to a progressive proportional series derived from a base module and its volumetric implications illustrated by the section.

Most significantly, an analysis of the plan of the *haram* reveals a progressive series of interlocked and overlapping squares. First there is the square plan of the prayer hall itself defined by the centerline of the eight columns. This is divided into nine equal squares that align with the edges of the columns. Another square inscribed by opposite edges of the columns defines a central square. When this is divided into nine equal squares we get the center square of the muezzin's lodge. This object, located directly under the dome at the center

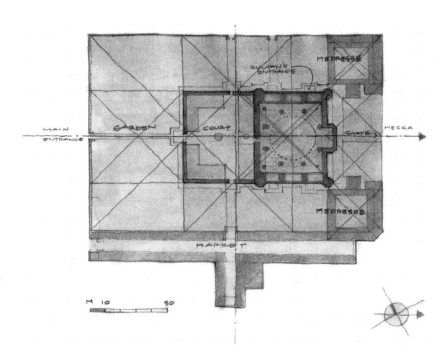

9.31

Geometry is a primary organizing and symbolic element at the Selimiye Mosque, as we have observed in the Islamic mosque in general, and Sinan's work in particular. The Selimiye complex, Edirne, site proportions

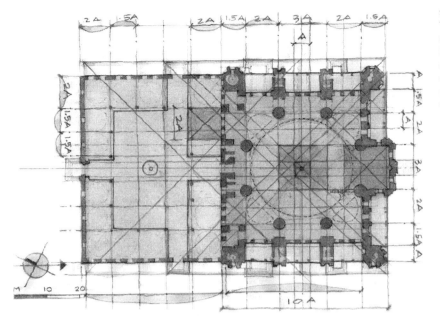

9.32
The plan of the *haram* reveals a progressive series of interlocked and overlapping squares. The Selimiye complex, Edirne, plan proportions of mosque and courtyard

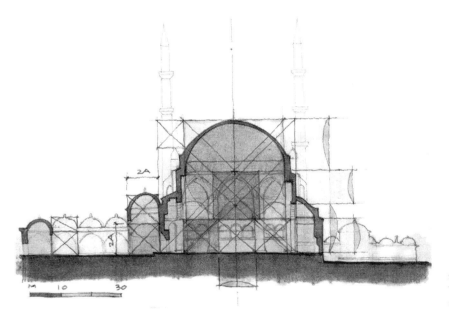

9.33
The Selimiye complex, Edirne, section proportions

of the space, is in turn divided into nine equal squares, defined by its nine white marble columns. At its center is an octagonal marble fountain. The wooden ceiling of the muezzin's lodge reveals further geometric subdivisions based on the square and overall there is an interwoven number progression. First of all, it too is divided into nine equal squares. The center panel, directly over the

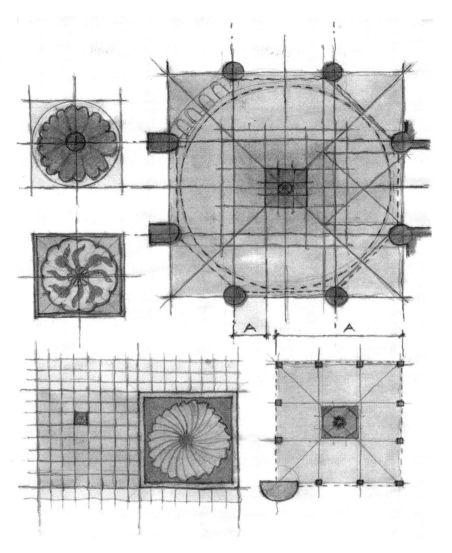

9.34

The Selimiye complex, Edirne, progressive geometry. Upper right: plan of mosque showing eight columns; lower right: plan of the muezzin's lodge showing fountain at the center; lower left: plan of the ceiling of the muezzin's lodge; upper left (two drawings), details of ceiling medallions.

fountain, features a single, relief wooden medallion, a "whorled circle,"[54] that suggests a spiral growth form. The other panels are subdivided into sixty-four squares. Within each is an eight-sided spiral floral pattern set within a twelve-sided medallion. Lastly at the center of this spiral the number 9 appears again in a final, small medallion.

The hemispherical dome is 31.5 meters in diameter and rests on eight massive columns.[55] The vertical ribbing on the columns reduces their visual impact, however, as do the shallow squinches located between columns. The red and white bands of stone on the arches further dissolve the solidity of the space, allowing the dome to dominate the space. Thirty-two windows are located at the base of the dome. The galleries that surround the central space are relatively thin in section and are skillfully integrated with the structure. Ground floor porches are inserted on three sides, which add to the unity of the

space and modulate the light entering it. It is a luminous, light-filled space, with large ground-floor windows that allow views to the surrounding gardens. Overall a spatial unity and colossal scale are achieved that was unprecedented in Ottoman architecture.

9.35
The Selimiye complex, Edirne, dome

Source: Photo by Aras Neftçi.

The Symbolism of Sinan's Late Works

I have suggested that the prevalent symbolic goal of sacred architecture was representations of the perfection of the divine cosmos. Islamic architecture, in particular because of its doctrinal iconoclasm, aimed to express divinity through non-iconographic imagery, space, structure, geometry, and light. It was an expression of piety for the patrons and arguably a spiritual exercise by the architects who created it, that attempted to represent aspects of God through the media of architecture. Its built form, space, and symbolism were intended to be revelatory, a threshold that mediated between the visible and the invisible, humans and god. The Sokollu Kadirga and Selimiye Mosques, some of the last works of an accomplished architect who was in his eighties when they were completed, illustrate many of the themes of the Islamic mosque in general, and the mature Ottoman mosque in particular.

As we have observed, the interior of the Ottoman mosque contained the most imagery and held the most symbolism.[56] However, exterior massing and articulation were essential elements that significantly contributed to its

Perfected Worlds

symbolic content and the symbolic agendas of its creators. First of all, the mosque was a centralized place – clearly established as a sacred center by the central dome and, in the case of the Selimiye, by the four remarkable flanking minarets.[57] It was a composition of formal elements, as at the Suleymaniye and Sokollu Kadirga, that through scale and placement, created a hierarchical, pyramidal mass. This, among other motifs, reflected the order and hierarchy of the Ottoman world. Friday Mosques, such as the Selimiye, were only built for Sultans, and thus served as potent podiums to express their political power and the dominance of the Ottoman Empire. It was through the appropriation and transformation of the architectural language of former empires and, in particular, the domed spaces of the Romans and Byzantines that symbols of power were, in part, authenticated.[58]

Even though political and cultural agendas defined many aspects of the Ottoman mosque, it is the theme of the paradise garden that is perhaps its ultimate symbolic content. This theme was introduced in the gardens and courtyards of mosque complexes – the gardens were a green oasis and, in the Ottoman city, one of the few green spaces available to the public. At the Selimiye green carpets of grass, gardens, and cedar trees create cool shady spaces of repose that directly communicate the peace and divinity of nature. Roses, symbolizing the Prophet Mohammed, were the preferred plant, a reinforcement of the theme of the primordial garden where contact with the divine was propitious. Part of the paradise garden imagery is, of course, water and fountains are an element essential to the ritual of entering the mosque. Men must wash themselves in a strictly proscribed sequential manner to achieve the requisite cleanliness for entering the sacred space of the mosque. (Bath houses are typically found outside the enclosed mosque precinct if a more thorough cleansing is necessary.) However, the *sardivan*, often located at the center of the entrance courtyard, is the most symbolically significant place of ablution and has achieved in some examples a remarkable degree of refinement and architectural expression. In the Ottoman mosque the *sardivan* typically interrupts the axial path to achieve a visual and symbolic dominance in the courtyard. This is particularly apparent at the Sokollu Kadirga where as one ascends the steps at the main entry an archway creates a view frame filled by the profile of its base and dominant roof – all of which underscores the importance of the ritual act of ablution.

The interior of the Selimiye is arguably the most unified space in Ottoman architecture, achieved, in part, by the skillful manner in which Sinan integrated the galleries with the space and suppressed their visual impact, a clear departure from his earlier works such as at the Suleymaniye. It is a complex space, however, with multiple visual and spatial directions subtly balanced. The muezzin's lodge, because of its unusual location directly underneath the dome, reinforces the centrality of the space. Its placement along the central axis of the complex mitigates, but does not obviate, the orientation of the space toward the *mihrab*. Its location also creates a rectangular prayer space in front of the *mihrab* apse that reinforces the cross-axial direction established by communal prayer.[59] The horizontal banding of the tiles and galleries inscribe this space while also creating horizontal visual tiers that lead one's view to the space above (which is reminiscent of the Sehzade). Lastly, the size of the muezzin's lodge is similar

to the *Kaaba* at the Great Mosque at Mecca, which, along with its location, suggests circumambulation.[60]

The Sokollu Kadirga, because of its smaller size and scale, offers a very different experience. The courtyard has significant spatial impact as one emerges from the shadow of the entrance stairs and, because it is twice the size of the mosque, the prayer hall appears small and compact. Here Sinan realized his most sophisticated and integrated resolution of a dome on a hexagonal baldachin to create a clearly centralized space – even though the plan is a cross-axial rectangle. This is accomplished, in part, by the galleries that, along with the *qibla* wall, inscribe a square centralized space, above which hovers the hemispherical dome. The light is much dimmer at the Sokollu Kadirga than at the Selimiye and there is significantly more decoration. Consequently, themes of the paradise garden dominate. Throughout the mosque are images of a cool oasis, from the ablution fountain to its dim interior. The floral designs of the tiles, "naturalistic without being realistic,"[61] depict an exuberant but cultivated garden, and also, the rich spectrum of color expresses the diversity of God's presence.[62] It symbolizes the paradise garden promised in the Koran, four gardens that are "watered by a flowing spring," filled with trees bearing "every kind of fruit," where "Virgins as fair as corals and rubies" are observed as one reclines on "green cushions and fine carpets."[63] The *muqarnas*, stalactites in the squinches, provide another image of a cool grotto, which is also depicted in the stalactites and prismatic geometry of the column capitals, a reference perhaps to the cave on Mt. Hira where Mohammed received the word of God. The original carpets would have added another layer of garden imagery, as well as the dome, which originally, we can assume, had rich, floral paintings.[64]

Throughout a self-contained verdant cosmos, a perfected (and divine) world is symbolized through words, scale, geometry, and light. The central medallions on the domes at both the Selimiye and Sokollu Kadirga urge one to believe that God creates and maintains this cosmos. Surrounding the space are the many names of God and his laws as revealed by the Prophet. The interior of the Sokollu Kadirga Mosque is distinguished by the preponderance and unity of its tile work, the most extensive application of tiles, with the exception of Rustem Pasa. The famous Iznik tiles, in brilliant "Bolu" red, blue, and green, flank the *mihrab* and decorate the dome pendentives and window heads. Floral patterns dominate, but there are also epigraphic tiles, both inside and outside the mosque. In the *haram*, tiles containing the names of Allah, Mohammed, the Four Caliphs, and the two sons of Ali are placed around the central space. At the *mihrab* a number of Koranic passages appear. The top cartouches state the first pillar of Islam, that there is only one God and that Mohammed is his Prophet. Underneath one of the last Suras of the Koran appears. Entitled "Oneness," it states, "God is One, the Eternal God. He begot none, nor was he begotten. None is equal to Him." Above the graceful niche of the *mihrab* is a passage from the Sura entitled "The Imrans," which discusses, among others, the Torah and the Gospels and their relationship to Islam. In an excerpted passage, a story about the Virgin Mary illustrates the generosity of God. Above the windows at the galleries the many names of God are listed. Outside, above the windows of the porch, the first Sura entitled "The Exordium" is reproduced in tile work. Along the entry sequence that is aligned with the axis which points toward Mecca, a devotional and exhortative narrative unfolds. Panels state the oneness of God, that the Prophet has made the world right, and that Muslims must pray. Over the entry door we read God's message of welcome and kindness. Inside the *haram*, as we have observed, the axis terminates with messages of God's oneness and generosity.

In contrast to the Sokollu Kadirga, the scale at the Selimiye unambiguously dwarfs the individual. However, this is not a space where God is mysteriously present, as in the Byzantine church, but one that underscores one's inability to perceive the divine. The Islamic solution to this condition is to simply submit oneself to God's elusive omnipotence. The word "mosque" (*masjid*) means a "place of prostration," an appropriate response to this concept of the divine. The size and scale of the space are such that one feels part of a much larger realm, and has entered the vastness and ubiquity of God. As Kuban states, it acts as "a catalyst in subduing him to the will of an omnipresent and omniscient God."[65]

Attendant to this vision of the oneness and enormity of God are representations of the multiplicity and complexity of the divine. Geometry is the most potent media to communicate this symbolic content, as explicitly expressed at both the Sokollu Kadirga and Selimiye. According to Seyyed Hossein Nasr, understanding Islamic geometry is the key to unlocking Islamic spirituality.[66]

The geometric elements of the archetypal mosque have symbolic content: the hemispherical dome reflects the unity of God, and its centrality establishes an *axis mundi*; the octagonal base symbolizes the faith's foundation of God, Muhammed, the Four Caliphs, Ali and his son; its square base represents the earth or material world; and lastly the stalactites mediate between the earthly and heavenly realms. The austerity of the architecture and its spatial and geometric purity, create an emptiness, a void, that does not presume to represent God, but instead creates an image of "spiritual poverty"[67] that can be bridged only through submission to God. According to Nasr, "The space of Islamic architecture is not the quantified space of Cartesian geometry but the qualified space related to sacred geometry and given order through the presence of the sacred."[68] It is an empty space to be filled with devotion, consecrated by repeatedly touching one's forehead to the ground.

At the Sokollu Kadirga, the repetition, superimposition, and translation of a standard spatial module create a self-referential, ordered model of the cosmos. As one traverses the entry path, geometric elements are introduced, repeated, amalgamated, and then synthesized in the rarefied space of the *haram*. Repeated proportions in plan, elevation, section, and volume create an integrated architectural language while pointing to a much vaster divine context. This is achieved through the interlocked geometry of a progressive number series. For example, the *mihrab* is divided into three parts, the dome base into six, and the dome itself into eighteen windows.

9.37
The Selimiye complex, Edirne, *muezzin mahfeli* (muezzin's lodge) and fountain

Source: Photo by Aras Neftçi.

At the Selimiye, applied geometry and themes of multiplicity perhaps reached their most potent expression. A series of scales – from the voluminous *haram* and its dome, down to the palm-sized wooden medallions of the muezzin's lodge ceiling – are interlocked in a manner reminiscent of the order of the natural world. One number series, based on an arithmetic progression of the number 8, weaves the elements together. In this context the central placement of the muezzin's lodge is logical – it stands at the center of a simultaneously expanding and contracting universe, its geometry both fracturing and coalescing – a potent image of infinity. At its very center is the equally unusual octagonal fountain. Here the theme of the paradise garden is reasserted, symbolizing a self-contained cosmos vivified by a flowing spring. Worshippers drink from tin cups placed there for this purpose, a recapitulation of pagan practices at healing springs that is uncharacteristic of Islam, but might be explained as a vestige of practices that the Turks brought when they migrated to Central Anatolia from the East.[69]

Sacred architecture has traditionally modulated the quality and intensity of the light that penetrates its walls and illuminates its interiors. It is a vessel that holds both light and shadow and the strategic placement of openings focuses perception and suggests movement inside its spaces. The special quality of light in sacred architecture often symbolized God and was believed to be a medium that could co-join humans with the divine. All the intertwined elements of the *haram* at the Sokollu Kadirga and Selimiye are placed within the luminous, ambient light of its space – perhaps its most subtle and compelling aspect. The Koran states: "God is the light of the heavens and the earth. His light may be compared to a niche that enshrines a lamp, the lamp within a crystal of star-like brilliance."[70] The mosque is a vessel for the subtle rendering of direct and ambient light. Its beacon, the minaret, is from the Arabic *al-manarah*, which means the "place of light."[71] Inside the mosque the light is subdued, a recreation of a cool grove – subtle and peaceful. The light, descending from the dome above, or filtered through thick walls, shimmering on the surface of tiles and illuminating the deep hues of the prayer carpets, creates a place of sublime repose. As described in the Koran, light is the medium of connection to God, "His light is found in temples which God has sanctioned to be built for the remembrance of His name . . . Light upon light; God guides to His light whom He will."[72]

The architecture of the Ottoman mosque is an amalgam of cultural forces, religious themes, and architectural traditions. What makes the late works of Sinan significant is his ability to synthesize such broad socio-political and religious agendas into an architecture that both expresses and transcends its time. Sinan worked within a highly circumscribed political and religious context and yet, his work is distinguished by invention, experimentation, and, certainly in the case of the Selimiye, inclusiveness that incorporated timeless religious themes. The results were lasting cultural artifacts of great subtlety and expressiveness. According to Necipoğlu, Sinan's works "transcend historical confinement and occupy a timeless present," and hold "inexhaustible reservoirs of 'ontological possibility.'"[73] Outside the classroom of the *madrasa* at the Sokollu Kadirga one reads that "prayer" is the "column" that holds up one's religion. This architectural metaphor suggests the reciprocity of the mosque and the act of devotion to God. At the Sokollu Kadirga and Selimiye complexes, the reciprocity of belief, ritual, and architectural expression is multivalent and complex – a culmination of the career of its enigmatic creator.

The meanings of Sinan's late works and the significance they may hold today, can be said to lie between, or even beyond, their multitudinous contexts, packed agendas, and diverse interpretations. Sinan's work, in part, is a product of a predominant lineage in sacred architecture – the application of domed spaces in service of representations of a perfected world. Derived from domestic models, domed spaces came to be associated with the cosmic archetype where contact with the divine (or divine ruler) was possible. Nero's Golden House, for example, appropriated these themes to present the emperor as an earthly incarnation of the sun god. His *Domus aurea* presents not only a direct structural precedent for the Pantheon, but an intriguing symbolic one as well.[74] The conflation of political authority and divine omnipresence, codified through architecture in Imperial Rome, found new expressions in the Byzantine Church. As we observed earlier, the Hagia Sophia created a complex cosmic model within which, and through the agency of ritual, the Emperor and the clergy made mysterious and portentous appearances. The Ottoman mosque, especially as interpreted by Sinan, may present clarified spatial and structural models, but it includes equally diverse and nuanced socio-political and religious symbolism.

Ottoman culture has been cited as being intensely visual, a position supported by the, at times, intense visual impact of its religious architecture. These were not static scenes, however, but rather dynamic spatial relationships and sequences, often supported by oblique distant views and serial spatial sequences. Decorative and epigraphic practices reached their height during Sinan's time. The choice of Koranic and Hadithic passages often reflected the religious sensibilities of their Sultanic patron, but also presented multiple readings and interpretations.[75] Approach, movement, and readings of the tableaux of surface decoration and epigraphy, were vivified and completed through communal rituals. In his last works Sinan was able to achieve a unified centralized and vertical cosmic space that simultaneously satisfied the requirements of the horizontal orientation of communal prayer. Unlike some of the other examples this study has examined, the Sokollu Kadirga and Selimiye complexes are active religious communities. During Friday services the men line up shoulder-to-shoulder, facing the *qibla* wall, while the imam moves from lectern, to *minbar*, to *mihrab* – all under the all-encompassing central dome. The symbolism and its meanings live on through contemporary uses and interpretations.

The plans of the Hagia Sophia and the Selimiye Mosque were said to have been revealed by God[76] – an expected assertion given their roles as providing a place where humans and their god might be connected. At the Selimiye, the octagonal scheme of the mausoleum is applied in service of the paradise garden themes ubiquitous to royal tombs. Sehzade's tomb was likened to the Garden of Eden and described by Sinan's biographer as a "paradise-like building."[77] Mohammed's "Night Journey" is also referenced at the Prince's tomb – and the Selimiye has been compared to the Dome of the Rock, where Mohammed's journey ended and he is believed to have ascended to heaven.[78] The Pantheon and the Hagia Sophia have been described in their times as replicas of the

"Dome of Heaven"[79] and Sinan's biographer described the Selimiye as the "Sphere of Heaven."[80] Just as the Dome of the Rock depicts a paradise garden at the center of the world, analogously the Selimiye Mosque presents a center that mediates between humans and their god – the fundamental role of sacred architecture.

Chapter 10

Conclusion

It is only with the heart that one can see rightly; what is essential is
invisible to the eye.

(Antoine de Saint-Exupéry)[1]

I began this book suggesting that religion, religious figures, symbolism, ritual,
and their architectural settings serve as mediators to connect humans with the
gods they worship, and the knowledge or understandings they seek. It is through
symbolism and ritual use that sacred architecture creates the intermediary zone
required by the religions it was built to serve. The symbolic content is elucidative,
often didactic and at times exhortative, and is designed to engender emotional
and sensual responses. In many cases the multifarious and complex "call" and
"response" of sacred architecture is designed to orient the religious aspirant in
the world – to clarify their spiritual, socio-political, and environmental "position."
In other words, the architecture "takes a position" to establish its "position in
the world."

I am primarily interested in contributing to a re-positioning of architecture
as profoundly sensual and as a media of elucidation and (at times) transformation. I have chosen the selective lens of sacred architecture in the belief that
it may be the most accessible means to do so. However, that does not imply or
suggest that architecture with other functions or cultural imperatives are bereft
of symbolic content or incapable of engendering sensual and meaningful experiences. It is particularly incumbent on contemporary culture (and its architects
and artists) to discover new expressions of enduring spiritual themes – perspectives that reveal the perennial condition of human consciousness, of which
we are all a part. This is particularly important in a contemporary setting where
the old worn-out hierarchies no longer work. However, this loss of a "sacralized
world" offers new possibilities for the sacred through new approaches and

incarnations of one of its most powerful mediums, architecture. The practice of hermeneutic retrieval is a promising means to bring contemporary perspectives to certain aspects and cultural artifacts of the past, and derive new interpretations that hold meaning for us today. Hermeneutic, homological, and integrative perspectives and methodologies serve to establish an intersubjective middle ground between the past and the present.

Throughout this book, I have positioned architecture as a cultural artifact and an expression of its social, political, economic, and environmental contexts. As a communicative media, sacred architecture contains and expresses a complex matrix of cultural, symbolic, mythological, doctrinal, and (in some cases) historical content. I have presented sacred architecture as an active agent that performs didactic, elucidative, and (in some cases) coercive roles, and have suggested that it is through use and ritual that architectural settings are completed and vivified. Furthermore, I have argued that the inclusion of haptic, kinesthetic, and multi-sensory experiences of architecture is essential to decipher its content and interpret its significance and meaning. Phenomenology, Buddhist philosophy, and Transcendentalism have all been put into the service (either implicitly or explicitly) of bringing attention to the "thingly-real" and the ephemeral, poetic, and immaterial aspects of architecture.

Shared Patterns of Mediation

The examples and case studies have been applied to provide clear, accessible, and direct illustrations of the roles played and responses encouraged (or produced) by sacred architecture and its ritual uses. Through examining the form, space, sequence, symbolism, and ritual uses of pan-cultural and trans-historical examples, certain shared patterns of sacred architecture have emerged, to which I now turn.

The media of architecture, as employed in examples as diverse as Paleolithic art and Carl Jung's house in Bollingen, demonstrated the potential of architecture to articulate symbolic content and elicit broadened existential understandings. The creative process and the resulting artifact were reciprocal in rendering what otherwise was inexpressible. "Stones," for Jung in particular, were a means to conceptualize both personal and archetypal questions and possible answers. Primary elements, such as earth and stone, materialized a broad range of content beginning with the earliest of architecture – effigy figures, earthworks, and burial mounds. The fundamental act of building between earth and sky, as a means to symbolically access ancestors and thus establish historical and political continuity, can be found, in multiple iterations, throughout the world. The simplicity and clarity of primordial examples, at least from a contemporary vantage point, help us to recognize the principal architectural act of delimiting place.[2] The clear articulation of place requires a separation from its immediate context, and thus the necessity of entry and passage. That spatial sequences can embody potent symbolic narratives is understandable given the double mediation of separation and connection often performed by sacred architecture. The sacred place itself, in all of its manifestations, is the goal of the journey and where contact with the divine (or what the divine represents) is believed to be portentous. As a place where "god dwells," it requires ordering commensurate with this role, and geometry and proportion have generally served in this capacity. And in the perfected worlds of cosmic archetypes represented by sacred architecture, all the components of place, path, and organization – as well as symbolic content, sensual engagement, and experience – are potently synthesized. The sacred place "delivers" the divine while simultaneously "connecting" to the divine – that is why sacred architecture has enjoyed its predominant and preeminent status for so long.

The Immaterial, Nature, and the Built Environment

I have suggested throughout this book that substantially understanding sacred architecture depends on recognizing the mediating roles it performed. However, I would like to expand this perspective by suggesting that even though it employed material means, its effects were essentially *immaterial*. In other words, the "thingly-real" experience of the sacred place engages us and leads to a type of "coition with the world." In religious or spiritual experiences, separation is eased – connection maximized. That is their power, and consequently the power appropriated and embodied by sacred architecture. The result is an essentially *im-mediate* (Latin, *immediatus*), or *unmediated* experience – the repositioning of oneself to others, the environment, and the transcendent, which has been a perennial concern of religion. It is in the capacity of the material setting to lead to immaterial experiences that the power of sacred architecture lays.

Unmediated experiences where unity with the divine is believed to have occurred, of course, do not depend on architectural settings and constitute part of the literature of mystical sects and practices. For example, the eighth-century Chinese poet Li T'ai-po describes the immediate presence of being in a natural setting in "Zazen in the Mountain":

> The birds have vanished into the sky,
> And now the last cloud drains away.
> We sit together, the mountains and me,
> Until only the mountain remains.[3]

Nature writers (so-called) often describe experiences of the wild that are transcendent and transforming (and at times employ architectural imagery to expand their points). In the words of Gary Snyder:

> Some of us have learned much from traveling day after day on foot over snowfields, rockslides, passes, torrents, and valley floor forests, by "putting ourselves out there" . . . For those who would seek directly, by entering the primary temple, the wilderness can be a ferocious teacher, rapidly stripping down the inexperienced or the careless. It is easy to make the mistakes that will bring one to an extremity. Practically speaking, a life that is vowed to simplicity, appropriate boldness, good humor, gratitude, unstinting work and

play, and lots of walking brings us close to the actually existing world and its wholeness.[4]

Barry Lopez describes engaging children in nature as follows:

> The door that leads to the cathedral is marked by a hesitancy to speak at all, rather to encourage by example a sharpness of the senses. If one speaks it should only be to say, as well as one can, how wonderfully all this fits together, to indicate what a long, fierce peace can derive from this knowledge.[5]

And Annie Dillard writes about a transformation of perception resulting from focused presence:

> It was sunny one evening last summer at Tinker Creek; the sun was low in the sky, upstream. I was sitting on the sycamore log bridge with the sunset at my back, watching the shiners the size of minnows who were feeding over the muddy sand in skittery schools. Again and again, one fish, then other, turned for a split second across the current and flash! The sun shot out from its silver side. I couldn't watch for it. It was always just happening someplace else, and it drew my vision just as it disappeared: flash, like a sudden dazzle of the thinnest blade, a sparkling over a dun and olive ground at chance intervals from every direction. Then I noticed white specks, some sort of pale petals, small, floating from under my feet on the creek's surface, very slow and steady. So I blurred my eyes and gazed towards the brim of my hat and saw a new world. I saw the pale white circles roll up, roll up, like the world's turning, mute and perfect, and I saw linear flashes, gleaming silver, like stars being born at random down a rolling scroll of time. Something broke and something opened. I filled up like a new wineskin. I breathed an air like light; I saw a light like water. I was the lip of a fountain the creek filled forever; I was ether, the leaf of the zephyr; I was fleshflake, feather, bone.
>
> When I see this way I see truly. As Thoreau says, I return to my senses.[6]

For Emerson, it was the moments of unmediated experience where divinity was most significantly engaged. Nature was the primary source for these engagements, an "organ through which the universal spirit speaks to the individual, and strives to lead back the individual to it."[7] His insistence on a more authentic and unmediated religion found its most potent expression in *An Address* to the Harvard Divinity School in 1838, where he castigated ministers for their over-reliance on scripture and the historical Christ. He recounts a service during which a snowstorm raged outside the windows of the church, where "the snowstorm was real; the preacher merely spectral."[8] Emerson goes on to state that "Preaching in this country . . . comes out of the memory, and not out of the soul,"[9] and "It is the office of a true teacher to show us that God is, not was; that

He speaketh, not spake."[10] In "Nature," Emerson states that a "lover of nature" engages in "intercourse with heaven and earth," and asks why one should not enjoy the "original relation to the universe," that is often described in scripture. Nature, which for Emerson was the entire phenomenal world, is the means to do so, where one can "come to look at the world with new eyes."

So how does this leave (or lead to) architecture? I would like to suggest two distinctions regarding the primacy of nature as the "temple" or "cathedral" where unmediated "unity" with the divine (within or without) is believed to be possible. First of all, we make distinctions between the natural and the built environments and, in doing so, fail to recognize that they are all environments. In other words, "natural" and "built" environments constitute the complete environment of which we are all a part. The materials and performance of any humanly made artifice are a product of, and contingent upon, the natural environment. Second, the built environment, as we observed in some of the previous examples, not only responded to its natural contexts but also aspired to replicate pertinent aspects of the natural world. As the architectural theoretician Norman Crowe states, "The man-made world is an alternative nature, so to speak, created by artifice and born as a human reflection of the wonder we find in the natural world – the heavens, the seasons, landscapes and seascapes, plants and animals."[11] Furthermore, as I suggested earlier, replications of the cosmos in sacred architecture were intrinsic to its mediating roles and served to explicate and elucidate the world and our place in it. However, as we have observed, these were not the only symbolic and communicative roles assigned to sacred architecture. In many examples, especially in important state architecture, socio-political, doctrinal, scriptural, and historical content were embodied. In this context we can move beyond Goethe's formal characterization of architecture as "frozen music" and describe it instead as "material culture." In doing so, we recognize why architecture has enjoyed its status as a pre-eminent cultural production and has played predominant symbolic roles for much of the history of human civilization. It is through understanding, to the best of our abilities, these often-complex roles, that new perspectives might be gained to inform how (and why) we build today.

Authenticity

The study of history and its architectural artifacts has value only in its capacity to provide lessons applicable to the problems we face today. They are not frozen artifacts that are of interest only as explanations of how we arrived at the present, disconnected from the thoughtful making of architecture and place. This historical compartmentalization reveals the prejudices of the scientific and positivistic orientation of our age that sees time and history as linear. Of course, time and events occur sequentially, but our relationship to the past and its artifacts is much more dynamic than this limited worldview suggests. The applicability of the strategies, formal relationships, and symbolic media learned from historical artifacts depends, in part, on valuing authenticity. One could argue that because significant sacred architecture is embedded in broad cultural and religious foundations that, by tradition, utilize a clearly articulated shared language; one might argue that they are more authentic than other, less agenda-driven examples. Of course, this depends on what values and definitions one applies to the question of authenticity.

I would argue that the most inauthentic architecture has little understanding regarding the contexts from which it emerged and upon which it is dependent. This includes idiosyncratic examples that are possible only if one is either ignorant or insensitive to one's own value systems. The one-size-fits-all moniker of "creativity," often applied indiscriminately in architecture and other design disciplines, serves as a means to ignore or circumvent the contexts within which we inevitably operate. I would also add, that just as unconscious fears and urges play themselves out in unhealthy ways in interpersonal relationships, an unreflective architecture is, at worst, built neuroses. In this context, recognizing our architectural intentions is essential to authentic design. It is only through establishing a critical relationship with our prejudices – a critical distance – that we may create places grounded in the multiple contexts of which they are a part. In other words, unrecognized personal prejudices tend to marginalize, trivialize, or obviate the environmental, social, physical, historical (and other) contexts, in the same way that narcissism truncates deep connections in relationships with others. Both are, by definition, self-referential.

Michael Benedikt provides a helpful context regarding authenticity when he outlines four essential elements of "realness" in architecture – "presence, significance, materiality, and emptiness." For Benedikt, a building has "presence" when it is both self-aware and "seems attentive to our presence"; "significance" when it engages us directly (instead of referring to something else); "materiality" when it uses materials appropriate to their specific qualities; and "emptiness" when it generously provides something, often ephemeral, beyond the confines of program and site.[12] Engaging and generous architecture have been themes throughout this book, but it is Benedikt's definition of "emptiness" that deserves to be expanded. I would like to suggest that our orientation and approaches need to be both "radical" (pertaining to fundamentals) and "extravagant" (transgressing boundaries).[13] Authentic architecture, like other authentic cultural outputs, is deeply embedded in its contexts in complex, multitudinous, and multivalent ways.[14] It leads both inward and outward. It is through interpreting past and contemporary architecture in an expansive, engaged, and non-dogmatic manner that we might discover the means to create a more authentic architecture. The Buddhist concept of "no self" does not deny our temporal, embodied consciousness; it simply repositions it within a much larger and interconnected context. And, as one's boundaries of self expand, so does one's engagement with others. Similarly, the more expansive and inclusive architecture is, the more its creation is a selfless act, and the more it can provide for multiple interpretations and generous interactions.

Architecture and Transformation

One danger in any study that features historical examples to illustrate the potency, significance, and meaning of architecture is that readers may misconstrue the examples as exemplars. That is not my intention. Even though at times I have been deeply moved, inspired, and instructed by the buildings and places included in this study, I am more interested in explicating the essential, engaging roles they perform. All of which is to reassert the cultural significance of architecture and, in this context, reposition our contemporary understandings of it. Each age builds its aspirations, authority, and, in some cases, neuroses. In significant examples, sacred architecture effectively serves to elucidate, inspire, and potentially transform. As Gadamer insists, "We do not encounter a work of art without being transformed in the process." If there is any reliable historical continuity in architecture, I would argue that it is its potential to engage, inform, and transform us.

Architecture, according to some proponents, has the ability (or, at least, potential) to improve us, to "change our life."[15] In this context, we might deepen our interpretive approaches through considering other self-improvement practices such as psychotherapy and Buddhist meditation practices. The discursive methodologies of the former and, in particular, the depth psychology of the Jungian tradition, aim to reveal formerly hidden aspects of our psyches as a means to bring greater integration and presumably meaning, purpose, and happiness to our lives. The latter depends on methodological attention to our thoughts, feelings, and bodily sensations (primarily through meditation), as a means to cultivate awareness of our habitual behavior patterns and pre-understandings. We read in the *Majjhima Nikaya, the Middle Length Discourses of the Buddha* of the Pali Canon, that the *dhamma* is a practical, not metaphysical "raft" though which one might "pierce through this net of conceptual projections in order to see things as they really are."[16] Both methods use the media of talk and observation (though in different amounts and applications) to reveal what was formerly hidden and thus aid in establishing broader contexts for one's life. Analogously, I suggest that it is the potential of architecture, as a material (not metaphysical) artifact, to assist those who are committed to a more substantial and authentic engagement with the world – where the world becomes "both brighter and less burdensome."[17]

Practices of hermeneutics, phenomenology, Buddhism, Transcendentalism, and psychotherapy can be vehicles that carry one to see and experience the world in expanded ways. It is my assertion that, in part, sacred architecture was often created in the hope or belief that, whether through inspiration, exhortation, or coercion, it would be a transformative agent. The power of architecture to touch, affect, instruct, and change one is, of course, a central theme of this study, but I would like to expand on this to suggest two issues relevant to contemporary concerns regarding the creation of meaningful, authentic architecture. First, the interpretive and reflective practices applied in this study have the potential to bring broader awareness to the multiple contexts, imperatives, and roles of architecture. The result may not be a "changed" mind, but one that has been broadened. Our fundamentally inclusive inquiries do not aim at "either–or" dichotomies, but "both–and" integrations. And, second, in this process of inquiry, there is the potential that we will be changed, will become more aware of our presumptions and intentions, and consequently the conceptualization and creation of a more substantially "context-embedded" architecture (in all of its forms) may be possible.

How might we frame approaches that respond to these revivified perspectives regarding the potent and deeply embedded roles architecture can play?

First of all, in the context of phenomenology and hermeneutics, we recognize that the most affective and effective architecture is one that "touches" us. When we say we "see" something, we usually mean we have some understanding of it – but when we say we are "touched" – by beauty, art, and architecture – we usually mean that we have been more deeply engaged by (and with) it, and understand it in deeper and broader ways. I am suggesting that if we are to create places that connect with us in this way, we need to change our perspectives regarding how (and why) we build. In essence, we need to build from the same place where we are most deeply affected. We need to incorporate our souls and hearts, as much as our intellects. We need to "make love" (an inherently creative act) when we "make architecture."

Of all the arts, historically significant architecture has the ability to hold the past and the present simultaneously, a true hermeneutic circle. And because we physically experience it with our bodies (most potently through ritual), "feel it," and are "touched by it," phenomenology comes into play. We may be "informed" by sixth-century descriptions of the history, use, and symbols of the Hagia Sophia, but we come to "understand" it when we stand in its central space on a particular day, at a certain time of our lives, and in relationship to others. Places like this do not deserve to be beaten into relative significance according to the social and political limitations of its time, and diminished by the cultural platform of our time. I would argue that the full contexts of the Pantheon, the Hagia Sophia, or the Selimiye help us to understand the positive *and* negative conditions *of* their time from our present position, but do not diminish their importance *to* our time. Religious architecture, like religion itself, can be misunderstood in the cultural relativism of contemporary culture. This study adopts the position that religion is not as much about "faith" or "belief" as our contemporary culture would have us believe, but actively engenders "transformation." Analogously, even though most of the examples in this study have played roles of reinforcing the faith and beliefs of their time, they also were agents and mediators that lead the lay and devout alike to see the world in different ways. That was (and is) their power.

I have included examples that were designed and built, in part, as models of the cosmos, as perfected worlds that represented the perfection attributed to the divine. However, this predominant emphasis should not limit our understandings and exclude the fact that sacred architecture is often messy, conflicted, and, at times, aggressive. What almost all examples share is the fact that at one or multiple levels, they are enticing and engaging. In this context, it would be inappropriate to hold them against some measurement of beauty because often they are not beautiful, at least according to the often-vague metrics of today. Nor do they always align with attributions of being peaceful or even meaningful – the embracing and comforting of its acolytes were not always the first agendas of sacred architecture (or religion). One only needs to spend an afternoon in the complex, confrontational, and contested spaces of the Church of the Holy Sepulchre to appreciate this. What places like these are, however, is enlivening – through a variety of means and media they confront and engage us, often viscerally. Because their separate nature brings us to a different physical place, they have the potential to lead us to a changed ontological position. I am not arguing that they are always or uniformly successful at this, but that this is a consistent, though typically unspoken, agenda. What this perspective suggests is that we can free ourselves from self-imposed notions of beauty in the making of architecture when we recognize the broader agencies and operations of the built environment. Anyway, ideals of perfection, like religious piety, typically mask deep internal contradictions, and are fraught with misunderstandings and danger.

Philosophical Foundations

Interpretations of architecture, to approach a modicum of comprehensiveness, need to synthesize multiple viewpoints, perspectives, and components. It is essential that any analysis or interpretation of the built environment recognizes the positions, presumptions, prejudices, and presuppositions we bring to any discursive, didactic, analytic, or design activity. However, it is equally important that we take a position. There need to be reasons for the particular choices we make. In this study, it is the sensual engagement, elucidative and transformative roles of sacred architecture, and the broadened perspectives that it can bring to contemporary culture and its artifacts that I am especially concerned with. It is the philosophical foundations upon which our efforts to build rest that are preeminent, not particular methodologies (though they can be helpful). As Gadamer insists, any "concentration on method can conceal much that art and history has to teach us."[18]

That said, taking my inspiration from the sign-posted way of Buddhism,[19] I next briefly outline elements that might comprise an engaging and authentic architecture.

First of all, we recognize that any significant architecture is rarely (if ever) neutral. Instead it has the ability to improve our individual and collective lives through facilitation, elucidation, and incorporation. This occurs at a number of different levels: it is functional – the architecture provides appropriate spaces for the activities it serves; it is healthy – the architecture supports the health and well-being of its users; it is experiential – the architecture offers uplifting, challenging, or calming places; it is elucidative – the architecture communicates implicit and explicit meanings that enrich our lives; and it is communal – the architecture provides places for shared activities and connections.

To further describe the often active engagements of architecture, its mediating roles can also be outlined, this time under two principal headings of *energizing* and *calming qualities*. The *energizing qualities* comprise *enticement*, *dynamic relationships*, and *reciprocal engagement*. Enticement is the ability of architecture to invite us to participate in the game of interactions with its surfaces and within its spaces. Even though it may not always make access easy, or usher us in gently, there is always a visual and spatial invitation to enter and engage in some form of discourse or intercourse. Entrances have the capacity to entrance us. Dynamic relationships occur at both formal and metaphysical levels. We have observed how spatial sequences and symbolic narratives were often put into the service of the multifaceted agendas of sacred architecture. However, there were often other articulate relationships upon which the potency of the place depended. For example, the act of building is often a mediation between the past and the present – a "constant interaction between our aims in the present and the past to which we still belong."[20] Other relationships are also at play in the form of the socio-political and cultural agendas often crystallized by the architecture. And in reciprocal engagement, the setting and its content are expanded and completed through ritual – from solitary prayer to communal processions. Here, the architecture provides the setting for the ritual and the ritual completes the symbolic meanings embodied by the setting.

The *calming qualities* necessary for efficacious architectural settings are *order*, *coherence*, and *beauty*. A defined order of the form, surfaces, spaces, and sequences of architecture is essential to its successful engagement and mediation. As we have observed in numerous examples, the application of geometry and proportion often served to create a unified whole for both formal and symbolic reasons. The coherence of the architecture is its effectiveness in establishing relationships between the participant and place and delivering its symbolic content. Even though the content may be occulted, nuanced, complex, or even contradictory, it is typically consistent, at a number of levels, with the overall agendas of the culture or religion it was built to serve. Similar to rhetoric, the "act of speaking well," the media of architecture is employed to "speak" clearly and cogently and, in this way, establish meaning.[21] Lastly, beauty is most likely the most difficult term to define but one where we have bounteous philosophical resources to lean upon. Beauty is not limited to formal and scenographic tableaux, but more importantly can be defined as the ability to lead one to perceive the intrinsic beauty of the world. For Plato, beauty mediated between the perceptual world and the ideal world of "forms." In the words of Gadamer, "the ontological function of the beautiful is to bridge the chasm between the ideal and the real."[22] It is both anagogical and transformational.

Broadened Contexts

We have observed that the center is not only the destination, but also a threshold that mediates between the known and the unknown – the mundane and the celestial. At Bollingen, symbols were rendered in surface, form, and space, and mediated between the past and future, the earthy and the spiritual, and led Jung to deeper understandings of himself and his place in the world. It was through the media of architecture and art that Jung negotiated the questions that he was presented with. After the death of his wife, he reflected that "it cost me a lot to regain my footing, and contact with stone helped me."[23] For Jung, the material of art and architecture led to the immaterial of deeper engagement and understanding. In essence, it mediated between present and future understandings. From a Buddhist perspective, once the vehicle (in our case, art and architecture) has served its purpose, it can then be discarded. In the *Majjhima Nikaya*, there is the well-known story that describes the raft of the *dhamma* as a vehicle for "passing over" to the other side. Once there, however, the raft should be abandoned, "being for the purpose of crossing over, not for the purpose of grasping."[24] Thoreau similarly describes the media of art as essentially a spiritual practice:

> The true poem is not that which the public read. There is always a
> poem not printed on paper, coincident with the production of this,

stereotyped in the poet's life. It is what he has become through his work. Not how is the idea expressed in stone, or on canvas or paper, is the question, but how far it has obtained form and expression in the life of the artist.[25]

This offers an intriguing perspective regarding the mediating role of architecture that allows us to simultaneously see it as an essential vehicle but one that only has value in its ability to lead us to new perspectives.

In the dominant Western concepts of linear time, past, present, and future are conceived as distinct separate entities and the passage of time as a relentless progression of autonomous events. Within these cultural bounds, one traverses their individual interval of time separately, the days parsed out by the quantified expectations of one's "life-span." In this context, others are viewed as occupying parallel trajectories, their starting and ending points different, their pasts and present individual and separate. It is easy to see how acquisitive and egocentric perspectives can emerge from these cultural assertions – and how alienating and stupefying it can be. I would posit that sacred architecture has a long and distinguished history of addressing and seeking to resolve these enduring paradoxes of the human condition. We have illustrated in examples as diverse as Neolithic burial mounds, Korean Zen Temples, and Ottoman mosques how time in sacred architecture is both collapsed and expanded. Here ancestors and the cosmos are embodied – are present – and the individual finds themselves part of a much larger context. The authority of sacred architecture to "speak" articulately depends, in part, on its success in embodying memory. Like the Greek goddess Mnemosyne, it derives its power from its ability to connect the present with the past.

Dependent on this, and other connections, is the establishment of critical relationships. Calibrating relationships within formal compositions is a common architectural design strategy. Through measure, proportion, and geometry, for example, we articulate the relationships between parts, as in the composition of elevations. What is often not considered are the immaterial relationships equally essential to an articulate architecture. I have noted that objects alone do not create meaningful connections – it is only through interaction, a dialectical dance, that the coition between one and the environment is possible. It is in this manner that the architectural setting is truly completed. In the dynamics of human relations seeing oneself not as much as singular but in relationship to others is the result of emotional maturity, and when one occupies this middle zone of interrelationship, the anxiety of maintaining rigid self-conceptions expand into a broader context. Analogously, a mature architecture selflessly created to create multivalent relationships with the world and others, is essentially polysyncretic – its presence dependent on the totality of its experience and meaning.

Visualizing architecture as a transducer offers another perspective in service of expanding a too often formally and visually prejudiced discipline. Antidotes to the presumptions we can bring to the creation of architecture are desperately needed in a built environment often dominated by self-referential, dislocated objects. Our prevalent ways of building may be rationalized by explaining them as contemporary cultural artifacts, but this is only one side of the relationship, which fails to recognize the ability of architecture to influence its cultural setting, a reciprocal relationship that has traditionally been part of its power. Repositioning architecture in this way may aid in transforming predominant values that are often uncritically held. As Thoreau reminds us,

> There are architects so called in this country, and I have heard of one at least possessed with the idea of making architectural ornaments have a core of truth, a necessity, and hence a beauty, as if it were a revelation to him. All very well from his point of view, but only a little better than the common dilettantism. A sentimental reformer in architecture, *he began at the cornice, not at the foundation.*[26]

Thoreau's insistence on authentic experience and essential places perhaps offers a foundation for a broadened context of architecture. That the mundane, the sensual and the ideal are integrated in his philosophy is not surprising given its Transcendentalist roots. Thoreau noted that "the shallowest still water is still unfathomable."[27] In the conclusion of *Walden*, he recalls an Indian parable that speaks about the relative positions of creative endeavors and the potential of art to effect transformation:[28]

> There was an artist in the city of Kouroo who was disposed to strive after perfection. One day it came into his mind to make a staff. Having considered that in an imperfect work time is an ingredient, but into a perfect work time does not enter, he said to himself, It shall be perfect in all respects, though I should do nothing else in my life. He proceeded instantly to the forest for wood, being resolved that it should not be made of unsuitable material; and as he searched for and rejected stick after stick, his friends gradually deserted him, for they grew old in their works and died, but he grew not older by a moment. His singleness of purpose and resolution, and his elevated piety, endowed him, without his knowledge, with perennial youth. As he made no compromise with Time, Time kept out of his way, and only sighed at a distance because it could not overcome him. Before he had found a stock in all respects suitable the city of Kouroo was a hoary ruin, and he sat on one of its mounds to peel the stick. Before he had given it the proper shape the dynasty of the Candahars was at an end, and with the point of the stick he wrote the name of the last of the race in the sand, and then resumed his work. By the time he had smoothed and polished the staff Kalpa was no longer the pole-star; and ere he had put on the ferule and the head adorned with precious stones, Brahma had awoke and slumbered many times. But why do I stay to mention these things? When the finishing stroke was put to his work, it suddenly expanded before the eyes of the astonished artist into the fairest of all creations of Brahma. He had made a new system in making a staff, a world with full and fair proportions; in which, though the old cities and dynasties had passed away, fairer and more glorious ones had taken their places. And now he saw by the heap of shavings still

fresh at his feet, that, for him and his work, the former lapse of time had been an illusion, and that no more time had elapsed than is required for a single scintillation from the brain of Brahma to fall on and inflame the tinder of a mortal brain. The material was pure, and his art was pure; how could the result be other than wonderful?[29]

Broadened environmental, temporal, and symbolic agendas in architecture are certainly not new – the Egyptians, at particular times and in often complex and multivalent ways, articulated expansive worldviews. The Late Kingdom Mortuary Temple of Queen Hapshepsut (Deir el-Bahri) in West Thebes incorporates its mountain backdrop and aligns its causeway with the ceremonial way at the Temple of Amun at Karnak across the River Nile. The aligned causeways of these

10.1

Thebes, general site plan showing alignment of causeways at Queen Hapshepsut's Mortuary Temple (Deir el-Bahri) and the Temple of Amun

Source: Drawing by Richard Tobias by permission of Oxford University Press.

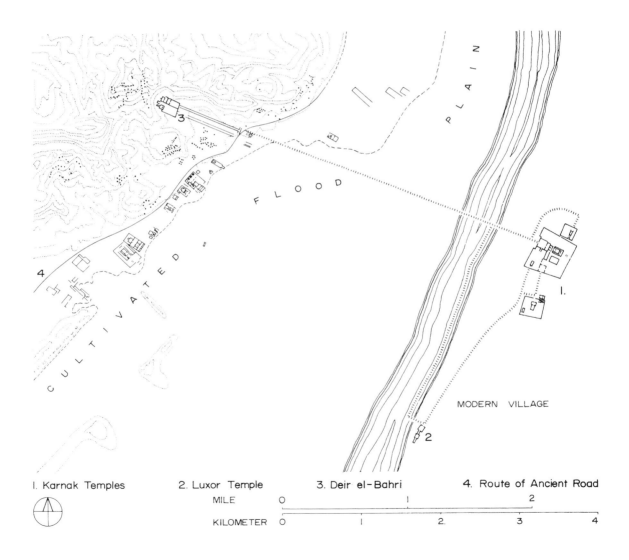

I. Karnak Temples   2. Luxor Temple   3. Deir el-Bahri   4. Route of Ancient Road

MILE   O   1   2

KILOMETER O   1   2.   3   4

two extensive temples occupy a space of over 3 miles, and the path at Queen Hapshepsut's Temple ascends three terraces by means of a series of ramps. The lower terraces were planted with myrrh trees and the final terrace included a colonnaded court flanked by chapels. The Queen's inner sanctum lay beyond, carved into the solid rock of the mountain. Once a year the Festival of the Valley was held during which Amun, the principal god of this time, symbolically journeyed from his temple in the east to the land of the dead in the west. In this way the aligned causeways mediated between the living and the dead; the participants and the immortal gods (including the queen). The temple also mediated between the Nile and the mountain and appropriated its vast environmental setting of earth, mountain, water, and sky. Its arboreal imagery replicated a primordial paradise garden, and thus mediated between the past, present, and future, deepened by the rituals of the Festival of the Valley. The result was a timeless place, that today still stretches across the Nile at a scale visible from space, and through architecture, symbolism, and meaning, articulates its place in the world.

As he straddled the worlds of life and death, corporal existence and nirvana, the Buddha told his disciples,

> Be lamps onto yourselves
> Rely on yourselves and do not depend on external help
> Hold fast to the truth as to a lamp
> Seek salvation alone in the truth.[30]

Emerson said: "Art is the path of the creator to his work," and, in the conclusion to "Nature," urges us to consider the following:

> Every spirit builds itself a house; and beyond its house a world; and beyond its world, a heaven. Know then, that the world exists for you. For you is the phenomenon perfect. What we are, that only can we see. All that Adam had, all that Caesar could, you have and can do. Adam called his house, heaven and earth; Caesar called his house, Rome; you perhaps call yours, a cobbler's trade; a hundred acres of ploughed land; a scholar's garret. Yet line for line and point for point, your dominion is as great as theirs, though without fine names. Build, therefore, your own world.[31]

A broadened context of architecture occupies an expansive territory that includes its power to engage, connect, inform, and transform. As a cultural artifact that embodies religious axioms and beliefs, incorporates historical and socio-political conventions, and facilitates individual and communal rituals, sacred architecture synthesizes experience, symbolism, and meaning. As I have argued, it traditionally served as an intermediary between humans and the gods that represented their collective aspirations for knowledge, understanding, and purpose. Recognizing this lineage offers potent foundations upon which to build – a lamp of inner light and illumination. Consequently, we may build, in the words of the Buddha, with "a heart so full of love it resembles space."[32] From a hermeneutic perspective, somewhere in between the multifarious forces, agendas, and incarnations of sacred architecture lies the "truth" of evocative, elucidative, and transformative architecture. In this in-between zone between the old and the new, the traditional and the innovative, the visceral and the cognitive, the emotional and the rational, lies the promise of timely, authentic, and meaningful architecture.

Chapter 11

Closing Thoughts

Personal Experiences of Place

11.1
Saint Benedict's Abbey, Vaals,
view of cemetery path

I had left the noon Good Friday service at Vaals and walked outside to the gardens behind the monastery. The voices of the monks, the sung mass expressing the sadness and loss symbolized by this holy day, still reverberated as I walked uphill along the wide tree-lined path. Ahead I could see the simple graveyard where van der Laan is buried. The day was overcast but suddenly the sun pierced a space between the clouds and illuminated the slice of earth where I stood. Shadows vibrated on the moss-covered surface of the path and the world was instantly vivified in a manner that struck me right in my chest. I started to cry. A few tears at first, then heaving sobs as I staggered upward. It was not sadness but a different kind of joy. I only stopped when I noticed one of the brothers behind me, a tall black-robed figure striding through the sun and shadow. We chatted briefly, my face unashamedly still wet with tears. A few days later we spoke again and he said that what I had experienced was God bursting into my heart and I agreed. The church, the mass, the path, the light and shadow – my apprehension and fatigue – all had coalesced at that moment. The sun parted the clouds and had opened my heart.

There have been other immediate experiences of place, which have revealed meanings that otherwise would have remained hidden.

Part of the *madrasa* of the Sulemaniye complex in Istanbul looks like a ruin. Its entrance is on a street lined with shops below the mosque. It seemed impossible to gain access to, but the more shopkeepers my assistants and I talked to, the more our hopes were raised. We learned that a man lived there with his family but that he didn't like visitors. We banged on the door – no response. We drank tea in a nearby shop and discussed ideas: perhaps he will pass this way today? Or one of his children will come out? Soon it seemed the entire street was helping us, but without success. Then just as we had given up and were walking away, someone shouted "He's here!" and, after an initially guarded conversation, he smiled and opened the door. Inside was a courtyard surrounded by cells that artfully stepped down the slope. The classroom was adjacent to the entrance, and on the inside of its dome were fragments of original paintings – colorful, twined plant forms. Finally, a clue that perhaps revealed what the dome at the Sokollu Kadirga would have originally looked like! I'm not sure, however, if I really understood it then, or when I tasted the ripe strawberry my friends had plucked from the garden in the courtyard – architecture and sweetness became one.

It is an odd thing to sing in a tomb, but the Tomb of Clytemnestra is a perfect place to do so. She was a victim at the end of a tragic cycle that completed the curse placed on the house of Atreus. The city of Mycenae was founded by Perseus and eventually passed into the hands of the house of Atreus where Clytemnestra lived in the palace with her husband Agamemnon. According to the popular story, she and her lover murdered him in his bath after he returned from the siege of Troy. She in turn was murdered by her son Orestes, who was then tormented by the Furies until Athena gave him reprieve. Adultery, murder, torments – tragic events resulting from human passion are part of who we are and of this ancient place. But the cool, rainy winter day that I was there, I sang joyfully. The hive-shaped *tholos* has wonderful acoustics for amplifying and reverberating an untrained voice like my own. And so a place built for quiet entombment and sealed by ritual and material is also, within a short span of cosmic time, a place of spontaneous, passionate, song.

My stays in Korean monasteries were intense periods of experiential-scholarly research paired with regular meditation practice. Throughout the day, I sketched, photographed, and observed, participated in the ritual life of the monastery, and meditated in the temples and my room. The first bell was rung at 3.00 a.m., a cadence of gongs produced by the rhythmic swinging of a massive wooden pole hung horizontally from the rafters of the Bell Tower, ending with seven measured rings – then silence. I would walk silently to the temple for the first service of the day, bowing and chanting with the monks. One stay was at Magok-sa, a small, remote monastery located in the mountains near Gongju. My simple room opened onto the river that bent around the main temple complex, and I would end the day meditating in front of the door, the silence deepened by the murmuring of the water. One night, at dusk, after the last bell was rung, I took a walk. While crossing the monastery's main bridge, I looked into the almost-still water and saw a school of orange carp, glowing in the subdued light, as they swam together. Suddenly the boundaries between myself, the fish, and all of which we are a part, lessened. Somewhere my embodied consciousness understood that the individual fish only exists as part of its larger context – and that when one dies, it is only one small part of a timeless whole. At that moment there was a silent recognition of the reciprocity of life and death, and a deeper understanding of my position in the world. Later, I came upon a small calico cat, staring intently at the water as it sat on a rock in the river. I paused, and we sat together, the cat and me, until . . .

The path may symbolize the journey, the pilgrimage, the spiritual quest, but it is the sacred place, the center in all its forms, that ultimately performs the role of leading one to another perspective, another way of being in the world. It points to other realities, to new centers and places. My research and writing, viewed from a hermeneutic perspective, are both objective and quantifiable interpretations of sacred architecture, and a path of deepening my own inner development and understandings. For me, the study, experience, and making of architecture, like any contemplative, engaging, and creative enterprise, provides potent opportunities for personal growth and expanded understandings.

I am most interested in what lies between. The spaces between past and future; objective and subjective; sensual and conceptual; material and immaterial – that are not one or the other, but both. The realm of ideas, Emerson reminds us, is one that endures, is timeless. And the sensual world provides the ever-present condition of coition with the environment of which we are inseparably joined. For me, the packed agendas of sacred architecture expands my intellect in space and time – and the "thingly-real" of their sensual enticement engages me in the moment-to-moment awareness of the surprising, amazing, and audacious experience of being alive and our shared human consciousness. It is in the in-between, in Gadamer's words, that "the work speaks to us as a work," and we might experience the dynamics of a living architecture, and can recognize the Buddhist perspective of the "deathless state" of the ever-present. In these moments boundaries collapse, past and present fuse, and separations of self dissolve. Other and I are one.

Any understandings I have gained regarding the meaning and significance of architecture have depended on the scholars who have walked the path before me, and the places where I have been privileged to spend memorable times. It is my hope that this book may offer encouragement to others along their own journeys of discovery, and that the built environment might be conceptualized and made better for it.

Notes

1 Introduction

1 Mircea Eliade, *Symbolism, the Sacred and the Arts*, ed. D. Apostolos-Cappadona, New York: Continuum Publishing Company, 1992, p. 107.
2 Psalms 13.1.
3 Psalms 10.1.
4 Genesis 3.24.
5 Matthew 7.14.
6 Hans-Georg Gadamer, *The Relevance of the Beautiful*, Cambridge: Cambridge University, 1986, p. 26.
7 See Dalibor Veseley, *Architecture in the Age of Divided Representation: The Question of Creativity in the Shadow of Production*, Cambridge, MA: MIT Press, 2004.
8 Gadamer, op. cit., p. 9.
9 Robert Mugerauer, referencing the work of Hans-Georg Gadamer, describes this middle ground as a "fusion of horizons, where the past and present contexts come together to make something new of living value." Robert Mugerauer, *Interpreting Environments: Traditions, Deconstruction, Hermeneutics*, Austin, TX: The University of Texas Press, 1995, p. xxxi.

2 The Middle Ground of Interpretation

1 David Abram, "The Invisibles," *Parabola,* Vol. 31, No. 1, Spring 2006.
2 Diane Ackerman, *A Natural History of the Senses*, New York: Random House, 1990, p. xvii.
3 Kent Bloomer and Charles Moore, *Body, Memory and Architecture*, New Haven, CT and London: Yale University Press, 1977, p. 33, and Juhani Pallasmaa, *The Eyes of the Skin: Architecture and the Senses*, London: Academy Editions, 1996., p. 29.
4 Ackerman, op. cit., p. xix.

5 The Dalai Lama, *The Universe in a Single Atom: The Convergence of Science and Spirituality*, New York: Random House, 2005, p. 169.

6 Steen Eiler Rasmussen, *Experiencing Architecture*, Cambridge, MA: MIT Press, 1959, p. 33.

7 According to Juhani Pallasmaa, "The senses define the interface" between us and our environment, but he also offers an appropriate inversion of the reciprocity of our senses and the environment when he states, "Architecture is the art of reconciliation between ourselves and the world, and this mediation takes place through the senses." Pallasmaa, op. cit., pp. 29 and 50.

8 Ibid., p. 48.

9 Ibid., p. 35.

10 Ibid., pp. 37–42.

11 David Abram, *The Spell of the Sensuous*, New York: Random House, 1996, p. 55.

12 Pallasmaa, op. cit., pp. 9–10.

13 Ibid., p.13.

14 Ibid., p. 22.

15 See David Levin, *Modernity and the Hegemony of Vision*, Berkeley, CA: The University of California Press, 1993.

16 Shunryu Suzuki, *Zen Mind, Beginner's Mind: Informal Talks on Zen Meditation and Practice*, New York and Tokyo: John Weatherhill, Inc., 1970, p. 78.

17 Joanna Richardson, Ed., *Selected Poems, Baudelaire*, Harmondsworth: Penguin Books, 1975, pp. 61–62.

18 Marcel Proust is often cited regarding the memories evoked by tea and "petites madeleines" he describes in *Du côté de chez Swaan* (*Swaan's Way*), 1913.

19 Abram, op. cit., p. 2.

20 Durmot Moran, *Introduction to Phenomenology*, London: Routledge, 2000, p. 4.

21 In the section entitled "The Temple" from *The Origin of the Work of Art*, Heidegger does specifically describe a typical "Greek Temple." The capacity of architecture to disclose aspects of its physical setting and reveal their ontological significance is perhaps his most important contribution. See Neil Leach, *Rethinking Architecture: A Reader in Cultural Theory*, London: Routledge, 1997, p. 98.

22 See Michael Hayes, Ed., *Architecture Theory Since 1968*, Cambridge, MA: MIT Press, 2000, p. 463.

23 Edmund Husserl, "Material Things in Their Relation to the Aesthetic Body," in *Ideas Pertaining to a Pure Phenomenology and to a Phenomenological Philosophy*, Book 2: *Studies in the Phenomenology of Constitution,* included in Donn Welton, Ed., *The Body: Classic and Contemporary Readings*, Oxford: Blackwell, 1999, p. 12.

24 According to Pallasmaa, Merleau-Ponty "pointed out an osmotic relation between the self and the world – they interpenetrate and mutually define each other – and emphasized the simultaneity and interaction of the senses." Pallasmaa, op. cit., p. 11.

25 Christian Norberg-Schulz points out that Heidegger was explicit in claiming that this essay was not "about architectural ideas," and that "Heidegger did not leave us any text on architecture." See Christian Norberg-Schulz, "Heidegger's Thinking on Architecture," in *Architecture: Meaning and Place, Selected Essays*, New York: Electa/ Rizzoli, 1988, pp. 39–48.

26 Christian Norberg-Schulz, *Genius Loci: Towards a Phenomenology of Architecture*, New York: Rizzoli, 1979, p. 5.

27 Ibid., p. 8.

28 Ibid., p. 6.

29 Alberto Perez-Gomez, *Built Upon Love: Architectural Longing after Ethics and Aesthetics*, Cambridge, MA: MIT Press, 2006, p. 109.

30 Ibid., p. 3.

31 Ibid., p. 5.

32 Ibid., p. 28.

33 The antidote for Perez-Gomez is love. Love describes a more fruitful orientation in the making and experience of architecture. Love describes the uplifting experience of beauty as the font of inspiration. Building with love also describes an ethical position and suggests a means to achieve connection and provide meaning. Love is physical attraction and desire to fully experience the beloved, and thus is temporal, a process of delay and fulfillment. Lastly, love is the carnal and the erotic, recognition of the body's experience of place and its potential to lead one to a deeper understanding of one's place and purpose in the world.

34 Perez-Gomez, op. cit., p. 100.

35 Pallasmaa, op. cit., p. 13.

36 Bloomer and Moore, op. cit., p. 76.

37 Also, quasi-objective renderings of Christian scripture, based on appropriations of select historical contexts, were being used to further particular ideological arguments.

38 Ken Wilber, *The Marriage of Sense and Soul*, in *The Collected Works of Ken Wilber*, Vol. 8, Boston: Shambhala Publications, 2000, p. 186.

39 Ibid.

40 See Abram for a succinct summary of intersubjectivity to which this section is indebted. Abram, op. cit., pp. 37–39.

41 See Wilber, op. cit., Chapter 9, and *A Sociable God*, Chapter 1, in *The Collected Works of Ken Wilber*, Boston: Shambhala Publications, 2000.

42 The German philosopher Hans-Georg Gadamer (1900–2002) earned his Doctorate in Philosophy at the University of Marburg under the supervision of Martin Heidegger. He spent most of his career teaching at the University of Heidelberg and played key roles in revitalizing and redefining philosophy in postwar Germany. His major work *Truth and Method* was published in 1960 and, in part, provided perspectives and approaches to history untainted by the misappropriations during the National Socialism dictatorship. Language as a media of communication and as a cultural artifact was a continuing theme in his work.

43 Hans-Georg Gadamer, *The Relevance of the Beautiful*, Cambridge: Cambridge University Press, 1986, p. 26.

44 Jean Grondin, *The Philosophy of Gadamer*, Montreal: McGill-Queen's University Press, 2003, p. 46.

45 Quoted in ibid., p. 48.

46 Gadamer, op. cit., p. 19. John Dewey presents a similar argument in *Art as Experience*, New York: G.P. Putnam's Sons, 1934/1980, pp. 7–8.

47 Adrian Snodgrass and Richard Coyne in *Interpretation in Architecture: Design as a Way of Thinking*, London: Routledge, 2006, also make this point. See p. 7.

48 Lindsay Jones, *The Hermeneutics of Sacred Architecture*, Vol. 1: *Monumental Occasions, Reflections on the Eventfulness of Religious Architecture*, Cambridge, MA: Harvard University Press, 2000, p. 29.

49 Ibid., p. 19.

50 Ibid., p. 10.

51 Robert Mugerauer, *Interpreting Environments: Traditions, Deconstruction, Hermeneutics*, Austin, TX: The University of Texas Press, 1995, pp. xxvi–xxxii.

52 Lewis E. Hahn, Ed., *The Philosophy of Hans-Georg Gadamer*, Chicago and La Salle, IL: Open Court Publishers, 1997, p. 34.

3 Practices of Connection

1 Hans-Georg Gadamer, *The Relevance of the Beautiful*, Cambridge: Cambridge University Press, 1986, p. 32.

2 As Lindsay Jones, referencing Gadamer, states, "every human experience in which people learn, grow, or otherwise allow themselves to be transformed in significant ways – including the experience of ostensibly religious art and architecture – is an occasion of hermeneutical interpretation." Lindsay Jones, *The Hermeneutics of Sacred Architecture*, Vol. 1: *Monumental Occasions, Reflections on the Eventfulness of Religious Architecture*, Cambridge, MA: Harvard University Press, 2000, p. 5.

3 Quoted in Lewis E. Hahn, Ed., *The Philosophy of Hans-Georg Gadamer*, Chicago and La Salle, IL: Open Court Publishers, 1997, p. 29.

4 See David Tracy, "Traditions of Spiritual Practice and the Practice of Theology," *Theology Today*, July 1998.

5 Robert D. Richardson, Jr., *Emerson: The Mind on Fire*, Berkeley, CA: The University of California Press, 1995, p. 250.

6 Quoted in ibid., p. 250.

7 Quoted in ibid., p. 258.

8 Brooks Atkinson, Ed., *The Complete Essays and Other Writings of Ralph Waldo Emerson*, New York: The Modern Library, 1950, p. 6.

9 Ibid., p. 88.

10 Ibid., p. 93.

11 Ibid., p. xxii.

12 From the journals of Ralph Waldo Emerson, quoted by Richardson, op. cit., p. 283.

13 Henry David Thoreau, *Walden*, ed. Gordon S. Haight, Roslyn, NY: Walter J. Black, Inc., 1942, p. 153.

14 In the *Majjhima Nikaya, the Middle Length Discourses of the Buddha*, the seven "Taints to be removed by developing" are described as follows.

> What taints Bhikkhus, should be abandoned by developing? Here a bhikkhu, reflecting wisely, develops the mindfulness enlightenment factor, which is supported by seclusion, dispassion and cessation, and ripens in relinquishment. He develops the investigation-of-states enlightenment factor . . . the energy enlightenment factor . . . the rapture enlightenment factor . . . the tranquility enlightenment factor . . . the concentration enlightenment factor . . . the equanimity enlightenment factor, which is supported by seclusion, dispassion, and cessation, and ripens in relinquishment.
>
> (Bhikkhu Nanamoli and Bhikkhu Bodhi (trans.), *The Middle Length Discourses of the Buddha: A Translation of the Majjhima Nikaya*, Boston: Wisdom Publications, 1995, 2.21, pp. 95–96)

The American Buddhist teacher Jack Kornfield outlines Theravada perspectives on the "Seven Factors of Enlightenment" in Joseph Goldstein and Jack Kornfield, *Seeking the Heart of Wisdom: The Path of Insight Meditation*, Boston and London: Shambhala Publications, 1987, pp. 61–77.

The two main schools of Buddhism are Theravada and Mahayana. Theravada, found mostly found in Southeast Asia, has traditionally been the more Orthodox. Mahayana expanded from India to Nepal, China, Korea, and Japan, and traditionally has been the more heterodox school. (A third school, an offshoot of Mahayana, is Tantra, and is found mostly in Nepal and Tibet.) Mahayana Buddhism arrived in China in the early sixth century, where it influenced, and was influenced by, Taoism and

Confucianism. Buddhism came to Korea in the sixth century, and to Japan, by means of China and Korea, in the early seventh century.

15 In his first sermon after achieving enlightenment, the Buddha outlined the "Four Noble Truths" – that life was "suffering" (or "unsatisfactory"), that the cause of suffering was grasping for self-protective desires and ignorance about connections outside our self, that overcoming the delusion of a separate self frees us from suffering, and that the "Eightfold Path" is the means to achieve this. The Eightfold Path comprises three categories – morality, which includes right speech, action, and livelihood; meditation, which includes right effort, mindfulness, and concentration; and wisdom, which includes right understanding and resolve.

16 Jack Kornfield and Paul Breitner, *A Still Forest Pool: The Insight Meditation of Achaan Chah*, Wheaton, IL: Quest Books, 1985, p. 51.

17 Reiho Masunaga, *A Primer of Soto Zen: A Translation of Dogen's Shobogenzo Zuimonki*, Honolulu: The University of Hawaii Press, 1971, p. 24.

18 Goldstein and Kornfield, op. cit., pp. 64–65.

19 Nancy Wilson Ross, Ed., *The World of Zen: An East–West Anthology*, New York: Random House, 1960, p. 117.

20 Quoted in *Inquiring Mind*, Vol. 25, No. 2, Spring 2009. Translation by Jane Hirshfield and Mariko Aratani.

21 Jones, op. cit., pp. 29 and 41.

22 Thoreau, op. cit., p. 39.

23 Paul F. Boller Jr., *American Transcendentalism 1830–1860: An Intellectual Inquiry*, New York: G.P. Putnam's Sons, 1974, p. 1.

24 From Emerson's Journal of 1837, quoted by Boller, op. cit., p. 33.

25 Emerson, "The Transcendentalist," in Atkinson, op. cit., p. 89.

26 Their interests, however, were not unrelated to European traditions, in particular Romanticism, which included aspects of philosophies of the "Orient." See Arthus Versiuis, *American Transcendentalism and Asian Religions*, New York: Oxford University Press, 1993, p. 7.

27 D. Lopez, Ed., *Buddhist Hermeneutics*, Honolulu: University of Hawaii Press, 1988, p. 3.

28 Ibid., p. 5.

29 Ibid., p. 2.

30 Ken Wilber, *The Marriage of Sense and Soul*, in *The Collected Works of Ken Wilber*, Vol. 8, Boston: Shambhala Publications, 2000, p. 192.

31 However, Norberg-Schulz's definition of place is almost entirely environmental, neglects other important considerations, and truncates the ability of his philosophy to address contemporary issues of place and meaning. See Christian Norberg-Schulz, *Genius Loci: Towards a Phenomenology of Architecture*, New York: Rizzoli, 1979, p. 6.

32 Ibid., p. 23.

33 Thoreau, op cit., p. 114.

34 Ken Wilber, *One Taste*, in *The Collected Works*, op. cit., p. 429.

4 Mediating Elements

1 Dalibor Veseley, *Architecture in the Age of Divided Representation: The Question of Creativity in the Shadow of Production*, Cambridge, MA: MIT Press, 2004, p. 8.

2 Karsten Harries provides a typology of symbols aligned with his theoretical interests (and not applicable to all examples). He cites *natural symbols* (the archetypal cave, stone, and cromlech), *conventional symbols* (commonly accepted forms such as the cross and the pyramid), the *authority of texts* (the relationship of religious texts and

sacred space, as in the Bible and the Gothic Cathedral), and lastly *play with symbols of the past* (as in post-modernist pastiche and pluralism). Karsten Harries, *The Ethical Function of Architecture*, Cambridge, MA: MIT Press, 1998, pp. 130–132.

3 The over-reliance on surface symbolism (or, one might argue, signs), is what ultimately makes the often, formal and symbolic mélange of post-modern architecture, in all of its forms, insubstantial.

4 However, formal and spatial evidence, though it has clear scholarly limitations, is an essential component of any study that aims to describe the experience and meaning of architecture. Unfortunately, formal analysis is often viewed as a goal and not a means to the analysis of architecture. An analysis of a symphonic performance, which addressed only the technical execution of the musicians to the exclusion of the historical context and contemporary interpretations of the work, to give just two examples, would obviously be incomplete. Furthermore, a strictly formal analysis is not unlike the swift and precise butchering of a hog – the parts may be efficiently revealed but the life (and soul) of the being are lost. (For this analogy I must give credit to my former colleague at Manchester Metropolitan University, Joe Jessop, who perhaps was thinking of Plato who states in *Timaeus and Critias* that objective approaches "cut nature at its joints, like a good butcher.")

5 C.G. Jung, Ed., *Man and His Symbols*, New York: Dell Publishing Co. Inc., 1968, p. 4.

6 Hans-Georg Gadamer, *The Relevance of the Beautiful*, Cambridge: Cambridge University Press, 1986, p. 31.

7 Ibid., p. 32.

8 Earl Baldwin Smith, *Architectural Symbolism of Imperial Rome and the Middle Ages*, Princeton, NJ: Princeton University Press, 1956, p. 3.

9 Rudolf Arnheim, *The Dynamics of Architectural Form*, Berkeley, CA: The University of California Press, 1979.

10 Stephen Holl, Juhani Pallasmaa, and Alberto Perez-Gomez, *Questions of Perception: Phenomenology of Architecture*, Tokyo: A + U: Architecture and Urbanism, 1994, p. 45.

11 From "Nature," in Brooks Atkinson, Ed., *The Complete Essays and Other Writings of Ralph Waldo Emerson*, New York: The Modern Library, 1950, p. 13.

12 From the *Upanishads*, quoted by Joseph Campbell, *The Hero with a Thousand Faces*, Princeton, NJ: Princeton University Press, 1949, p. 22.

13 Ibid., FN 21, p. 104.

14 Adapted from the *Sutta-nipata*. Jack Kornfield and Gil Fronsdal, trans., *Sulta-nipata: The Teachings of the Buddha*, Boston: Shambhala Publications, 1993, p. 30.

15 Lindsay Jones, *The Hermeneutics of Sacred Architecture*, Vol. 1, Cambridge, MA: Harvard University Press, 2000, p. 98.

16 Ibid., p. 99.

17 See William MacDonald, *The Pantheon*, Cambridge, MA: Harvard University Press, 1976.

18 William H. Coldrake, *Architecture and Authority in Japan*, London: Routledge, 1996, p. 3.

19 In the words of Lindsay Jones:

> Built forms, irrespective of contemporaneous textual evidence, can tell us a great deal more about empirical, historical religious sentiments and priorities than scholars have been willing to concede. Architecture is a peculiar sort of cultural production, but it need not, as the disparaging assignation "mute text" implies, be judged as inherently lower, weaker or crippled documentary resource to which one retreats only in the absence of the certainty that written texts alone can provide.
>
> (Jones, op. cit., p. xxv)

20 John 14.6.

21 John 10.9.

22 Timothy 2.5.

23 Thomas Barrie, *Spiritual Path – Sacred Place: Myth, Ritual and Meaning in Architecture*, Boston: Shambhala Publications, 1996, pp. 166–180.

24 Pier Vitebsky, *The Shaman, Voyages of the Soul: Trance, Ecstasy, and Healing from Siberia to the Amazon*, Boston: Little Brown and Co., 1995, pp. 60–61.

25 David Abram, *The Spell of the Sensuous*, New York: Random House, 1996, p. 7.

26 Ibid., p. 95.

27 Luke 24.13–16.

28 Luke 24.31. Herman Hesse also eloquently describes the process of revelation in *The Journey to the East*. Here the narrator, a member of a secret society, embarks on a sacred quest, only to lose his companions and his faith along the way. Only years later does he find his way back, though at first he is blind to God. His guide, the "servant" Leo, leads him on a lengthy, circuitous walk through the city, "by way of the strangest and most capricious detours," a walk that could "have been done in a quarter of an hour," but instead took all morning. Finally he arrives at the destination, and is ushered into the great hall of The League, where his blindness is lifted and hubris dissipated when Leo is revealed as its President.

29 Herman Hertzberger, *Lessons for Students in Architecture*, Rotterdam: Uitgeverij 010 Publishers, 1991, p. 32.

30 Aldo van Eyck, Herman Hertzberger, Addie van Roijen-Wortmann, and Francis Strauven, *Aldo van Eyck, Hubertus House*, Amsterdam: Stichting Wonen, 1982, p. 45.

31 Robert Mugerauer, *Interpreting Environments: Traditions, Deconstruction, Hermeneutics*, Austin, TX: The University of Texas Press, 1995, p. 119.

32 Christian Norberg-Schulz, *Intentions in Architecture*, Cambridge, MA: MIT Press, 1965, p. 179.

33 Christopher Alexander, *A Pattern Language*, New York: Oxford University Press, 1977, p. xiii.

34 Holl *et al.*, op. cit., p. 45.

35 The archetypal marking of a center has been much discussed by Mircea Eliade and others.

36 René Daumal, *Mount Analogue: A Novel of Symbolically Authentic Non-Euclidean Adventures in Mountain Climbing*, trans. Roger Shattuck, Boston: Shambhala Publications, 1992, p. 5.

37 George Michell, *The Hindu Temple: An Introduction to Its Meaning and Forms*, Chicago: The University of Chicago Press, 1977, p. 61.

38 See Barrie, op. cit.

39 Pilgrimage, a tradition employed by all of the world's major faiths, is an elongated journey that traverses a middle ground from the profane to the sacred. The temporal nature of the journey aids the pilgrim in spiritual preparation. The approaches, gateways, thresholds, passages, and spaces of sacred architecture often recreate the pilgrimage path through a rich spatial sequence and symbolic narrative. Pilgrimage is a journey that symbolizes passage from one mode of being to another. In Christianity, pilgrimage is a sacred time during which the three-fold path of purgation, illumination, and union are traversed. During the Middle Ages Christian pilgrimage became firmly established and highly codified through the belief in the redemptive power of relics and the architecture that housed them. The principal destinations were Jerusalem, Rome, and the Cathedral of Saint James in Santiago de Compostella. Four routes led from Northern and Eastern France; and along the way important churches were built and monasteries established.

40 The birth of the Buddha, in some traditions, falls on the first full moon in May and

corresponds to the mythical time of his miraculous birth to Queen Maya in the Lumbini Gardens. It is a time when Buddhists celebrate the Buddha's last rebirth as the Sakyamuni Buddha and his enlightened state at birth. The Jewish Passover, also a spring festival, celebrates the "passing over" of the plagues that God inflicted on the Egyptians as recounted in Exodus, and the deliverance of Jews from slavery. It is a joyful holiday that symbolizes emancipation and rebirth. Christian Easter celebrations are similarly linked to scripture and are a time of symbolic death and rebirth. All of these are heirs to spring festivals that date from pre-history, and reflect the environmental and symbolic "rebirth" of the earth from the "death" of winter.

41 Ritual has always served the purpose of allaying anxiety, from annual rituals associated with the harvest, to daily religious observances. Because anxiety is part of the "human condition," we need rituals to bridge our separateness, to feel connected to something beyond ourselves, and to establish a sense of purpose to our lives. According to Spiro Kostof, "Public architecture at its best [is] . . . a setting for ritual that makes each user, for a brief moment, a larger person that he or she is in daily life, filling each one with the pride of belonging." Spiro Kostof, *A History of Architecture: Settings and Rituals*, New York: Oxford University Press, 1985, p. 41.

42 A term that Lindsay Jones uses.

43 Peter Nabokov and Robert Easton, *Native American Architecture*, Oxford: Oxford University Press, 1989, p. 361.

44 The Telesterion at Eleusis, for example, was dedicated to the Goddess Demeter and provided a potent setting for the Cult of Eleusis and the performance of the Eleusinian mysteries.

45 Genesis 28.17.

46 Analogous examples are found in Pharaonic Egypt and Medieval Japan. In Egyptian mythology, the first people emerged from a divine oasis, the "first place" of primordial time where humans and the gods were not separated. This was represented by the hypostyle halls characteristic of Late Kingdom Pylon Temples through reference to the sacred grove where Isis gave birth to Horus, a symbol of fecundity and resurrection. In the hypostyle hall massive stone columns in the form of lotus buds and flowers supported a stone roof, the underside of which was painted to depict a starry night sky. Pure Land Buddhism in late Medieval Japan visualized an idealized post-mortem paradise garden set in the west and "surrounded with golden nets, and all round covered with lotus flowers made of all the precious things." The royal family built the Phoenix Hall of Byodo-in, near Kyoto, during a time when their political authority was being eclipsed by the military. This Shinden Style pavilion is set on the western shore of a pond in an extensive stroll garden and features a gilded statue of the Amida Buddha on a lotus flower dais surrounded by murals and architecture that symbolize the western paradise of The Pure Land.

47 The village of Conques is built on the slopes of a remote valley of the Dourdou River – the word *conque* from *cirque* means "cavity" which succinctly describes its environmental setting.

48 Charlemagne had a special affinity for Conques and its young saint, and was said to have visited many times. As the word of miracles spread, the pilgrims increased and the coffers of the church grew. In the tenth century the cult statue of Saint Foy was begun, and today can be seen in the adjacent museum. It is a strangely androgynous, gold-leafed figure, decorated with gems and glass, and slightly reclining on a small throne. It is not the only artifact in the museum, however, which displays an astonishing array of riches.

49 Pilgrims typically traveled in large groups for both safety and camaraderie.

5 Symbolic Engagements

1 From a letter of 1947. Gerhard Adler, *Selected Letters of C.G. Jung, 1909–1961*, Princeton, NJ: Princeton University Press, 1953, p. 77.

2 Karsten Harries, *The Ethical Function of Architecture*, Cambridge, MA: MIT Press, 1998, p. 136.

3 Juhani Pallasmaa, *The Eyes of the Skin: Architecture and the Senses*, London: Academy Editions, 1996, p. 43.

4 Carl Gustav Jung (1875–1961) was the protégé of Sigmund Freud, but came to distinguish himself from his older mentor and found a distinctive school of analytical psychology. Jung's "depth psychology" refers to his interest in exploring what he came to call "the unconscious" – the hidden or repressed aspects of the psyche. Jung's analysis employed the interpretation of dream symbolism, a process of interpreting archetypal symbols to bring understanding to one's life that was, in part, a hermeneutical exchange. It is interesting to note that the grandfather for whom he was named converted to Protestantism after immersing himself in the writings of Schleiermacher, the founder of hermeneutics.

5 Spiro Kostof, *A History of Architecture: Settings and Rituals*, New York: Oxford University Press, 1985, p. 21.

6 The movements and times of arrival of the migrating herds were mysterious and therefore preparation, enactment, and conclusion of the hunt became a ritualized activity. The ritualization of the hunt had multiple symbolic components: to "guarantee" the abundance of the animal gods and "secure" their return; to "resolve" the paradox of death providing life; to expiate the "sin" of killing the god; to objectivize the act of killing the "father figure"; or simply to appease the animal gods. As far as we know, only humans have the need to address the paradox of killing another being so that one may have life. It is a potent combination; a life-sustaining god that must die at our hands, and it has been the fuel burned by the arts since symbolism was first given life by our hands.

7 Jacob Bronowski, *The Ascent of Man*, Boston: Little, Brown and Company, 1973, p. 54.

8 According to Joseph Campbell, caves such as Lascaux were settings for ritual initiations. Here "shamans" guided young men from being boys to hunters. Rituals were enacted which illustrated the importance, danger, and excitement of hunting the great bulls, and the skills needed to become useful members of the hunting parties.

9 Attributed to Margaret Naumburg in the 1940s.

10 Jung called it *The Red Book* as it came to be bound in red leather. Inside were a collection of paintings and text that were the result, in part, of Jung's inner work during the time he was "confronting the unconscious."

11 Jung defined the Collective Unconscious as follows:

> Besides these we must include all more or less intentional repressions of painful thoughts and feelings. I call the sum of all these contents the "personal unconscious." But, over and above that, we also find in the unconscious qualities that are not individually acquired but are inherited, e.g., instincts as impulses to carry out actions from necessity, without conscious motivation. In this "deeper" stratum we also find the . . . archetypes . . . The instincts and archetypes together form the "collective unconscious." I call it "collective" because, unlike the personal unconscious, it is not made up of individual and more or less unique contents but those which are universal and of regular occurrence.
>
> (From the *Structure and Dynamics of the Psyche*, cited in A. Jaffé, Ed., *Memories, Dreams, Reflections*, by C.G. Jung, New York: Random House, 1961, pp. 401–402)

12 Jaffé, op. cit., p. 196.

13 Ibid., p. 199.

14 There have been many architects in the Jung family. Jung's daughter Gret married a Baumann, which means builder, and a number of Baumanns have been architects. Jung's only son, Franz, failed at medical school, but went on to be a successful architect in Zurich, after qualifying in the offices of his cousin in Stuttgart. Deirdre Bair, *Jung: A Biography*, Boston: Little, Brown and Company, 2003, pp. 318–20. Daniel Baumann, an architect who currently practices in Zurich, hosted the author at Bollingen.

15 Robert Mugerauer, *Interpreting Environments: Tradition, Deconstruction, Hermeneutics*, Austin, TX: The University of Texas Press, p. 16.

16 Clare Marcus, *The House as Symbol of Self*, Berkeley, CA: Conari Press, 1995.

17 Jaffé, op. cit., p. 21.

18 Jung came to see Freud's inability to satisfactorily analyze the dream and his reluctance to fully engage Jung in his own dreams as the beginnings of their eventual professional and personal split.

19 Jaffé, op. cit., pp. 158–159.

20 Ibid., p. 174

21 Ibid., pp. 173–175.

22 Deirdre Bair, *Jung: A Biography*, Boston: Little, Brown and Company, 2003, p. 299.

23 Jung's first choice for property was an island on Lake Zurich, which was the site of the former monastery of St. Gallen that included a revered hermitage of St. Meinrad. The purchase was apparently blocked by the local community who viewed the site as sacred and therefore inappropriate for the controversial "mind doctor." The site Jung eventually bought in 1922 had also been held by the monastery, but apparently had less significance as the sale went through. Bair, op. cit., p. 322. As recounted by Barbara Hannah:

> It was not easy . . . to find the right site. He remained true to the upper Lake of Zurich, which even now has remained real country with few houses on its shores. It proved so difficult to find the right piece of land that he even thought of buying some land above Bollingen which had a magnificent view of the lake and the mountains . . . but he never really meant to build anywhere but on the shore of the lake for, as he said in Memories, "It was settled from the start that I would build near the water."
>
> (B. Hannah, *Jung, His Life and Work: A Biographical Memoir*, New York: G.P. Putnam's Sons, 1976, p. 147)

24 There was a train line and road nearby when Jung purchased the land. Jung, who did not drive a car until later in life, often took the train, but his preferred means was to sail a small sailboat from his house in Kusnacht. As recalled by Barbara Hannah, the rail line actually served as an effective boundary between his land and the outside world.

25 Jaffé, op. cit., p. 226.

26 Marcus Vitruvius Pollio wrote:

> It was the discovery of fire that originally gave rise to the coming together of men, to the deliberative assembly, and to social intercourse. And so, as they kept coming together in greater numbers into one place, finding themselves naturally gifted beyond other animals in not being obliged to walk with faces to the ground, but upright and gazing upon the splendour of the starry firmament, and also being able to do with ease whatever they choose with their hands and fingers, they began in that first assembly to construct shelters. Some

made them of green boughs, others dug caves on mountainsides, and some, in imitation of the nests of swallows and the way they built, made places of refuge out of mud and twigs.

(Vitruvius, *The Ten Books of Architecture*, trans. M. Morgan, New York: Dover Publications, Inc., 1960, pp. 38–39)

Marc-Antoine Laugier described the virtues of the primitive hut in his *Essay on Architecture* published in 1753 (in a manner reminiscent of Vitruvius), and argued that it provided an exemplar applicable to the creation of principles of architectural style and composition. He states that: "All the splendors of architecture ever conceived have been modeled on the little rustic hut I have just described. It is by approaching the simplicity of this first model that fundamental mistakes are avoided and true perfection is achieved" (W. Herrmann and A. Herrmann (trans.), *An Essay on Architecture by Marc-Antoine Laugier*, Los Angeles: Hennessey and Ingalls, Inc.,1977, p. 12).

27 T. Hayashiya, M. Nakamura, and S. Hayashiya, with Joseph P. Macadam (trans.), *Japanese Arts and the Tea Ceremony*, New York/Tokyo: Weatherhill/Heibonsha, 1974, pp. 29–30.

28 This letter was written in 1965, five years after the building was completed. Christine Bochen, Ed., *The Courage for Truth: The Letters of Thomas Merton to Writers*. Quoted in Robert Lipsey, "'How I Pray is Breathe': Thomas Merton in the Hermitage Years," *Parabola*, Vol. 31, No. 1, Spring 2006.

29 Jaffé, op. cit., p.160.

30 E.A. Bennet, *Meetings with Jung*, Zurich: Daimon, 1985, p. 118.

31 Jaffé, op. cit., p. 223.

32 The courtyard provided the privacy that Jung depended on at Bollingen. His introverted personality needed periodic seclusion, and the walls and loggia that surrounded the courtyard effectively blocked views from the lake. A gateway to the courtyard is even overlooked by a small window in the loggia. When the weather was warm enough, Jung often cooked over the fireplace in the loggia.

33 Aniela Jaffé, Ed., *C.G. Jung: Word and Image*, Princeton, NJ: Princeton University Press, 1979, p. 136. Jung also had this statement carved on his tombstone.

34 Jaffé, *Memories*, op. cit., p. 195.

35 Sacred sites such as at Angkor and Borobudur have been described as built mandalas. In the case of the latter, a circumambulating path passes through a series of gateways and passages until reaching the top and sacred center of this important Buddhist pilgrimage site.

36 Jaffé, *Memories*, op. cit., p. 196.

37 Ibid., p. 196.

38 Elijah had appeared in the fantasies of Jung's inner work and represented "intelligence and wisdom." Ibid., pp. 181–182. Elijah is the messianic figure, described in the final chapter of the Old Testament and represents the emergence of higher consciousness. Malachi 4.5.

39 Goethe was a consistent reference point for Jung and family stories suggested that he was related to this important eighteenth-century German philosopher, scientist and statesman, though this lineage was never proven. See Jaffé, *Memories*, op. cit., pp. 35–36n and p. 234. See also Bair, op. cit., pp. 650–651n.

40 Jaffé, *Memories*, op. cit., pp. 183–184.

41 Wayfarers and travelers were under Jupiter's protection.

42 Mercury, also called Hermes, was also known as the messenger god and an interpreter. The term hermeneutics is derived from Hermes. A. Snodgrass and R. Coyne, *Interpretation in Architecture: Design as a Way of Thinking*, London: Routledge, 2006, p. 12.

43 The origins of this carving are described in detail in a letter to Ignaz Tauber in 1960. Gerhard Adler, *Selected Letters of C.G. Jung, 1909–1961*, Princeton, NJ: Princeton University Press, 1984, p. 196.

44 Jaffé, *Memories*, op. cit., p. 226.

45 Ibid., p. 31.

46 A quote from the fourteenth-century alchemist Arnaldus de Villanova.

47 They were also employed as memorials to the patrons of their cities.

48 According to the myth, Asclepeius learned to bring the dead back to life through the medium of the Gorgon's blood. Zeus saw this as a challenge to the gods and killed him, but he was transformed into stars and so became a god himself.

49 An important early center was located on the Aegean island of Kos.

50 The Asklepeion was built below the acropolis site of Pergamon at a place that had been known before Hellenistic times as a healing site. It was during the reign of Hadrian, however, that its function as a hospital took its most complete and potent form. The enclosed complex was entered by means of a sacred way and propylon and included a library, theater, a cylindrical temple dedicated to Asclepeius, baths built around a sacred spring, and a cylindrical treatment building.

51 Jaffé, *Memories*, op. cit., p. 233.

52 Mugerauer, op. cit., pp. 16 and 19.

53 Adler, op. cit., p. 190.

54 In his clinical work, he often led patients to understand what they were experiencing in the present as a means to confront their psychic disturbances. E.A. Bennet recalled a conversation where

> [Jung] referred to the comfort a patient got from an idea that his illness was because of something in the past, in the parents perhaps. But he has the illness now. If a man has a bullet in his leg he may find out who shot the bullet, but he has it in his leg and it is this which must be dealt with.
>
> (Bennet, op. cit., p. 28)

This recalls a teaching of the Buddha in the Sutta 63 of the *Majjhima Nikaya*.

55 Quoted in Claire Dunn, *Carl Jung: Wounded Healer of the Soul*, New York: Parabola Books, 2000, p.108.

56 Bennet, op. cit., p. 27.

57 Hannah, op. cit., p. 199.

58 It was paired with his house in Kusnacht, which served as an outer manifestation of Jung's persona and was the setting of his outer-directed professional and familial life. The Bollingen house, in contrast, allowed Jung to explore the hidden, unconscious, mythological, and timeless aspects of his being. As Mugerauer states, "Together the two houses strengthened each dimension of Jung's personality and made an opening for the integration that they now memorialize." Mugerauer, op. cit., p. 26.

59 Bennet, op. cit, p. 99.

60 According to Jung, another manifestation of Mercury was as Merlin of the Grail Legend who came to be associated the "spiritus mercurialis . . . the sought-after arcanum of the alchemists." Jaffé, *Memories*, op. cit., p. 313

61 According to Mugerauer, Jung's building of Bollingen "made an opening for the gradual manifestation of and integration with the timeless." Mugerauer, op. cit., p. 27.

62 Jaffé, *Memories*, op. cit., p. 355.

63 Ibid., p. 237.

64 Gaston Bachelard, *The Poetics of Space*, trans., Maria Jolas, Boston: Beacon Press, 1969, p. 6.

65 When the author visited Bollingen with family members, this was the only inaccessible room.

66 Introduction to "The Religious and Psychological Problems of Alchemy," in Violet Staub de Laszlo, *The Basic Writings of C. G. Jung*, New York: The Modern Library, 1959, p. 446.

67 Marcus, op. cit., p. 50.

6 Earth and Sky

1   *New York Times* obituary of Jaquetta Hawkes by Mel Gussow, March 21, 1996.

2   Mircea Eliade, *A History of Religious Ideas*, Vol. 1, *From the Stone Age to the Eleusinian Mysteries*, trans. William Trask, Chicago: The University of Chicago Press, 1978, p. 13. Italics in original.

3   Ibid., p. 115.

4   Ibid., p. 13.

5   Spiro Kostof, *A History of Architecture: Settings and Rituals*, 2nd edn., New York: Oxford University Press, 1995, p.23.

6   Eliade, op. cit., p. 13.

7   As an amalgam of the birth channel, the cave also symbolized places of rebirth, often accompanied by initiatory rituals. Dreams set in caves suggest a desire to explore the hidden depths of the psyche. H. Biederman, *Dictionary of Symbolism: Cultural Icons and the Meanings Behind Them*, New York: Meridian/Penguin Group, 1992.

8   Kostof, op. cit., p. 35.

9   Ibid.

10 Ibid., p. 240.

11 According to Lindsay Jones, the history of architecture contains a "fabulous abundance and diversity of extravagant religio-architectural manifestations of the fascination, fear and awe of death – tombs, vaults, sepulchers and sarcophagi, morgues, mausoleums, gallows and graves." Lindsay Jones, *The Hermeneutics of Sacred Architecture*, Vol. 1: *Monumental Occasions, Reflections on the Eventfulness of Religious Architecture*, Cambridge, MA: Harvard University Press, 2000, p.153.

12 Ibid., p. 180.

13 Ibid., p. 173.

14 Agrarian cultures produced cults of the dead and necropolises in part because of the connection between the cycles of life and death in the vegetative and human worlds. Eliade, op. cit., p. 116.

15 Ibid., p. 123.

16 According to Rodney Castleden, "The tombs and stone circles [of the British Isles], prove that they had a developed technology, strength of purpose and elaborate and deeply-held system of beliefs." Rodney Castleden, *The Stonehenge People: An Exploration of Life in Neolithic Britain 4700–2000 BC*, London and New York: Routledge, 1990, p. 5.

17 Eliade, op. cit., p.123.

18 Jones, op. cit., p. 159.

19 Castleden, op. cit., p. 185.

20 As Castleden suggests, burial mounds were enduring symbols of "people living in a half-tamed landscape, seeking to forge a covenant with continuity with their short-lived ancestors and with unknown generations to come." Castleden, op. cit., p. 190.

21 Richard Saul Wurman, *What Will Be Has Always Been: The Words of Louis I. Kahn*, New York: Access Press/Rizzoli, 1986, p. 151.

22 Brooks Atkinson, Ed., *The Complete Essays and Other Writings of Ralph Waldo Emerson*, New York: The Modern Library, 1950, p. 670.

23 Quoted in Richard Hayman, *Riddles in Stone: Myths, Archaeology and the Ancient Britons*, London and Rio Grande, OH: Hambledon Press, 1997, p. 193.

24 Castleden, op. cit., p. 156.

25 According to James Loewen. American high school history books are notorious for their selective histories, with many pre-Columbian and non-European events mis-represented or excised. See James W. Loewen, *Lies My Teacher Told Me: Everything Your American History Book Got Wrong*, New York: The New Press, 1995.

26 Our maps demonstrate this, with their dearth of references to ancient sites. In contrast, English Ordnance Survey maps carefully note earthworks, stone circles, Roman roads and forts, and other markings from their pre-English past (though the English have their own selective history).

27 Peter Nabokov and Robert Easton, *Native American Architecture*, New York and Oxford: Oxford University Press, 1989, p. 97.

28 George Milner, *The Moundbuilders: Ancient Peoples of Eastern North America*, London: Thames and Hudson, 2004, pp. 44–45.

29 Nabokov and Easton, op. cit., p. 101.

30 Ibid., p. 96.

31 According to George Milner, the public

> latched onto a singularly strange idea: the existence of a separate race of mound-builders. Fantastic stories flourished in the near absence of solid data, which were slow in coming, and an unwillingness to pursue the little information that was available. Many thought that the moundbuilders originated in distant corners of the world. Others believed they were Native Americans, but an earlier people who had the misfortune of being pushed out by barbarians, who were, in turn, displaced by waves of European settlers. Here was a convenient justification – if one was really needed – to take land that was only thinly populated.
>
> (Milner, op. cit., p. 15)

32 Thanks to John Hancock, Professor of Architecture and Project Director of the Center for the Electronic Reconstruction of Historical and Archeological Sites, College of Design, Architecture, Art and Planning, the University of Cincinnati, for this infor-mation. See *Earthworks: Virtual Explorations of the Ancient Ohio Valley*, CD-ROM, 2007.

33 The Adena were named for an estate where a mound was excavated in 1901. See Milner, op. cit., p. 60.

34 Susan L. Woodward, Susan and Jerry N. McDonald, *Indian Mounds of the Middle Ohio Valley: A Guide to Adena and Ohio Hopewell Sites*, Blacksburg, VA: The McDonald and Woodward Publishing Company, 1986, p. 2.

35 E.G. Squier and E.H. Davis, *Ancient Monuments of the Mississippi Valley: Comprising the Results of Extensive Original Surveys and Explorations*, Washington, DC: The Smithsonian Institution, 1848, p. 47.

36 Ibid., p. 67.

37 Squier and Davis placed Fort Hill and other earthwork enclosures of its type under the category of "Works of Defense," and speculated about how they may have served as defensive enclosures.

38 Across the Scioto River is the Hopeton Earthworks where a large circle and square earthwork connected to the shoreline by parallel embankments suggests connections between these two sites.

39 Both genders were represented in mound sites. Milner, op. cit., pp. 91–92.

40 See Milner, op. cit., p. 64.

41 Today Mound City is a national park, its federal ownership a legacy of a former use as a World War I training and detention center. It was during its time as Camp Sherman

that twelve mounds were leveled and the rest damaged. However, subsequent excavations have revealed valuable artifacts, and it was fully restored and a declared a national monument in 1923.Today it is adjacent to a Federal Prison, the Chillicothe Correctional Institution; its razor wire enclosing an inner ground of another type, but perhaps just as succinctly describing the age in which it was built and the culture that built it.

42 Milner, op. cit., p. 92.
43 Eliade, op. cit., pp. 11–12.
44 Milner, op. cit., p. 79.
45 Attributed to Vaclav Havel.
46 Jones, op. cit., p. 181.
47 Atkinson, op. cit., pp. 670–671.
48 Attributed to Big Thunder of the Wabanakis Nation. T.C. McLuhan, *Touch the Earth: A Self-Portrait of Indian Existence*, New York: Simon & Schuster, 1971, p. 22.
49 McLuhan, op. cit., p. 29.

7 The Sacred Path and Place

1 Edward Conze, Ed., *Buddhist Scriptures*, London: Penguin Books, 1959, p. 232.
2 Thomas Barrie, *Spiritual Path – Sacred Place: Myth, Ritual and Meaning in Architecture*, Boston: Shambhala Publications, 1996, pp. 111–115.
3 According to Lawrence Sullivan, "To better understand a specific work of sacred architecture it needs to be set against the general context of sacred architecture." From the Foreword to Lindsay Jones, *The Hermeneutics of Sacred Architecture*, Vol. 1, *Monumental Occasions: Reflections on the Eventfulness of Religious Architecture*, Cambridge, MA: Harvard University Press, 2000, p. xv.
4 Mircea Eliade, *Patterns in Comparative Religion*, London: Sheed and Ward, 1958, pp. 367–385.
5 A quote misattributed to St. John of the Cross, but actually penned by a translator in his introduction to the "Ascent of Mt. Carmel."
6 Religious beliefs are often symbolized through ritual and typically there is a reciprocal relationship between the rituals and the architectural setting through which belief, ritual, and architecture are interwoven. According to Joseph Campbell, "A ritual is an enactment of a myth." Analogously, religious architecture is essentially "built myth," that both symbolizes a culture's belief systems of its time and accommodates and facilitates the enactment of shared rituals.
7 See Barrie, op. cit.
8 Lauren Artress, *Walking a Sacred Path*, New York: Berkeley Publishing Group, 1995, p. 52.
9 The center at Amiens is marked in a curious way – it is inscribed with the names of the four master builders.
10 Artress, op. cit. pp. 97–98.
11 George Michell, *The Hindu Temple: An Introduction to Its Meaning and Forms*, Chicago: The University of Chicago Press, 1977, p. 66.
12 The author gratefully acknowledges the translation of the Chinese characters by Dong-il, a Sami Monk at Tongdo-sa.
13 There are twelve temple buildings, including the Main Temple, which date from a range of eras. The monastery was significantly damaged during the Japanese invasions of the sixteenth century and many of its buildings have been re-built numerous times.
14 Kusan, *The Way of Korean Zen*, trans. Maritine Bachelor, Boston: Weatherhill, pp. 11–12.

15 Ibid., p. 14.

16 Only recently has Buddhism enjoyed a revival, and today approximately 25 percent of Koreans are Buddhists. The major monasteries belong to the Chogye Order, the largest of contemporary Buddhist sects in Korea. The monasteries are popular tourist destinations – in part because many are located in mountainous national parks. However, even though one sees young and old visiting the monasteries, most of the worshippers are old women. Today many monasteries are active monastic communities, as well as being national treasures and World Heritage Sites.

17 Theravada, the more orthodox branch of Buddhism, stresses the historical Sakyamuni Buddha.

18 Heo Gyun, *Korean Temple Motifs: Beautiful Symbols of the Buddhist Faith*, trans. Timothy Atkinson, Pajubookcity Munbal-li Gyoha-eup, Paju-si, Gyeonggi-do: Dolbegae Publishers, 2000, English version 2005, p. 292.

19 The concept of a non-fixed self is most directly illustrated by the body, which is subject to the constant change of aging and the inevitable decline, sickness, and death. However, Buddhists also view consciousness as ever changing – feelings of pleasure, discomfort, anger, fear, and love come and go, as well as beliefs, ambitions, and goals.

20 *What is Korean Buddhism?*, Seoul: Jogye Order of Korean Buddhism, 2004, p. 209.

21 Robert Buswell, *The Zen Monastic Experience*, Princeton, NJ: The Princeton University Press, 1992, p. 154.

22 Ibid., p. 160.

23 The walled enclosures of Korean monasteries are more symbolic than practical. Unlike Medieval Japan, where there were protracted civil wars and monasteries often served as refuges, Korea had no large-scale internal conflicts until the twentieth century. When monasteries were suppressed during the Joseon Dynasty and attacked by Japanese invaders in the sixteenth century, it was on a scale when any walls were superfluous.

24 Monasteries can range from a small community of Bhikkus (male monks) or Bhikkunis (female monks) to a large resident community and an extensive complex of historically significant structures. The three most significant monasteries in Korea are named the Triple Jewels, according the Buddhist terminology that describes the *Buddha*, *Dhamma* (teachings), and *Sangha* (community of monks). Songgwang-sa, located in Jogyesan Provincial Park in Jeollaman-do province (in Southwest Korea) was founded in 867 CE and is dedicated to the *Sangha*, the followers of the Buddha. Haein-sa, located in Gayasan National Park in Gyeongsangbuk-do province (in Southeast Korea) was founded in the ninth century and includes buildings that house wood blocks for printing the Tripitaka Koreana, the Buddhist sutras, rules, and commentaries, and therefore is dedicated to the *dhamma*, the teachings of the Buddha. Tongdo-sa, located in Gyeongsangnam-do province (in Southwest Korea), is dedicated to the Buddha and contains a main hall that looks over a stupa that is believed to contain a bone from the relics of the Sakyamuni Buddha.

25 Gyun, op. cit., p. 287.

26 Thomas Byrom (trans.), *The Dhammapada: The Sayings of the Buddha*, New York: Vintage Books, 1976. The *Dhammapada* was written in Pali (the canonical language of its time and location), sometime in the third century BCE. *Dhamma* can be translated as "truth" and *pada* as "path."

27 Guardian figures of this type are often found at the entrances to monasteries. Gyun, op. cit., p. 32.

28 Ibid., p. 308.

29 Ibid., p. 277.

30 These guardian figures are identified by the sword, dragon, pagoda, or lute that they hold, and are said to dwell on Mt. Meru – the symbolic center of the world.

31 The monastery's atypical orientation was most likely the result of the topography, though all of the main temple buildings face in the auspicious southern direction.

32 One the left it states, "Many different people live here and so need to live in harmony." On the right, "The way to live in harmony is to follow the rule."

33 The Bell Tower is an essential component of monasteries, where drums, gongs, and bells perform practical and symbolic functions. The life of monks is regulated by daily schedules and annual calendars. The monk's day begins with the sounds of these instruments at 3.00 a.m. played by designated monks and calling the monastic community to the 3.30 a.m. service. A large drum, hung on its side from the rafters, is beaten with wooden sticks, calling the creatures of the earth to hear the *dhamma*. A cloud gong is rung, calling the creatures of the sky; a wooden fish drum, calling all creatures of the water; and, lastly, a massive cast-iron bell is chimed by monks swinging a large wooden pole, symbolically calling all beings suffering in hell realms.

34 Barrie, op. cit., pp. 119–125.

35 Denise Patry Leidy and Robert A.F. Thurman, *Mandala: The Architecture of Enlightenment*, Boston: Shambhala Publications, 1997.

36 The *Lotus Sutra*, or *Sutra of the True Dharma (Which Resembles a White Lotus)*, is the most important Mahayana text. Here the Buddha is no longer limited to a historical figure (as in Theravada), but is an omniscient and omnipresent being at the center of a vast cosmic paradise. Within this cosmology, *Bodhisattvas* occupy separate worlds to guide others to enlightenment. The T'ien-T'ai, or Lotus School, was a sect founded in China in the sixth century CE on the principles of this sutra. John Bowker, Ed., *The Oxford Dictionary of World Religions*, Oxford: Oxford University Press, 1997, pp. 587–589. See also Gyun, op. cit., p. 291.

37 Leidy and Thurman, op. cit., p. 26. According to Leidy, Eight Bodhisattva Mandalas are "among the earliest and most widespread examples of mandala imagery in Asia."

38 The temples to the Medicine, Sakyamuni, and Amitabha Buddhas of the first courtyard, Vairocana, Avalokitesvara, and Maitreya of the second courtyard, and Ksitigarbha and Disciples of the third courtyard.

39 See Buswell, op. cit., pp. 51–52, for a description of the layout of Songgwang-sa and Gyun, op. cit., pp. 285–294.

40 See Barrie, op. cit., Chapter 6, for a complete discussion of the symbolism of Medieval Japanese Zen Buddhist monasteries.

41 Korean culture has been significantly influenced by the hierarchical stratification of Confucianism.

42 See Kusan, op. cit., p. 40.

43 Lindsay Jones suggests that even though sacred architecture "evokes a range of disparate meanings from the heterogeneous constituency that is experiencing it," it also can be understood as providing two "overlapping and contradictory codes" that appeal to both "lay" and the "elite" participants and "engender drastically different 'low' and 'high' (or popular and elite) readings." Jones, op. cit., pp. 31–32.

44 Gyun, op. cit., p. 25.

45 The One-Pillar Gate is often called the "mountain gate" and monks entering the monastery are said to "enter the mountains." See Buswell, op. cit., p. 70.

8 Ordering the World

1 Richard Padovan, *Proportion: Science, Philosophy, Architecture*, London: E & FN Spon, 1999, p. 60.

2 Lindsay Jones, *The Hermeneutics of Sacred Architecture: Experience, Interpretation,*

Comparison, Vol. 2, *Hermeneutical Calisthenics: A Morphology of Ritual-Architectural Priorities*, Cambridge, MA: Harvard University Press, 2000, p. 48.

3   Mircea Eliade, *A History of Religious Ideas*, Vol. 1, *From the Stone Age to the Eleusinian Mysteries*, trans. William Trask, Chicago: The University of Chicago Press, 1978, pp. 70–73.

4   In the Sumerian legend, the world is first ordered by Marduk after he slays Tiamet and splits her corpse in two. In the Egyptian origin myth, the "first place" appears when a sacred mound or lotus appears in the primordial waters – one becomes two.

5   As canonized and administered by the Brahmin priesthood.

6   From the *Upanishads*.

7   Brahma is the creator god who is so omnipotent and omnipresent that he is beyond all worship and thus there are few temples dedicated to him.

8   The square form of the mandala symbolizes the order of the earth – its cardinal points and the positions of the zodiac.

9   The two most important configurations are the 64 and 81 square mandalas, and most late Hindu temples, however detailed, correspond to this system.

10 George Michell, *The Hindu Temple: An Introduction to Its Meaning and Forms*, Chicago: The University of Chicago Press, 1988, p. 71.

11 Ibid., p. 73.

12 Isaiah 40.22. See also E. Baldwin Smith, *The Dome: A Study in the History of Ideas*, Princeton, NJ: Princeton University Press, 1950, p. 86.

13 Kings I, 6.2–3.

14 Isaiah 11.12.

15 Kings I, 6.16–21.

16 Kings I, 6.23–24.

17 Kings I, 6.5–6.

18 Kings I, 8.12–13.

19 The term Shinto comes from the Chinese *Shentao* and means the "way of the gods," and "mystic rules of nature."

20 The diurnal pattern of day and night was the first subdivision, followed by the phases of the moon, the waxing and waning of the yearly cycle of the sun, and the patterns of the movements of the planets and stars. Early architecture served as a bridge between worlds – most importantly between earth and sky – and was built to replicate the divine order of the cosmos.

21 Robert Lawlor, *Sacred Geometry: Philosophy and Practice*, London: Thames and Hudson, 1982, p. 6.

22 Padovan, op. cit., p. 15.

23 This concept is related to the Greek philosophers, from Pythagoras to Neo-Platonists, who viewed the world as governed by an omniscient intelligence, an intelligence that was also reflected in the human mind, making it possible to comprehend the cosmic order. See Richard Tarnas, *The Passion of the Western Mind: Understanding the Ideas That Have Shaped Our Worldview*, New York: Ballentine Books, p. 47.

24 Padovan, op. cit., p. 18.

25 Ibid., p. 33.

26 Ibid., p. 34.

27 Ibid., p. 38.

28 Vitruvius, *The Ten Books of Architecture*, trans. Morris Hicky Morgan, New York: Dover Publications, Inc., 1960, p. 72.

29 The geometry corresponds to the squaring of the circle, where the circumference of the circle equals the perimeter of the square upon which it is superimposed.

30 Vitruvius, op. cit., p. 75.

31 Adrian Snodgrass also describes it as essentially informed by Stoic philosophy. See

Adrian Snodgrass and Richard Coyne, *Interpretation in Architecture: Design as a Way of Thinking*, London: Routledge, 2006.

32 Desmond Lee, trans., *Plato: Timaeus and Critias*, New York: Penguin Books, 1963, p. 29.

33 Plato's maternal great-grandfather.

34 Lee, op. cit., p. 37.

35 *Plato: Apology, Crito, Phaedo, Symposium, Republic,* trans., B. Jowett, ed. Louise Ropes Loomis, Roslyn, NY: Walter J. Black, Inc., 1942, p. 398.

36 Padovan, op. cit., p. 106.

37 Lee, op. cit., p. 44. Italics in original.

38 Lawlor, op. cit., p. 80.

39 Ibid.

40 This golden sectional growth spiral is a form that is found in nature – most notably in the cross-section of a nautilus shell, but also in many plants and animals. See Georgy Doczi, *The Power of Limits: Proportional Harmonies in Nature, Art and Architecture,* Boston: Shambhala Publications, 1981.

41 It was not until the fifteenth century that a complete pattern book of Medieval Masonic practices was written by Mathes Roriczer and Lorenz Lechler, which documented techniques of drawing and layout utilized by the secret societies of the master masons.

42 They were typically drawn to scale on parchment to show to the patrons of the cathedral, and laid out at full scale on tracing floors. Parchment was often reused, scraped clean (or palimpsested), and then drawn on again. In one extant French example, the façade of a church is still apparent, even though the sheet was palimpsested and reused as a church book. In the palimpsest, shadows of each of the layers of marks are still visible on the sheets, each showing an aspect of the integrated totality – the media that joined the theoretical with the material.

43 Erwin Panofsky, *Gothic Architecture and Scholasticism: An Inquiry into the Analogy of the Arts, Philosophy, and Religion of the Middle Ages,* New York: Penguin Books, 1951, pp. 44–45.

44 Claude Bragdon, *The Beautiful Necessity: Seven Essays on Theosophy and Architecture,* Wheaton, IL: Quest Books, 1910, p. 88.

45 Ibid., p. 69.

46 Master builders were forbidden to work outside the order, a further impetus for the systematic application of their architectural program. See Kenneth John Conant, *Carolingian and Romanesque Architecture 800–1200,* Harmondsworth and New York: Penguin Books, 1959, p. 226.

47 This led to the important development of repetitive, rib-vaulting that anticipated the Gothic to follow. Conant, op. cit., p. 229.

48 Henri Gaud and Jean-François Leroux-Dhuys, *Cistercian Abbeys: History and Architecture,* Cologne: Konemann, 1998, p. 34.

49 The first monastery was founded by St. Bernard in 1098 at Cîteaux, from which the Cistercians got their name. The order quickly spread, and some of its early monasteries such as Pontigny and Fontenay, located in the Burgundy region of Northern France, are enduring artifacts of their beliefs and the architecture built to serve them. Pontigny was founded in 1114 and its abbey church, one of the order's oldest, was also one of its largest. Its basilican plan, generated from a square module, comprises low groin-vaulted aisles that flank a rib-vaulted nave, and lead to a sanctuary distinguished by eleven radiating chapels. Each component, built in this order, became increasingly complex – a progression from the dark Romanesque aisles, to the two-tiered arcades and expressed structure of the nave, to the exuberance of the sanctuary. The overall effect is stunning, a synthesis of clarity of plan, structure, and proportion. According

to Conant, "The whole effect of the interior is of extraordinary calm and religious serenity, virginal in sweetness and purity." Conant, op. cit., p. 231.

50 Lawlor, op. cit., p. 6.

51 See Doczi, op. cit., p. 8.

52 The abbey church at Pontigny is similarly generated from the square, both in plan and section.

53 The abbey church of Le Thoronet in Southern France, for example, is renowned for its acoustic qualities.

54 The precision of the acoustics of Cistercian churches was not limited to proportions alone, but was often exactly tuned. At Fountains Abbey, in England, clay jars were placed strategically in the nave as a means of dampening its reverberations. Gaud and Leroux-Dhuys, op. cit., p. 61.

55 Lee, op. cit., pp. 73–74.

56 Spiro Kostof, *A History of Architecture: Settings and Rituals*, 2nd edn., New York: Oxford University Press, 1995, p. 325.

57 Rudolf Wittkower, *Architectural Principles in the Age of Humanism*, New York and London: W.W. Norton & Company, 1971, p. 117.

58 Simon Unwin, *Analysing Architecture*, 3rd edn., London and New York: Routledge, 2009, p. 236.

59 Wittkower, op. cit.

60 Vitruvius, op. cit., p. 13.

61 Wittkower, op. cit.

62 Born in 1502, Palladio trained as a mason, but was led to architecture through his study of Vitruvius and the ruins of ancient Rome. Mathematics, number, and proportion figured prominently in his architecture and theory, as documented in his *Four Books of Architecture*.

63 Elsewhere, Palladio's proportioning system was applied to the dimensioning of the rooms that flank the central space.

64 Padovan, op. cit., p. 15.

65 Humans intuitively visually measure the physical environment and structure their understanding of it through size relationships – an outcome of evolutionary physiology – the ability to accurately measure distance and form a coherent pattern from disparate parts is endemic to human physiology. According to van der Laan, there are two basic ways that we perceive and measure our environment: ordering by size; and arranging by type of size. One of van der Laan's formal explorations documented a random collection of stones that were arranged from smallest to largest, or grouped in rows of similarly sized stones from smallest to largest. Each utilized a base module of the smallest stone, and arranged them either arithmetically or harmonically – the foundation of any proportioning system.

66 Quoted in Padovan, op. cit., p. 358.

67 Dom H. van der Laan, *Architectonic Space: Fifteen Lessons on the Disposition of the Human Habitat*, trans. Richard Padovan, Leiden: E.J. Brill, 1983, p. 173.

68 Ibid., p. 66.

69 Richard Padovan, from an article published in *The Architect*, May, 1986.

70 Similar to Le Corbusier's *Modular*, his system has two interrelated geometric progressions – one twice the measure of the other. Together they form an interwoven volumetric series that contain Fibonnaci golden sectional numbers and another progression of "plastic numbers." However, the *Modular* has no limits as the plastic number does.

71 Van der Laan, op. cit., p. 182.

72 Alberto Ferlenga and Paola Verde, *Dom Hans van der Laan: Works and Words*, Amsterdam: Architectura & Natura, 2001.

73 Jonathan Glancey, *RIBA Journal*, January, 1986.

74 Van der Laan, op. cit., p. 54.

75 Ferlenga and Verde, op. cit., p. 12.

76 Lindsay Jones argues that "the 'mechanisms of architecture,' which depend on a two-fold juxtaposition of order and variation of conformity with and departure from expectations, requires that all (successful) architecture, even that produced by the most fiercely individualistic designers, is rule bound." Jones, op. cit., p. 47.

77 Padovan, op. cit., p. 35.

78 Ibid., p. 74.

79 Van der Laan, op. cit., p. 175.

80 Ibid., p. 75.

81 Ibid., p. 27.

82 Ibid., p. 175.

83 Ibid., p. 61.

84 Ibid.

85 Psalms. 119.62, and Psalms 119.164.

86 Van der Laan, op. cit., p. 67.

9 Perfected Worlds

1 Mircea Eliade, *The Sacred and the Profane: The Nature of Religion*, trans. William R. Trask, San Diego: Harcourt Brace Jovanovich Publishers, 1959, p. 22.

2 According to Lindsay Jones, such "cosmic articulations are virtually always the beginning of an architectural event's significance rather then a summation of its total significance." Lindsay Jones, *The Hermeneutics of Sacred Architecture: Experience, Interpretation, Comparison*, Vol. 2, *Hermeneutical Calisthenics: A Morphology of Ritual-Architectural Priorities*, Cambridge, MA: Harvard University Press, 2000, p. 44.

3 See Jones, op. cit., p. 26.

4 E. Baldwin Smith, *The Dome: A Study in the History of Ideas*, Princeton, NJ: Princeton University Press, 1950, p. 6.

5 Ibid., p. 6.

6 Hadrian's Pantheon replaced previous temples on this site. Even though the Pantheon completely replaced its predecessor, Hadrian chose to restore its inscription at the entry portico, which reads, M AGRIPPA L F COSTERTIVM FECIT "Marcus Agrippa, the son of Lucius, three times consul, built this." William MacDonald, *The Pantheon: Design, Meaning, and Progeny*, Cambridge, MA: Harvard University Press, 1976, p. 13.

7 According to William MacDonald, the Pantheon "is one of the most important buildings for the history of architecture ever erected." William MacDonald, *The Architecture of the Roman Empire*, Vol. 1, *An Introductory Study*, New Haven, CT: Yale University Press, 1965, p. 95.

8 The history of architecture is one of spatial and symbolic possibilities optimized by contemporary materials and structural technology. Most of its early history is distinguished by massive, load-bearing materials that have distinct spatial limitations. The prodigious building programs of the Egyptians and the Greeks were bound, for the most part, by the limitations of massive trabeated construction. It was the Romans, however, who, through structure and technology, transformed the spatial possibilities of architecture and consequently expanded the medium of symbolism. In Roman architecture we find resonances between structure, material, and meaning.

9 They did not invent the arch, vault, and dome, but through applied technology were able to significantly exploit these basic elements of architectural construction. Nor

did they invent concrete, it had been known since the second century BCE, but were the first to exploit its possibilities. Roman concrete, in particular, was the catalyst for their ability to dramatically expand the spatial possibilities of architecture and thus the creation of a powerful medium for symbolic content.

10 Some elements are more recent. The paving, for example, dates from the nineteenth century, though it includes original pieces and is believed to accurately depict the original floor. See MacDonald, *The Pantheon*, op. cit., p. 100.

11 The 142-ft in diameter hemispherical dome rests on a massive cylindrical base and rises to an oculus at its apex created by a 2ft-thick ring of hard-burnt bricks set in strong mortar. This was possible due to the Romans' understanding of the structural forces exerted by a dome and the application of cast-in-place concrete. The 5,000 tons of weight exerted by the dome is counteracted by a 23ft-thick concrete tension ring at its base.

12 John Stamper outlines four different theories regarding the deities represented in the rotunda. The planetary deities, outlined above, appear to be the most plausible, given the celestial orientation of the building. However, some have suggested that deities associated with the family of Augustus were arranged there. Others have suggested that the twenty-eight coffers in each ring of the dome indicate a lunar orientation of the space. Lastly, it has been suggested that any reference to the gods was subservient to the pure geometry of the space. John Stamper, *The Architecture of Roman Temples: The Republic to the Middle Empire*, Cambridge: Cambridge University Press, 2005, pp. 200–201.

13 Kostof, *A History of Architecture: Settings and Rituals*, 2nd edn, New York and Oxford: Oxford University Press, 1995, p. 218.

14 Statues of Augustus and Agrippa also occupied niches in the entry portico, a symbolic integration of past and present – gods and emperor.

15 Stamper, op. cit., p. 203.

16 MacDonald, *The Architecture of the Roman Empire*, op. cit., p. 119.

17 Imperial emperors were often worshipped as gods, and in the eastern part of the empire Hadrian was known as Hadrian-Zeus. Stamper, op. cit., p. 202.

18 MacDonald, *The Architecture*, op. cit. p. 111.

19 MacDonald, *The Pantheon*, op. cit., p. 11.

20 Wim Swaan, *The Gothic Cathedral*, New York: Park Lane, 1985, p. 265.

21 It also may have benefited from the earlier and smaller church of Sergius and Bacchus, also built by Justinian and located nearby, though this has never been definitively established.

22 J.G. Davies describes this church as a "cross-domed basilica," basilical on the ground floor and cruciform at the gallery level. J.G. Davies, *The Origin and Development of the Early Christian Church*, New York: Philosophical Library, 1953, p. 69.

23 Kostof, op. cit., p. 264.

24 The Second Council of Nicaea in 787 actually regulated the position and placement of all icons. The Virgin, archangels, angels, apostles, and saints had specific locations assigned to them in the architectural space, with Christ Pantocrator ("Ruler of All") located at the center of this cosmogram. Peter and Linda Murray, *The Oxford Companion of Christian Art and Architecture*, Oxford and New York: Oxford University Press, 1996, pp. 73–74.

25 Eliade, op. cit., pp. 61–62.

26 Kostof, op. cit., p. 264.

27 Davies, op. cit., p. 71.

28 Smith, op. cit., p. 4.

29 Smith, op. cit., p. 90.

30 Kostof, op. cit., pp. 262–263.

31 Gülru Necipoğlu, *The Age of Sinan: Architectural Culture in the Ottoman Empire*, Princeton, NJ: Princeton University Press, 2005, p. 14.

32 Robert Hillenbrand, *Islamic Art and Architecture*, London: Thames and Hudson, 1999, p. 264.

33 As Dogan Kuban states:

> The 16th century Ottoman culture had no place for an examination of the objective world in itself . . . The material world is an encumbrance to be disparaged – in theory, if not in practice. Man serves Allah and the Sultan." Thus there was no place in Ottoman culture for the discourses that in many ways define the Italian Renaissance, and therefore historians are left primarily with the works themselves and any surviving court records. Additionally, the reluctance to record the personalities, activities, and lives of the figures that created and led Ottoman culture truncates the ability of historians to place the architecture in its cultural and religious context.
>
> (D. Kuban, *Sinan's Art and Selimiye*, Istanbul: The Economic and Social History Foundation, 1997, p. 11)

The Italian Renaissance dominates architectural histories of this period and Renaissance architecture typically is positioned as the defining era of European and world architecture. Even Turks are not very knowledgeable about the legacy and importance of Ottoman architecture and Sinan's significant contributions to it. See also Necipoğlu, op. cit., p. 128.

34 Ibid., p. 14.

35 The most direct account of Sinan's life is a vague prose poem by a man simply known as Sai. A passage from this relatively short accounting of a long and productive life reveals its superficial nature:

> Then this humble and sinful servant of the all-compassionate God, chief architect Sinan, son of Abdülmennan, came as a devsirme during the reign of the deceased Sultan Selim, the sword of Islam, son of Sultan Bayezid, the mercy and blessing of God be upon him and attained the honor of learning the glory of Islam and faith and the service of great and humble men, and at the time of the deceased Sultan Suleyman, the soldier of Islam, became a Janissary and took part in the Rhodes and Belgrade campaigns, participated in the Mohacs campaign as a light dragoon, and was promoted to infantry captain for new recruits.
>
> (Quoted in Kuban, op. cit., p. 29)

36 The Ottoman Empire emerged from a fragmented collection of Anatolian Turcoman emirates following the fall of the Selcuks in the mid-thirteenth century. Its beginnings are traced to a local ruler named Osman – from which we get the term Ottoman – who, beginning in the 1290s, started to expand his territory beginning from an area near the Anatolian city of Sogut. His son is credited with capturing the important Byzantine cities of Iznik and Bursa in the 1330s, and subsequent Ottoman sultans continued the expansion of the empire until it began a protracted decline, which started in the seventeenth century and lasted until the Turkish Republic was founded in 1923.

A series of sultans ruled an increasingly organized and prosperous empire – many distinguished both by their military conquests and their building programs. Murat I captured Edirne in 1362, the beginning of a march that eventually led to Vienna. Mehmet II captured Constantinople in 1453, and named the new capital Istanbul. This was the last Byzantine holding that had tenuously survived as an island in Ottoman territory. His son Beyazit II succeeded him in 1481 and ruled until 1512 when his son Selim I forced him to abdicate. Selim I, known as "The Fierce" locally, as "The Grim" to Europeans, earned this nickname for his extensive military campaigns that greatly enlarged the empire. After his death he was succeeded by Suleyman the Magnificent in 1520, who ruled for the next forty-six years, arguably the height of Ottoman power. The decline of the Ottoman Empire began with the accession to the throne of Selim II, after Suleyman died in 1566.

37 According to Robert Hillenbrand, "Ottoman architecture is first and foremost an architecture of mosques." The Ottoman mosque is arguably the height of development of this building type and was heir to a 1,000-year period during which the faith expanded at a phenomenal rate. When Mohammed founded Islam in the sixth century, its architectural implications were undefined, except for the practice of praying in the direction of Mecca. The principal elements of the archetypal mosque developed from this essential practice plus the requirements for communal prayer and the reading of Islam's holy books, the Koran, the word of God through His intermediary Mohammed, and the Hadith, the sayings of the Prophet himself. Every mosque is required to face toward Mecca and the *mihrab*, a niche in the *qibla*, the wall closest to Mecca, underlines this axis. Its direction established, the second requirement for communal prayer is provided by the *haram*, the prayer hall. This is typically a rectangular space with an orientation transverse to the Mecca axis, in part because of the practice of praying shoulder-to-shoulder and the importance given to being as close to the *mihrab*, and thus Mecca, as possible. The third requirement for all to hear the word of God and His Prophet, is satisfied by a number of interior elements of the mosque – the *minbar*, an often elaborate stairway that serves as a "pulpit" for the imam, the *muezzin mahfeli*, a raised platform where the muezzin provides responses to the imam's words for the congregation, and a *kursi*, a lectern that is used for similar purposes.

The other principal elements of the mosque accommodate other essential functions. A courtyard is typically located on the entrance side of the building and provides an enclosed anteroom to the *pishtaq*, the main entrance to the *haram*, and a space for the *sardivan*, the fountain for ritual ablution. A minaret, the tower from which the muezzin traditionally ascended five times a day to sing the call to prayer (before the contemporary use of loudspeakers), is typically located at one of the front corners of the mosque, though some mosques have multiple minarets. Depending on the mosque, there may be other architectural components provided for specific purposes. *Madrasas*, or Koranic schools, tombs, gardens, toilets, and bathhouses may be part of the complex. The Ottoman *külliye*, or mosque complex, is distinguished in part by the breadth of functions it provided. At the Suleymaniye *külliye* in Istanbul, for example, in addition to its magnificent mosque surrounded by gardens, there are tombs, *madrasas*, public baths, a hospital, a soup kitchen, a hostel, and even a wrestling ground, all within a unified urban plan. See Robert Hillenbrand, *Islamic Architecture: Form, Function and Meaning*, New York: Columbia University Press, 1994.

38 See Kuban, op. cit., p. 55, for a further discussion of formal and spatial precedents.

39 See Necipoğlu, op. cit., pp. 17–19.

40 Ibid., p. 28.

41 Ibid., p. 20.

42 Ibid., p. 39.

43 The conservative orthodoxy of Suleyman suppressed the T-shaped plans associated with the religious rituals of Sufism and favored centralized plans more conducive to communal prayer. Necipoğlu, op. cit., p. 102.

44 See Kuban, op. cit., p. 50, for his modular analysis of a number of early Ottoman mosques.

45 Necipoğlu, op. cit., p. 205.

46 Ibid., p. 215.

47 The design of the Sokollu Kadirga was begun in 1569.

48 John Rogers, *Sinan*, London and New York: Oxford Centre for Islamic Studies, 2006, p. 55.

49 As observed earlier, a similar condition is found at the Suleymaniye mosque complex in Istanbul.

50 Today the *madrasa* still functions as a Koranic secondary school for boys, and the *tekke* as a secondary school for girls. Most days the cadence of the recitation of the Koran by the students echoes the cadence of the components of the architecture.

51 For further discussion, see Necipoğlu, op. cit., p. 103. Hillenbrand describes three principal characteristics of the mosque: the first is this building type's flexibility of function and use. The non-hierarchical relationship of spaces results in an architecture that is adaptable and can serve numerous functions. The second is the suppression of decoration of the exterior. He argues that this is the result of specific passages in the Hadith that suggest that the Prophet disapproved of ostentatious exteriors, and that mosques were typically located in dense urban settings where views of the exterior were limited. The third is an emphasis on the interior spaces where most of the decorative elements were placed. These include "floral, geometric and epigraphic" components – abstracted planiform motifs, interlocking geometries that determined the measure and proportions of both architectural and decorative elements, and expressive calligraphy which communicated principal Islamic personages, practices, and sacred writings. Hillenbrand, op. cit.

52 Henri Stierlin suggests that Armenian refugees first saw Cistercian churches early in the second millennium. Henri Stierlin, *Turkey: From the Selcuks to the Ottomans*, Cologne: Taschen, 1998, pp. 72–75.

53 N.J. Dawood (translated with notes), *The Koran*, London: Penguin Books, 1997, p. 308.

54 Necipoğlu, op. cit., p. 251.

55 The overall dimensions of the mosque are 68 meters $\times$ 100 meters and the *haram* measures 36 meters $\times$ 46 meters. The dome is 31.5 meters in diameter, exceeding the Hagia Sophia by 0.5 meters (though the latter rises 12 meters higher).

56 Oleg Grabar states that there are five major decorative themes of the mosque: (1) human and animal figures, which are very rare; (2) architectural elements such as the use of stalactites (*muqarnas*), on minarets, columns, and dome squinches; (3) geometry; (4) writing in the form of "Koranic passages, eulogies to builders, or triumphal inscriptions"; and (5) vegetal elements. Oleg Grabar and Derek Hill, *Islamic Architecture and Its Decoration, AD 800–1500*, London: Faber and Faber, 1964, pp. 79–81.

57 The use of four flanking minarets is also found at the Hagia Sophia (two of which were designed by Sinan), which has a similar but less self-contained profile as the Selimiye. The Sultanahmet ("Blue") Mosque in Istanbul also employs a similar composition of minarets, but adds two more at its courtyard. The Suleymaniye has four prominent minarets, but they are located at the four corners of the courtyard and at the Sehzade, there are minarets on either side of the *son cemaat mahalli*. It was only the mosques built by the sultans or their relatives that could have more than one minaret, and so the other mosques such as the Sokollu Kadirga were limited to one. The 71-meter-high minarets at the Selimiye are the highest of Sinan's works and it was the first time that he used four minarets at the four corners of a mosque.

58 See Necipoğlu, op. cit., p. 83, for further discussion.

59 The men line up shoulder-to-shoulder facing the *qibla* wall during communal prayers.

60 It has also been suggested by Gunkut Akin that the geometry corresponds to a mandala pattern, a logical assumption given the contacts between Asia, Persia, and Ottoman Turkey at this time. This is most apparent at the muezzin's lodge. Its

nine-square plan fragments into 64 – both mandala patterns. See Gunkut Akin, "The Muezzin Mahfeli and Pool of the Selimiye Mosque in Edirne," in *Muqarnas – An Annual on Islamic Art and Architecture*, Vol. 12, Leiden: E.J. Brill, 1995, pp. 63–83.

61 Kuban, op. cit., p. 35.
62 Seyyed Hossein Nasr, *Islamic Art and Spirituality*, Albany, NY: The State University of New York Press, p. 54.
63 Dawood, op. cit., pp. 376–378.
64 The plaster and surface decorations are not original.
65 Kuban, op. cit., p. 65.
66 Nasr, op. cit., p. 59.
67 Ibid,. p. 46.
68 Ibid., p. 45.
69 Akin, op. cit., pp. 63–83.
70 Dawood, op. cit., p. 249.
71 Nasr, op. cit., p. 51.
72 Dawood, op. cit., p. 249.
73 Necipoğlu, op. cit., p. 16.
74 Smith, op. cit., p. 82.
75 Necipoğlu, op. cit., pp. 106–107.
76 Ibid., p. 241.
77 Ibid., p. 207.
78 The inside surfaces of the Dome of the Rock include an image of the Tree of Paradise.
79 Smith, op. cit., p. 11.
80 Necipoğlu, op. cit., p. 252.

10 Conclusion

1 Antoine de Saint-Exupéry, *Le Petit Prince*, Paris: Gallimard, 1943, Ch. 21.
2 Primordial also means primary, an appropriate way to conceptualize prehistoric architecture.
3 Sam Hamil, *Banished Immortal: Visions of Li T'ai-po*, Fredonia, NY: White Pine Press, 1987.
4 Gary Snyder, *The Practice of the Wild*, San Francisco: North Point Press, 1990, p. 23.
5 Barry Lopez, *Crossing Open Ground*, New York: Vintage Books, 1989, p. 151.
6 Annie Dillard, *Pilgrim at Tinker Creek*, New York: Harper and Row, 1974, pp. 31–32.
7 Brooks Atkinson, Ed., *The Complete Essays and Other Writings of Ralph Waldo Emerson*, New York: The Modern Library, 1950, p. 34.
8 Peter Turner, Ed., *Nature and Other Writings, Ralph Waldo Emerson*, Boston: Shambhala Publications, 1994, p. 71.
9 Ibid., pp. 72–73.
10 Ibid., p. 73.
11 Norman Crowe, *Nature and the Idea of a Man-Made World*, Cambridge, MA: MIT Press, 1985, p. 7.
12 Michael Benedikt, *For an Architecture of Reality*, New York: Luman Books, pp. 32–56.
13 I am indebted to Henry David Thoreau for this expanded definition of "extravagant."
14 When I say "authentic cuisine," traditional dishes from clearly defined regions may come to mind, but that would be an assumption based on the most common use of this term. When the term "traditional" is applied to any cultural output it is implicitly understood as communal, not individual, and that is a distinction helpful to this argument. Current contemporary cuisines (so-called "fusion cuisine"), may be equally authentic, but simply use different boundaries for the contexts they appropriate. The

key to defining authenticity is the degree of recognition of the contexts from which they emerge, either pre- or post-facto, and a determination regarding the appropriateness of their application.

15 In Lindsay Jones' words.
16 Bhikku Nanamoli and Bhikkhu Bodhi (trans.), *The Middle Length Discourses of the Buddha: A Translation of the Majjhima Nikaya*, Boston: Wisdom Publications, 1995, p. 40.
17 Hans-Georg Gadamer, *The Relevance of the Beautiful*, Cambridge: Cambridge University Press, 1986, p. 26.
18 Ibid., p. xi.
19 For this section I adopted the organization of the Theravada "Seven Factors of Enlightenment" as outlined by Joseph Goldstein and Jack Kornfield in *Seeking the Heart of Wisdom: The Path of Insight Meditation*, Boston: Shambhala Publications, 1987, pp. 61–77.
20 Gadamer, op. cit., p. 49.
21 See ibid., p. 17, for a further discussion.
22 Ibid., p. 15.
23 Aneila Jaffé, Ed., *Memories, Dreams, Reflections, by C.G. Jung*, New York: Random House, 1961, p. 175.
24 Nanamoli and Bodhi, op. cit., p. 228.
25 Henry David Thoreau, *Walden*, ed., Gordon S. Haight, Roslyn, NY: Walter J. Black, Inc., 1942, p. 70.
26 Ibid., p. 301. Italics in original.
27 From *A Week on the Concord and Merrimack Rivers*, quoted with commentary in Alan D. Hodder, *Thoreau's Ecstatic Witness*, New Haven, CT: Yale University Press, 2001, p. 192.
28 The source of this passage is unknown and it has been suggested that it is an amalgam of the Hindu, Confucian, and Taoist readings Thoreau was immersed in at this time. See Hodder, op. cit., p. 205.
29 Thoreau, op. cit., pp. 350–352.
30 From the *Mahaparinibbana Sutta*.
31 Atkinson, op. cit., p. 42.
32 Quoted in a *dhamma* talk by Vipassana teacher Sharon Salzberg.

Bibliography

Abram, D., *The Spell of the Sensuous*, New York: Random House, 1996.

Ackerman, D., *A Natural History of the Senses*, New York: Random House, 1990.

Adler, G., *Selected Letters of C.G. Jung, 1909–1961*, Princeton, NJ: Princeton University Press, 1953/1984.

Akin, G., "The Muezzin Mahfeli and Pool of the Selimiye Mosque in Edirne," in G. Necipogulu (ed.) *Muqarnas: An Annual on Islamic Art and Architecture*, Vol. 12, Leiden: E.J. Brill, 1995.

Alexander, C., *A Pattern Language*, New York: Oxford University Press, 1977.

Arnheim, R., *The Dynamics of Architectural Form*, Berkeley, CA: The University of California Press, 1979.

Artress, L., *Walking a Sacred Path*, New York: Berkeley Publishing Group, 1995.

Atkinson, B. (ed.), *The Complete Essays and Other Writings of Ralph Waldo Emerson*, New York: The Modern Library, 1950.

Bachelard, G., *The Poetics of Space*, trans. M. Jolas, Boston: Beacon Press, 1969.

Bair, D., *Jung: A Biography*, Boston: Little, Brown and Co., 2003.

Barrie, T., *Spiritual Path – Sacred Place: Myth, Ritual and Meaning in Architecture*, Boston: Shambhala Publications, 1996.

Benedikt, M., *For an Architecture of Reality*, New York: Lumen Books, 1992.

Bennet, E.A., *Meetings with Jung*, Zurich: Daimon, 1985.

Biederman, H., *Dictionary of Symbolism: Cultural Icons and the Meanings Behind Them*, New York: Meridian/Penguin Group, 1992.

Bloomer, K. and Moore, C., *Body, Memory and Architecture*, New Haven, CT: Yale University Press, 1977.

Boller, P., *American Transcendentalism 1830–1860: An Intellectual Inquiry*, New York: G.P. Putnam's Sons, 1974.

Bowker, J. (ed.), *The Oxford Dictionary of World Religions*, Oxford and New York: Oxford University Press, 1997.

Bragdon, C., *The Beautiful Necessity: Seven Essays on Theosophy and Architecture*, Wheaton, IL: Quest Books, 1910.

Bronowski, J., *The Ascent of Man*, Boston: Little, Brown and Co., 1973.

Burl, A., *Rings of Stone: The Prehistoric Stone Circles of Britain and Ireland*, London: Frances Lincoln Publishers Ltd., 1979.

—— *Great Stone Circles*, New Haven, CT: Yale University Press, 1999.

Buswell, R., *The Zen Monastic Experience*, Princeton, NJ: Princeton University Press, 1992.

Byrom, T., trans., *The Dhammapada: The Sayings of the Buddha*, New York: Vintage Books, 1976.

Campbell, J., *The Hero with a Thousand Faces*, Princeton, NJ: Princeton University Press, 1949.

—— *The Mythic Image*, Princeton, NJ: Princeton University Press, 1974.

Castleden, R., *The Stonehenge People: An Exploration of Life in Neolithic Britain 4700–2000 BC*, London: Routledge, 1990.

—— *Neolithic Britain, New Stone Age Sites of England, Scotland and Wales*, London: Routledge, 1992.

Coldrake, W., *Architecture and Authority in Japan*, London: Routledge, 1996.

Conant, K., *Carolingian and Romanesque Architecture, 800–1200*, Harmondsworth: Penguin Books, 1959.

Conze, E. (ed.), *Buddhist Scriptures*, London: Penguin Books, 1959.

Crowe, N., *Nature and the Idea of a Man-made World*, Cambridge, MA: MIT Press, 1985.

Dalai Lama, *The Universe in a Single Atom: The Convergence of Science and Spirituality*, New York: Random House, 2005.

Daumal, R., *Mount Analogue: A Novel of Symbolically Authentic Non-Euclidean Adventures in Mountain Climbing*, trans. R. Shattuck, Boston: Shambhala Publications, 1992.

Davies, J.G., *The Origin and Development of the Early Christian Church*, New York: Philosophical Library, 1953.

Dawood, N., trans., *The Koran*, London: Penguin Books, 1997.

De Laszlo, V.S., *The Basic Writings of C. G. Jung*, New York: The Modern Library, 1959.

Dewey, J., *Art as Experience*, New York: G.P. Putnam's Sons, [1934] 1980.

Dillard, A., *Pilgrim at Tinker Creek*, New York: Harper and Row, 1974.

Doczi, G., *The Power of Limits: Proportional Harmonies in Nature, Art and Architecture*, Boston: Shambhala Publications, 1981.

Dunn, C., *Carl Jung: Wounded Healer of the Soul*, New York: Parabola Books, 2000.

Eliade, M., *Patterns in Comparative Religion*, London: Sheed and Ward, 1958.

—— *The Sacred and the Profane: The Nature of Religion*, trans. W. Trask, San Diego: Harcourt Brace Jovanovich Publishers, 1959.

—— *A History of Religious Ideas*, Vol. 1, *From the Stone Age to the Eleusinian Mysteries*, trans. W. Trask, Chicago: The University of Chicago Press, 1978.

—— *Images and Symbols: Studies in Religious Symbolism*, Princeton, NJ: Princeton University Press, 1991.

—— *Symbolism, the Sacred and the Arts*, ed. D. Apostolos-Cappadona, New York: Continuum Publishing Company, 1992.

Ferlenga, A. and Verde, P., *Dom Hans van der Laan: Works and Words*, Amsterdam: Architectura & Natura, 2001.

Freeley, J. and Cakmak, A., *Byzantine Monuments of Istanbul*, Cambridge: Cambridge University Press, 2004.

Gadamer, H.-G. *The Relevance of the Beautiful*, Cambridge: Cambridge University Press, 1986.

—— *Truth and Method*, 2nd edn., trans. J. Weinsheimer and D. Marshall, New York: Continuum Publishing Company, 1996.

Gaud, H., and Leroux-Dhuys, J., *Cistercian Abbeys: History and Architecture*, Cologne: Konemann, 1998.

Goldstein, J. and Kornfield, J., *Seeking the Heart of Wisdom: The Path of Insight Meditation*, Boston: Shambhala Publications, 1987.

Goodwin, G., *A History of Ottoman Architecture*, London: Thames and Hudson, 1971.

Grabar, O. and Hill, D., *Islamic Architecture and Its Decoration, AD 800–1500*, London: Faber and Faber, 1964.

Grondin, J., *The Philosophy of Gadamer*, Montreal: McGill-Queen's University Press, 2003.

Gyun, H., *Korean Temple Motifs: Beautiful Symbols of the Buddhist Faith*, trans. T. Atkinson, Pajubookcity Munbal-li Gyoha-eup, Paju-si, Gyeonggi-do: Dolbegae Publishers, 2000, English version, 2005.

Hahn, L.E. (ed.), *The Philosophy of Hans-Georg Gadamer*, Chicago and La Salle, IL: Open Court Publishers, 1997.

Hamil, S., *Banished Immortal: Visions of Li T'ai-po*, Fredonia, New York: White Pine Press, 1987.

Hannah, B., *Jung, His Life and Work: A Biographical Memoir*, New York: G.P. Putnam's Sons, 1976.

Harries, K., *The Ethical Function of Architecture*, Cambridge, MA: MIT Press, 1998.

Hayashiya, T., Nakamura, M., and Hayashiya, S., *Japanese Arts and the Tea Ceremony*, trans. J. Macadam, New York/Tokyo: Weatherhill/Heibonsha, 1974.

Hayes, M. (ed.), *Architecture Theory Since 1968*, Cambridge, MA: MIT Press, 2000.

Hayman, R., *Riddles in Stone: Myths, Archaeology and the Ancient Britons*, London and Rio Grande, OH: Hambledon Press, 1997.

Herrmann, W. and Herrmann, A. (trans.), *An Essay on Architecture by Marc-Antoine Laugier*, Los Angeles: Hennessey and Ingalls, Inc., 1977.

Hertzberger, H., *Lessons for Students in Architecture*, Rotterdam: Uitgeverij 010 Publishers, 1991.

Hertzberger, H., Van Roijen-Wortmann, A., and Strauven, F., *Aldo van Eyck: Hubertus House*, Amsterdam: Stichting Wonen, 1982.

Hillenbrand, R., *Islamic Architecture: Form, Function and Meaning*, New York: Columbia University Press, 1994.

——— *Islamic Art and Architecture*, London: Thames and Hudson, 1999.

Hodder, A.D., *Thoreau's Ecstatic Witness*, New Haven, CT: Yale University Press, 2001.

Holl, S., Pallasmaa, J., and Perez-Gomez, A., *Questions of Perception: Phenomenology of Architecture*, Tokyo: A + U: Architecture and Urbanism, 1994.

Husserl, E., "Material Things in Their Relation to the Aesthetic Body," in *Ideas Pertaining to a Pure Phenomenology and to a Phenomenological Philosophy, Book 2: Studies in the Phenomenology of Constitution*, in D. Welton (ed.), *The Body: Classic and Contemporary Readings*, Oxford: Blackwell, 1999.

Jaffé, A. (ed.), *Memories, Dreams, Reflections, by C.G. Jung*, New York: Random House, 1961.

——— *C.G. Jung: Word and Image*, Princeton, NJ: Princeton University Press, 1979.

Jones, L., *The Hermeneutics of Sacred Architecture*, Vol. 1, *Monumental Occasions: Reflections on the Eventfulness of Religious Architecture*, Cambridge, MA: Harvard University Press, 2000.

——— *The Hermeneutics of Sacred Architecture: Experience, Interpretation, Comparison*, Vol. 2, *Hermeneutical Calisthenics: A Morphology of Ritual-Architectural Priorities*, Cambridge, MA: Harvard University Press, 2000.

Jung, C.G. (ed.), *Man and His Symbols*, New York: Dell Publishing Co. Inc., 1968.

Kindross, L., *The Ottoman Centuries: The Rise and Fall of the Turkish Empire*, New York: Morrow Quill Paperbacks, 1977.

Kornfield, J. and Breitner, P., *A Still Forest Pool: The Insight Meditation of Achaan Chah*, Wheaton, IL: Quest Books, 1985.

Kornfield, J. and Fronsdal, G., trans., *Sutta-nipata: The Teachings of the Buddha*, Boston: Shambhala Publications, 1993.

Kostof, S., *A History of Architecture: Settings and Rituals*, New York and Oxford: Oxford University Press, 1985; 2nd edn., 1995.

Kuban, D., *The Arts of Islam and the East*, Vol. 7, Ann Arbor, MI: The Freer Gallery of Art and the Smithsonian Department of the History of Art, 1968.

—— *Sinan's Art and Selimiye*, Istanbul: The Economic and Social History Foundation, 1997.

Kusan, *The Way of Korean Zen*, trans. M. Bachelor, Boston and London: Weatherhill, 1985.

Lawlor, R., *Sacred Geometry: Philosophy and Practice*, London: Thames and Hudson, 1982.

Leach, N., *Rethinking Architecture: A Reader in Cultural Theory*, London: Routledge, 1997.

Leidy, D. and Thurman, R., *Mandala: The Architecture of Enlightenment*, Boston: Shambhala Publications, 1997.

Levin, D., *Modernity and the Hegemony of Vision*, Berkeley, CA: The University of California Press, 1993.

Loewen, J., *Lies My Teacher Told Me: Everything Your American History Book Got Wrong*, New York: The New Press, 1995.

Lopez, B., *Crossing Open Ground*, New York: Vintage Books, 1989.

Lopez, D. (ed.), *Buddhist Hermeneutics*, Honolulu: Hawaii University Press, 1988.

Lundquist, J., *The Temple: Meeting Place of Heaven and Earth*, London: Thames and Hudson, 1993.

MacDonald, W., *The Architecture of the Roman Empire*, Vol. 1, *An Introductory Study*, New Haven, CT and London: Yale University Press, 1965.

—— *The Pantheon: Design, Meaning, and Progeny*, Cambridge, MA: Harvard University Press, 1976.

McLuhan, T., *Touch the Earth: A Self-portrait of Indian Existence*, New York: Simon & Schuster, 1971.

Mainstone, R., *Hagia Sophia: Architecture, Structure and Liturgy of Justinian's Great Church*, London: Thames and Hudson, 1988.

Marcus, C., *The House as Symbol of Self*, Berkeley, CA: Conari Press, 1995.

Masunaga, R., *A Primer of Soto Zen: A Translation of Dogen's Shobogenzo Zuimonki*, Honolulu: The University of Hawaii Press, 1971.

Michell, G., *The Hindu Temple: An Introduction to Its Meaning and Forms*, Chicago: The University of Chicago Press, 1977/1988.

—— *Architecture of the Islamic World: Its History and Social Meaning*, London, Thames and Hudson, 1978.

Milner, G., *The Moundbuilders: Ancient Peoples of Eastern North America*, London: Thames and Hudson, 2004.

Moran, D., *Introduction to Phenomenology*, London: Routledge, 2000.

Mugerauer, R., *Heidegger's Language and Thinking*, Atlantic Highlands, NJ: Humanities Press International, Inc., 1988.

—— *Interpreting Environments: Tradition, Deconstruction, Hermeneutics*, Austin, TX: The University of Texas Press, 1995.

Murray, L. and Murray, P., *The Oxford Companion of Christian Art and Architecture*, Oxford: Oxford University Press, 1996.

Nabokov, P. and Easton, R., *Native American Architecture*, New York: Oxford University Press, 1989.

Nanamoli, B., *The Middle Length Discourses of the Buddha: A Translation of the Majjhima Nikaya*, trans. B. Bodhi, Boston, Wisdom Publications, 1995.

Nasr, S., *Islamic Art and Spirituality*, Albany, NY: The State University of New York Press, 1987.

Necipoğlu, G., *The Age of Sinan: Architectural Culture in the Ottoman Empire*, Princeton, NJ: Princeton University Press, 2005.

Norberg-Schulz, C., *Intentions in Architecture*, Cambridge, MA: MIT Press, 1965.

—— *Existence, Space and Architecture*, New York: Praeger Publishers, 1971.

—— *Genius Loci: Towards a Phenomenology of Architecture*, New York: Rizzoli, 1979.

—— *Architecture: Meaning and Place*, New York: Rizzoli, 1980.

—— *Meaning in Western Architecture*, New York: Rizzoli, 1980.

—— "Heidegger's Thinking on Architecture," in *Architecture: Meaning and Place: Selected Essays*, New York: Electa/Rizzoli, 1988.

Padovan, R., *Proportion: Science, Philosophy, Architecture*, London: E & FN Spon, 1999.

Pallasmaa, J., *The Eyes of the Skin: Architecture and the Senses*, London: Academy Editions, 1996.

Panofsky, E., *Gothic Architecture and Scholasticism: An Inquiry into the Analogy of the Arts, Philosophy, and Religion of the Middle Ages*, New York: Penguin Books, 1951.

Perez-Gomez, A., *Built Upon Love: Architectural Longing after Ethics and Aesthetics*, Cambridge, MA: MIT Press, 2006.

Plato, *Timaeus and Critias*, trans. D. Lee, New York: Penguin Books, 1963.

Rasmussen, S., *Experiencing Architecture*, Cambridge, MA: MIT Press, 1959.

Richardson, J. (ed.), *Selected Poems: Baudelaire*, Harmondsworth: Penguin Books, 1975.

Richardson, R., *Emerson: The Mind on Fire*, Berkeley, CA: The University of California Press, 1995.

Rogers, J., *Sinan*, London and New York: Oxford Centre for Islamic Studies, 2006.

Ross, N. (ed.), *The World of Zen: An East–West Anthology*, New York: Random House, 1960.

Rykwert, J., *On Adam's House in Paradise*, New York: The Museum of Modern Art, 1972.

Saint-Exupéry, A. de, *Le Petit Prince*, Paris: Gallimard, 1943.

Scarre, C., *Monuments and Landscape in Atlantic Europe: Perception and Society during the Neolithic and Early Bronze Age*, London: Routledge, 2002.

Smith, E.B., *The Dome: A Study in the History of Ideas*, Princeton, NJ: Princeton University Press, 1950.

—— *Architectural Symbolism of Imperial Rome and the Middle Ages*, Princeton, NJ: Princeton University Press, 1956.

Smith, H., *The Religions of Man*, New York: Perennial Library, Harper and Row, 1958.

Snodgrass, A., and Coyne, R., *Interpretation in Architecture: Design as a Way of Thinking*, London: Routledge, 2006.

Snyder, G., *The Practice of the Wild*, San Francisco: North Point Press, 1990.

Squier, E. and Davis, E., *Ancient Monuments of the Mississippi Valley: Comprising the Results of Extensive Original Surveys and Explorations*, Washington, DC: The Smithsonian Institution, 1848.

Stamper, J., *The Architecture of Roman Temples: The Republic to the Middle Empire*, Cambridge: Cambridge University Press, 2005.

Stierlin, H., *Turkey: From the Selcuks to the Ottomans*, Cologne: Taschen, 1998.

Stratton, A., *Sinan*, New York: Charles Scribner's Sons, 1972.

Suzuki, S., *Zen Mind, Beginner's Mind: Informal Talks on Zen Meditation and Practice*, New York and Tokyo: John Weatherhill, Inc., 1970.

Swaan, W., *The Gothic Cathedral*, New York: Park Lane, 1985.

Tarnas, R., *The Passion of the Western Mind: Understanding the Ideas That Have Shaped Our Worldview*, New York: Ballentine Books, 1993.

Tavernor, R., *On Alberti and the Art of Building*, New Haven, CT: Yale University Press, 1998.

Thoreau, H., *Walden*, ed. Gordon S. Haight, Roslyn, NY: Walter J. Black, Inc., 1942.

Turner, P. (ed.), *Nature and Other Writings, Ralph Waldo Emerson*, Boston: Shambhala Publications, 1994.

Unwin, S., *Analysing Architecture*, 3rd edn., London and New York: Routledge, 2009.

Van der Laan, D., *Architectonic Space: Fifteen Lessons on the Disposition of the Human Habitat*, trans. R. Padovan, Leiden: E.J. Brill, 1983.

Versiuis, A., *American Transcendentalism and Asian Religions*, Oxford: Oxford University Press, 1993.

Veseley, D., *Architecture in the Age of Divided Representation: The Question of Creativity in the Shadow of Production*, Cambridge, MA: MIT Press, 2004.

Vitebsky, P., *The Shaman, Voyages of the Soul: Trance, Ecstasy, and Healing from Siberia to the Amazon*, Boston: Little, Brown and Co., 1995.

Vitruvius Pollio, M., *The Ten Books of Architecture*, trans. M. Morgan, New York: Dover Publications, Inc., 1960.

Von Simpson, O., *The Gothic Cathedral*, Princeton, NJ: Princeton University Press, 1956.

Wilber, K., *The Collected Works of Ken Wilber*, Boston: Shambhala Publications, 2000.

—— *The Marriage of Sense and Soul*, in *The Collected Works of Ken Wilber*, Vol. 8, Boston and London: Shambhala Publications, 2000.

—— *One Taste*, in *The Collected Works of Ken Wilber*, Vol. 8, Boston and London: Shambhala Publications, 2000.

Wittkower, R., *Architectural Principles in the Age of Humanism*, New York and London: W.W. Norton & Company, 1971.

Woodward, S., McDonald, J., and McDonald, S., *Indian Mounds of the Middle Ohio Valley: A Guide to Adena and Ohio Hopewell Sites*, Blacksburg, VA: The McDonald and Woodward Publishing Company, 1986.

Wurman, R.S., *What Will Be Has Always Been: The Words of Louis I. Kahn*, New York: Access Press/Rizzoli, 1986.

Index

Figures in **bold** refer to illustrations.

Dillard, Annie 215
Diocletian, Emperor 57
disconnections 1
dislocation 1
divine, the: connection to 214; definition
     6; directive of the 132, 134–6, **134**;
     re-connection with 3; representations
     of the 168; separation from 1; unity
     with 216
Dogen Zenji 33
dolmen **86**, 87
domes 169, 179; Caracalla baths 169;
     Hagia Sophia 174; Ismihan Sultan and
     Sokollu complex, Kadirga 192–3;
     mosques 185, 187, 208; Pantheon
     171, 172, 179, 252n11; Selimiye
     complex, Edirne 203, **204**
dynamic relationships 220–1

earth, the 12, 101–2
earthworks 81, 84; Native American 12,
     91–102, **93**, **94**, **95**, **96**, **97**, **99**, **100**
economy 149
Edirnekapi Mihrimah Sultan Mosque
     (Istanbul, Turkey) 197–8 *see also* Sinan
effigy figures 12, 81, 91
Egypt 136–7, 224–5, **224**, 238n46
Elements (Euclid) 143
Eliade, Mircea 1, 78, 81, 81–2, 86–7, 98,
     104, 167–8, 176
Ely Cathedral (England) 143, **143**
Emerson, Ralph Waldo 30, 31–2, 35, 36,
     38, 89–90, 215–6, 225, 229
empathy 19, **19**, 137
emptiness 217
engagement 19–20, **19**, 35, 217, 220–1
English narrative gardens 20
enlightenment 36, 44–5, 114
enticement 220
entry sequences **117**, 197, 201, 206, 220
Escale (France) 82
Eucharist, the 49, **175**, 176, 177
Euclid 143
eurythmy 149
existence 44
experience 8, 11, 12, 22, 151; auditory
     16; Jung on 76; multi-sensory 11, 14,
     15, 16–20; personal 13, 228–30;
     unmediated 214–6
Eyck, Aldo van 50

Faust (Goethe) 71

feminine, the 72
feng shui 114
Fibonacci Spiral, the 141, **142**
Fiechter, Ernst 66
Florence **147**, 148, **148**, 170
Fontenay (France) 250n52
form 45, **45**
Fort Hill 96, 244n37
Fountains Abbey 250n54
Freud, Sigmund 65, 240n18
funerary architecture 81, 85, 87–9, **88**,
     89

Gadamer, Hans-Georg 7–10, 26–7, **27**,
     28, 29, 218, 220, 221, 229, 233n42
Ganges, the 49, 52
gardens 205, 209, 238n46
gateways **115**, 116, **117**, 118, **120**, **121**,
     122, **124**, 125, 127, 201, 237n39
geometric progression 153
geometric relationships 137
geometry 12, 41, 77, 101, 110, 127, 132,
     144, 173–4, 176, 207, 221; Islamic
     207–8; Medieval 143; Platonic 139,
     144; practice of 136–7; progressive
     202–3, **203**, 208–9; sacred 140; sacred
     practices 133; of the square 133–4,
     133, 143, 146–7, 196–7, 201–3,
     248n29
Ggantija (Gozo) 83, **84**
Goethe, Johann Wolfgang von 71, 216,
     241n39
Golden House of Nero 210
Golden Section, the 137, 140, 141, **142**,
     143
Gospels 1, 47
Gothic proportioning systems 142–5, **143**,
     144, 146
Great Mosque (al-Masjid al-Haram)
     (Mecca) 110–1
Great Mosque (Bursa, Turkey) **19**
Great Stupa (Sanchi) 111–2, **111**
Grønjaegers Høj 87
Gudea, King of Lugash 135

Hadith, the 183, 210
Hadrian, Emperor 169, 172, 173, 252n17
Hagia Sophia (Istanbul) 12, 46, 173–8,
     173, **175**, **177**, 178, 210, 219,
     255n55, 255n57
haiku 34
hajj 105, 110

symbolic places 12

symbolism 6, 12–3, 35; architectural 5,
    39; cosmic 168; definition 6;
    embodying 8–9; Harries' typology
    235n2; importance of 41–2, 43–4;
    Jung House 66–9, 221; mandalas
    69–70; mediation 41; paths 107–8,
    125–31; phenomenology 23–4; role
    11–2; sacred architecture **43**; Sinan
    179, **204–11**, **206**, **208**; surface
    236n3; understanding 41–2

symbols: definition 41; mediation 44–5; of
    power 62

symmetry 140, 149, 151

Taoism 1, 67
taste 18–9
Telesphoros **72**, 73, 77
Ten Books of Architecture (Vitruvius) 137–8
territorial restriction 5
texture 41
Thebes 224–5
theoretical approaches 7–10
Theravada sect, Forest Lineage School 33
thingly-real, the 22, 35, 77, 213, 214,
    229
Thoreau, Henry David 32, 35, 37, 38, 67,
    221–2, 223–4
thresholds 50, 53, 77, 118, 127, 221,
    237n39
Timaeus and Critias (Plato) 138, 140, 143,
    144
time 110, 222
Tongdo Zen Buddhist monastery (Korea)
    12, **44**, 113–31, 168; architecture
    114–8; Bell Pavilion 123, **123**, 247n33;
    bridges 118, **118**; courtyards 120,
    127; devas **122**; gateways **120**, **121**,
    122, 123, **124**, 127; hierarchical
    organization 127, 131; main temple
    123, **124**, 125, 127, **128**, 129–31,
    130; orientation 247n31; path as
    mediator 118–25; plan **119**; stupa
    129, 131; symbolism 125–31, **130**,
    167; use 131
touch 17
transcendental idealism 30
transformation 217–20; architecture and
    75–9; labyrinths and 110

trans-historical perspectives 9, 11
trial 105
trickster, the **71**, 72
truth 27
Truth and Method (Gadamer) 26
tympanum 107; Saint Foy, Conque 57,
    58, 59, **59**, 60

unconscious, the 64–6, 68, 239n11
understanding 133, 137
Unitarianism 35
unmediated experience 214–6
Upanishads, the 44

Vaals see Saint Benedict's Abbey, Vaals
van der Laan, Hans 81, 137, 150–1, 168,
    250n65 see *also* Saint Benedict's
    Abbey, Vaals
Varenasi 56
vastu purusha mandala 133–4, **133**
vastu-vidya, the **133**
Vatican II 162
Via Dolorosa (Jerusalem) 105–7, **105**
Villa Capra 149
Villard de Honnecourt 144, **144**
visual, power of the 17
Vitruvian Man, the 138, 146
Vitruvius 67, 137–8, 140, 149, 151, 166,
    240n26, 250n62

Walden (Thoreau) 32, 35
walls 151
Waterhouse, John William **2**
Way of the Pilgrim, The 49
Wells Cathedral (United Kingdom) **43**
West Kennet Avenue (England) 103–4
West Kennet Long Barrow (Wiltshire,
    United Kingdom) 88, **89**
wholeness 37
Wilber, Ken 26, 37, 38
Winchester Cathedral 108
Wittkower, Rudolf 141, 147, 149
Wolff, Toni 76

Yeats, William Butler 90
yoga 3

Zen Buddhism 33, 107, 127
ziggurats 51, 84

eBooks – at www.eBookstore.tandf.co.uk

A library at your fingertips!

eBooks are electronic versions of printed books. You can store them on your PC/laptop or browse them online.

They have advantages for anyone needing rapid access to a wide variety of published, copyright information.

eBooks can help your research by enabling you to bookmark chapters, annotate text and use instant searches to find specific words or phrases. Several eBook files would fit on even a small laptop or PDA.

NEW: Save money by eSubscribing: cheap, online access to any eBook for as long as you need it.

Annual subscription packages

We now offer special low-cost bulk subscriptions to packages of eBooks in certain subject areas. These are available to libraries or to individuals.

For more information please contact webmaster.ebooks@tandf.co.uk

We're continually developing the eBook concept, so keep up to date by visiting the website.

www.eBookstore.tandf.co.uk

19774882R00160

Printed in Great Britain
by Amazon